TRUMPET CALL

of

REFORMATION

TRUMPET CALL
of
REFORMATION

by

Oliver Read Whitley

THE BETHANY PRESS – ST. LOUIS, MO.

Library of Congress Catalog Card Number: 59-13169

Printed in the United States of America

To Lois

ACKNOWLEDGMENTS

The indebtedness of the writer to others, for intellectual stimulation and for interest in the subject matter contained here, is immeasurable. Many, in countless ways, have made this book possible. To Paul E. Becker, at one time minister of University Christian Church in Des Moines, Iowa, I am grateful for his sustaining interest in the problems of young people. To Luther W. Stalnaker, late Dean of Liberal Arts at Drake University, I owe my zest for things intellectual. He was a teacher with a great gift for inspiring a truly Socratic love of knowledge. To Dean Liston Pope, Professors Roland H. Bainton, and H. Richard Niebuhr of Yale University, I owe my interest in the subject discussed in the book. I am indebted to Professor Kenneth W. Underwood of Wesleyan University for many stimulating insights given when he taught a course in Sociology of Religion at Yale. To Professor John Sirjamaki of the University of Minnesota, formerly of Yale, I owe the awakening of my intense interest in American culture as a field of study. My indebtedness to numerous writers and scholars in sociology of religion is made clear in the first chapter.

A special word of thanks is due to two students who served as student assistants in the Department of Sociology of Religion at Iliff School of Theology while the book was being written—David Wyatt, who helped in typing and editing in the early stages of the work, and Thomas E. Wood, minister, First Christian Church, Thornton, Colorado, who did yeoman service in helping to prepare the manuscript in its final form. To the Bethany Press and its Director, Darrell Wolfe, go my thanks for the Bethany Book Award, and for the excellent help given in preparing the manuscript for publication.

A special word of thanks goes to several colleagues and friends who read the manuscript in various stages of its development and made helpful suggestions. G. Edwin Osborn and Dean Stephen J. England of Phillips University offered cogent criticisms of the work while I was on the faculty there. Professors Walter Sikes and F. E. Rector of Christian Theological Seminary made valuable criticisms of an earlier version. None of these persons is responsible for conclusions reached or for interpretations given. For these the author must accept full responsibility.

To my wife goes the dubious honor of having listened endlessly to the ideas contained herein. Without her love and care during a long period of illness which preceded the writing, this book would not have been written. Finally, I am grateful for a religious heritage in which this kind of inquiry can be carried on freely.

DENVER, COLORADO

April, 1959

INTRODUCTION

This study of Disciples of Christ undertakes to use a frame of reference which is, broadly speaking, socio-cultural. It is designed to apply the concepts and insights of a particular social science, sociology, to the understanding of the growth and development of a religious movement.

The study is in part conceived as a contribution to what Joachim Wach calls "the self-interpretation" of a religious movement. Speaking specifically of the sect, Wach writes, "a full understanding of its character cannot be achieved except by careful consideration of its self-interpretation, a methodological requirement which holds true for the study of all religious groups."[1] We intend to take a careful look at the way in which Disciples interpreted their own development, to examine the historical data and documents of the movement from the standpoint of their sociological significance.

Self-understanding is extremely important. What the members of a religious group think of themselves, the way in which they interpret the events in their heritage, can tell us a great deal about a religious movement. Long ago the American sociologist, W. I. Thomas, set forth a principle which is relevant here. Said Thomas, "if men define situations as real, they are real in their consequences." Applied to the present object of interest, this means that what Disciples have defined as the meaning of their history has had important influences upon the subsequent development of that history. Men respond as much to the meaning which events have for them as they do to objective aspects of those events. We behave as members of a particular religious group, in part at least, in terms of how we interpret the heritage which we share, that is, in terms of how we see ourselves. What is more, it appears that self-understanding is relevant to some of the tensions and strains that beset any religious movement. The parties in disagreement appear to this observer in large part to be supporting conflicting definitions of the historical significance of their movement in the religious world.

Second, this study is designed as a contribution to the use of sociological and cultural concepts in the interpretation of some aspects of social change in a religious group. Speaking of the treatment of religion in sociological thought one interpreter, Kingsley Davis, writes, "In general, the present generation of social scientists appears to be neglecting the subject. It is especially on the systematic level—the theory of religion as a social phenomenon—that little work is being done."[2] Many sociologists, perhaps reflecting their own values in their choice of topics for research, have ignored religion. This is in part because they have developed an interest in other aspects of societal life, and in part, no doubt, because they feel that religion is not of crucial importance in understanding society. At any rate, the present generation of social scientists is not devoting any considerable attention to the subject of religion.

Studies of particular religious groups—sects, churches, cults, and the like—made from the perspective of sociology are not plentiful. One may find a few articles occasionally in the journals, and even rarely a book. There are, of course, numerous tracts and books which are designed to glorify and applaud the accomplishments of a particular group, but few studies, the chief object of which is to understand and describe, leaving the glorification and applause to others.

That religious groups, like any other group that is being studied, should be interpreted from as many perspectives as possible needs no argument. Whatever may throw any conceivable light upon the subject should be exhaustively explored. The sociological point of view is, to be sure, only one particular approach. It does not claim to be the only approach or even the ultimate one. But certainly it may be claimed that unless other approaches are supplemented and filled in with the sociological one, an incomplete understanding of a religious group emerges.

At this point it may be helpful to contrast the *earthly* and the *spiritual,* the *visible* and the *invisible* church. The sociologist, obviously, is concerned with the earthly and the visible church, and not, except indirectly, with its theological and mystical counterpart, the spiritual or invisible church. Moreover, it is not the business of the sociologist to inquire into truth or falsity in theological matters. The sociologist begins at the point of saying that, however things may be in the heavenly kingdom, however things appear theologically, they objectify or institutionalize themselves in ways that are visible and can be observed in the behavior of men.

Thus, whatever else it may be, the religious group is a group with a visible, observable, earthly history. The sect, church, cult, or religious group is a human social institution; it has a *natural,* earthly history. As a human social institution the religious movement may be meaningfully studied and viewed in exactly the same way as other social institutions. A significant contribution to the understanding of a religious movement can be made by viewing it as a social institution, as influencing and being influenced by the surrounding society and culture.

Much evidence will be cited from the historical documents of Disciples to show how pervasive has been the influence of the United States' society and culture upon this religious movement. Indeed, a great deal of what is said will tend to support a generalization made by the rural sociologists Kolb and DeBrunner. "The church has had to submit to social and economic factors more often than it has conquered them."[3]

However, no implication that the influence was all one way is intended. Perhaps it will be a healthy and needed corrective to the extravagant claims that are often made for the influence of religious belief and life to have it pointed out that religious life is often unable to withstand the pressure of its mileu. Yet this is not at all to deny that religious groups do influence their social environment and act as agents in changing it.

Third, the study which follows is conceived as a contribution to the present and growing emphasis upon the development of a genuine ecumenical church, and the barriers which stand in the way of its realization. The most far-seeing of our modern religious leaders are beginning explicitly and urgently to recognize what sociologists and church historians have been saying for some time—that nontheological factors have often caused or perpetuated divisions in the churches which would not or need not have occurred otherwise.[4]

It will no longer do for churches to claim exemption from the operation of psychological, social, and cultural factors, for the more we claim to be exempt from the influence of these factors, the more we reveal the operation of these factors in our particular case. The search for nontheological factors in division is of paramount importance to the future of the ecumenical church. It would not be extravagant to claim that unless we pursue this inquiry faithfully, speedily, and critically, the ecumenical church *has* no future. The self-understanding of a religious movement, of which we spoke earlier, is the basis for that humility without which mutual understanding is impossible, and without mutual understanding there can be no ecumenical church.

CONTENTS

CHAPTER I

The Formative Years of a Religious Movement: the Sect-to-Denomination Process

Quite a number of . . . . [denominational church histories] bear a strong resemblance, as interpreters of the religious history of America, to a map of the Baltimore & Ohio as done by the cartographers of the Pennsylvania system. Other churches are seen through a glass darkly, if at all. To Methodists, Francis Asbury is shown as the "lonely horseman"—so lonely, in fact, that the impression is gained that he was the only saddlebag preacher who ever crossed the Appalachian mountains. But another volume will demonstrate that it was Alexander Campbell who, single-handed, evangelized what has become the Middle West. Many such denominational histories call to mind the immortal comment of Mr. Dooley on Theodore Roosevelt's book about the Rough Riders. Mr. Dooley remarked that it should have been called "Alone in Cuba."[1]

Halford E. Luccock, when he wrote the above paragraph, apparently had in mind that many denominational histories are written from a more than slight ethnocentric bias. Sociologically, his idea expresses also the fact that denominational histories are often written without an adequate understanding of the cultural and social forces which bring certain leaders to the fore, and which motivate the formation of new groups and institutions. This has been apparent to students in the field for some time.

A basic frame of reference for any sociological study of a religious group is the realization that "The effort to distinguish churches primarily by reference to their doctrine and to approach the problem of church unity from a purely theological point of view appeared to be a procedure so artificial and fruitless that . . . (one) . . . is compelled to turn from theology to history, sociology, and ethics for a more satisfactory account of denominational differences."[2] Theology and religious belief, while they cannot be interpreted entirely from an economic or political point of view, certainly cannot be dissociated from the social circumstances which condition and influence them. There is no question but that social traditions, the basic cultural heritage of a people, as well as economic interest, have an influence in the determination of what a group regards as religious truth.

Religion, to be sure, may supply the energy, the goal, and the motivation of sect-formation, but "social factors no less decidedly supply the occasion, and determine the form the religious dynamic will take. Were spiritual energies to develop unchecked they would scarcely issue in the formation of such denominations as now compose Christianity."[3] To argue that the present groups which make up Christendom are, each in its own way, the result of profound spiritual forces, with which social and economic influences have had little or nothing to do, is, at the present stage of our knowledge, to seem somewhat naïve.

One way to discover the ways in which social, economic, and political factors have influenced the origins and development of religious movements is to employ the concepts of the sect, denomination, and church, as these have been refined by various sociologists.

Troeltsch begins with a twofold division, classifying religious groups into "churches" and "sects." The church, as J. M. Yinger suggests in his summary of the Troeltsch tradition, "is a religious body which recognizes the strength of the secular world, and . . . accepts the main elements in the existing balance of power and thus attempts to remain in a position where it can get a hearing. It is built therefore on compromise; it is mobile and adaptive; it claims universality. . . . A church tries to organize the forces of society on whatever level they are found and to control them for its own stated ends."[4]

The sect, on the other hand, places a distinct emphasis upon a literal obedience to the "commands" of the Synoptic Gospels. It is a small, radical, voluntary type of association, invariably involving the so-called lower classes, that is to say, groups of people who have been left behind in the struggle for wealth and social position, and whose needs have not been met by the existing religious and other institutions. There is here a noticeable strain of individualistic perfectionism and asceticism, though very often this is oriented toward a correction of the social "wrongs" which the disinherited group may have suffered. The sect tends to be either hostile or indifferent to the state, and shows a marked dislike for the ecclesiastical "powers that be." Troeltsch gives a list of the characteristic traits of the sect, which includes lay Christianity, personal achievement in ethics and religion, radical fellowship of love, religious equality and brotherly love, the separation of religion from the economic struggle by laying stress on the ideal of poverty and frugality, a dislike of official spiritual guides and theologians, and finally a recurring appeal to the New Testament and the "primitive church."

Yinger, interpreting the Troeltsch view in terms of "power struggle," points out that there are two modal types of the "church," based on a distinction concerning the relative achievement of universality. First, there is the group which has a relatively high degree of success in realizing universality, best illustrated by the Catholic church of the thirteenth century. Second, there are other groups, less successful in achieving universality, but still to be classified as churches, because they accept the existing societal structure. Such churches fail to get universality because of such factors as geographic and class boundaries, and the failure to incorporate at least a token representation of sectarian elements. They are thoroughly conventional and respectable, and thus have gone far along the road to compromise. Here one might mention Lutheranism, and, to a lesser degree, the Church of England, and Methodism.

One can establish a similar differentiation for the sect type. At one extreme is the purely personal, unorganized religious experience of a group whose only ties at the time are a common religious need and feeling. At the other extreme is the group which in the second and third generations undergoes a profound transformation leading it to take on some of the characteristics of the church type. There is a recognizable tendency for sects to undergo this shift in emphasis in almost every instance. Such a shift is "partly simply a matter of age, partly the result of a different interpretation of the best way to meet the dilemma which faces the search for influence, and partly a reflection of a changing socio-economic position in the group. These are closely related. . . . The history of the church abounds with the stories of radical sect groups which shifted gradually into respectable denominations or churches."[5]

The religious group, in its search for influence, faces a very real dilemma. If it insists upon too great conformity to the religious ideal, the chances of persecution or neglect by the secular society are great. Yet if it does not make demands on behalf of its ideals, the group can have no influence. The attempt to deal with the question of how to gain influence and still hold to the group's ideals produces many changes in the original character of a religious movement.

H. Richard Niebuhr characterizes the sect and the church in somewhat the same manner, though he states the contrast in slightly different terms. The church, he says, is the *inclusive* type, which tends to think of itself as the educational and sacramental agency for an entire parish, community, or nation; the sect is an *exclusive* type, which tends to have rather rigid requirements for membership, and concentrates upon missionary and disciplinary functions. The church, according to Niebuhr, is either "organically related to the state or closely identified in practice with the established social order," whereas the sect is usually "critical of or antagonistic to prevailing political and economic institutions."[6]

The key to the church's relation to the general community mores is accommodation, but the sect has a tendency to be rigoristic. The church emphasizes a religious doctrine of salvation, and the participation of individuals in the means of grace, through its offices, but for the sect, conduct rather than minute points of doctrine and faith is the most important consideration. This means that the church requires a priestly and professional leadership, together with some kind of hierarchy of organization; in contrast to this, the sect favors a lay leadership and a democratic type of organization.

Still within the same general framework of explanation and definition is Robert E. Park's characterization of the sect in sociological terms. His view is, however, couched more in terms of the in-group, out-group relationship, the "over-againstness" of the sect type. A sect, says Park,

> is a religious organization that is at war with the existing mores. It seeks to cultivate a state of mind and establish a code of morals different from that of the world about it, and for this it claims divine authority . . . . It invariably seeks to set itself off in contrast with the rest of the world. The simplest and most effective way to achieve this is to adopt a peculiar form of dress and speech . . . . Persecution tends to dignify and sanctify all the external marks of the sect to maintain them.[7]

The sect, moreover, develops under recognizable and definite conditions, which are similar for all institutions like it; it has a sociological structure predetermined by characteristic processes and direction of development. In short, the sect has a natural history which can be described and explained sociologically.

> Sects have their origin in social unrest to which they give direction and expression in forms and practices that are largely determined by historical circumstances; movements which were at first inchoate impulses and aspirations gradually take form; policies are defined, doctrine and dogmas formulated; and even-

tually an administrative machinery and efficiencies are developed to carry into effect policies and purposes.[8]

Park also mentions the accommodative process which, as we have seen, appears in other views. When the sect accommodates itself to the rival organizations in the field at the time, that is, when it becomes tolerant and tolerated, it moves toward the denomination type. It is important to notice that the sect is involved in a rather clearly defined process. Each sect begins as the "first crystallization of every doctrine." An idea, if it is destined to have any influence at all, is "predestined to define itself in the more specific form of the sect, to become later a party, a school, or a church."[9] All faiths and beliefs pass through this sectarian phase, whether they are political, intellectual, or religious. For our purposes it is significant that in modern times "religious sects and social movements have had their origin in crowd excitements and spontaneous mass movements. The very names which have been applied to them . . . suggest . . . their origin in ecstatic or expressive crowds."[10]

Elmer T. Clark, in discussing the concept of the sect, lays a predominant emphasis upon the economic factor in its rise. Thus, he says,

> In the background of nearly all sects there is a strong economic influence. These groups originate mainly among the religiously neglected poor, who find the conventional religion of their day unsuited to their social and psychological needs . . . . Finding themselves ill at ease in the presence of an effete and prosperous bourgeoisie, their emotional natures unsatisfied by middle-class complacency, their economic problems disregarded by those who have no such problems to meet, and their naive faith and simple interpretations smiled upon by their more cultured fellows, the poor and ignorant revolt and draw apart into groups which are more congenial. They elevate the necessities of their class—frugality, humility, and industry—into moral virtues, and regard as sins the practices they are debarred from embracing.[11]

Wesley, who was himself involved in the origin and growth of one of the most influential religious groups of our time, the Methodists, recognized the importance of the economic factor in the process of religious revival. "I fear," he said, "wherever riches have increased, the essence of religion has decreased in the same proportion. Therefore I do not see how it is possible, in the nature of things, for any revival of true religion to continue long. For religion must necessarily produce both industry and frugality, and these cannot but produce riches. But as riches increase, so will pride, anger, and love of the world. . . ."[12] The inference from this rather pessimistic view that the religious group, at its birth, carries the seed of its own destruction, would seem to be that in order to be truly religious one must be poor. One may doubt the absolute truth of this, but it is evident that Wesley was perhaps more prophetic than even he himself realized. The unquestioned truth to which he points is that as members of a group rise in the social and economic scale, their religious expression may become more opulent and ornate, but by the same token less effective as a motivating life force.

Yet we must be careful not to assert a narrow economic interpretation of history. The complex ways in which beliefs, habits, and customs are intertwined in human behavior do not lend support to exclusively economic explanations.

In the rise of the sect, there is also an evident "spiritual" need. Emotions are given free rein, and this is somehow associated with the divine agency. The particular views of the group are taken with an almost fanatical seriousness, in which is involved the belief that the group is the true beloved of God and protector of true religion. It is at this point that the sectarian mind views the cause of disaffection as theological, concerned with the discovery of new "truth," or with the alleged neglect by the established churches of what is regarded as maintaining the "integrity of the Bible," or "restoring the church to its Apostolic purity." In the group which we propose to examine, this restoration motif is of the utmost importance.

The significance of the second generation in the development of the sect toward its inevitable status as a "denomination" is not overlooked by Clark.[13] With this second generation the need for indoctrination of the young in the cardinal principles of the movement arises; but those who must be *taught* the doctrines and practices (because they do not have access to the original experiences or revelations which gave them birth) hardly ever hold to these beliefs with the same fervor and devotion as those who first enunciated them. When thrift and industry begin to enable some of the group to rise economically, some of the reasons for the sectarian revolt tend to disappear, and what the fathers condemned, the children embrace, at first tentatively and with some misgivings, but later with enthusiasm. The sect, in short, becomes a denomination.

The economic influence operates directly or indirectly in a number of ways to help effect this transformation. To begin with, an increase in wealth tends to lessen the appeal of frontier simplicity. When the process has gone far enough, expensive and elaborate church edifices begin to appear, and the people who worship in them are better dressed, expect more dignified services, with less emotional sermons, music of professional quality, and highly trained ministers. The class distinctions of the secular world enter into the gates of the Most High, which means that the social life of the church accommodates more completely with the things of "this world."

In the second place, when the group grows in influence and numbers, this increasing "bigness" tends to undermine the democratic spirit, and to make necessary an increasing complexity of ecclesiastical organization. A need arises for general officers, various boards to handle the many enterprises of the church and supervise its programs, and a money-raising mechanism to get funds for the benevolent activities. Some kind of hierarchy, whether official or unofficial, is needed to be responsible for getting things done efficiently. This means ecclesiastical politics, and perhaps jealousies and distrust. A good many people, remembering the simplicity of the beginnings of the group, may be uncomfortable in the presence of all this machinery, which is certainly not "authorized" by the Scriptures; this may be the source of unrest, and could conceivably lead later to the formation of a new sect.

In the third place, when the members of a group begin to reach a higher educational level, this tends to lead to modifications in items of doctrine and belief, in type of religious expression regarded as "normal" and approved, and in ways of "reaching" people, in order to bring them into the group. Symptomatic of this is the controversy over "fundamentalism" and "modernism," which reached its heights in the battle over evolution. So furious did this become that one can almost imagine the limp, defenseless body of Charles Darwin being dragged from one end of the so-called Bible Belt to the other. It is even reported that one minister held up a copy of *The Origin of the Species* during his sermon, and fulminated as follows, "I have been preaching against this book for twenty years, and thank God I have never read a word of it!"

Be that as it may, however, the obvious fact is that with an increasing number of educated parishioners sitting in the pews on a Sunday morning, the old emotional, "speak as the spirit moves you" type of preaching will not do. As the sect moves toward the denomination, its ministers and leaders no longer boast of their humble origins and strict adherence to the literal words of Scripture, but they increase in sophistication and training. The older emphasis upon a "conversion experience" as a prerequisite to becoming a church member quietly slips away; it is replaced by a more dignified and, indeed, less embarrassing appeal to the social and cultural, as well as spiritual, advantages of belonging. The attempt to reach the children by constant Bible reading is replaced by an emphasis upon the latest and most "effective methods of religious education," which, like their counterpart in the secular realm, are "pupil-centered," rather than "content-centered."

Clark has provided us with an interesting and suggestive classification of sects in American society. Since the group we are studying falls within one of these categories, it will be helpful to list these briefly.

1. *The Pessimistic Sects.* These are typical groups of the disin-

herited, in final despair of obtaining through social processes the benefits they seek. . . .

2. *The Perfectionist Sects.* These seek holiness, personal perfection of life, or freedom from the temptations and "desires of the flesh." . . .

3. *The Charismatic Sects.* These bodies seek "gifts," the "spirit of prophecy," the "blessing," and spiritual enduements of various kinds. They are perfectionists of a radical order.

4. *The Communistic Sects.* These groups withdraw from "the world" into colonies where they secure the social approval which is denied them elsewhere and where they engage in economic experiments. . . .

5. *Legalistic Sects.* . . . A group of sects which stress certain rules, objective forms, observances, or "things" which can be definitely performed as essential to the true religion. . . . These sects derive their rites or taboos from some portion of the Bible and usually look upon themselves as the . . . restorers of primitive Christianity. . . .[14]

6. *Egocentric Sects.* These have physical comfort, personal exhilaration, and freedom from pain, disease, and ennui as their objectives. . . .

7. *Esoteric Sects.* These are devotees of the mystic. They espouse doctrines into which one needs to be initiated.[15]

This classification of the sects in America centers upon the most obvious goals and purposes toward which the given group directs its efforts, and in this manner is useful for the task of social analysis.

We should remember, however, that no group fits any such classification completely and exactly. Many of the sect-type groups are complex in origin and purposes, and cannot be adequately understood in this abstract fashion. Clark's classifications are nevertheless valuable and they give us general pictures of the sect phenomenon in America. There are clear-cut examples in our history of each of the types given.

A similar caution must be observed in attempting to distinguish between the sect and the church or denomination. Clark's point here is well taken. "Sectarianism is a matter of spirit rather than of form, organization, or size, hence it is not possible to closely define the term 'sect.' . . . In view of the gradual passing of the sect into a church, a process which rarely begins until the second generation and may require several generations for its completion, it is plain that there is no clear-cut line between the two. A definition is accordingly difficult or impossible to formulate in terms which include all the elements of the sect and exclude all those of the church; . . . All . . . claim to be churches and all repudiate the term sect as applied to themselves."[16]

Bearing this in mind, it is useful to note that there are certain general characteristics, one or more of which invariably are to be observed in the orgin and development of the sect. Clark lists several of these, which may also be found in most of the other literature on the subject. The first two of these characteristics have figured prominently in our discussion thus far. First, the sects are refuges for the poor, for those left behind in the economic and social struggle. Second, the sects are usually characterized by a Puritan morality. This is, in certain respects, conditioned by a lack of financial resources which prevents many thing from being called virtues, since the sect members could not affort them.

In addition to these traits of the sect, five others should be briefly mentioned. One of these is that the sect is often a refuge for the emotionally starved. Many persons do not find in so-called "respectable" churches the kind of emotional outlet they find is necessary for them. They are eager to find some place which will answer their "spiritual need," or fill the void in their lives. The sect, then, in this respect is a form of social catharsis. Another of the marks of the sect is the craving for objectivity. The desire for freedom is so much a part of the cultural configuration in American society that it is simply assumed that everyone desires freedom with a great burning passion. This, as Clark points out, is simply not true. On the contrary, what many persons want is some kind of outward observance or rite which they can perform, and not have to think too much about it. In the group which we are studying this craving for objectivity can be seen in its negative aspect in the formula, "where the Scriptures speak, we speak; where the Scriptures are silent, we are silent."

The term "conservatism" affords still another way of describing the sect. It is really remarkable that so many groups have been started which propose to restore the ancient order of things or to return to the faith once and for all handed down to the saints. At the beginning of many sects there is an evident suspicion of things modern in faith and belief, and a confident, sometimes militant, attitude which says that the old ways are the best. In the sects with millenarian ideas we note the further characteristic of an interest in the bizarre and the fantastic. Of course, to the persons accepting this sectarian tradition the matter is deadly serious. The attempt to find all the elements of modern history in Daniel and Revelation and to identify the Beast numbered 666 with whomever is the most disliked leader of the day is to these people a question of the utmost significance.

The last trait of the sect is one which is basic to the attempt to study the religious group sociologically. When we examine the history of almost any of the sects, we find that with the passage of time they go through the cycle of accommodation until finally they are really churches or denominations and not sects. This has run through our whole consideration of the nature of the sect, and it is certainly one of the key notions to be kept in mind. What is involved is that the sect, if it is successful in maintaining its existence, tends to lose the distinctive principles which gave it birth, that is, which set apart the group from others in the first place, and to take on many of the traits of the surrounding society and culture.

A useful typology of religious movements has also been developed by Howard Becker.[17] Four basic types are suggested. The first, the ecclesia, is basically similar to Troeltsch's concept of the *church*. In its fullest development, the ecclesia attempts to amalgamate itself with the state and the dominant classes. One does not *join* the ecclesia; he is *born into* it. The ecclesia is a social organization which attaches a great deal of importance to the means of grace, the official system of doctrine and organization. By the very nature of its aims, the ecclesia is committed to a policy of adjusting its ethics to the ethics of the surrounding culture.

Sharply contrasting with the ecclesia is the sect. Among the characteristics of the sect are its smallness, the elective nature of membership, its exclusiveness, its emphasis upon rigid moral demands, the tendency to demand some particular kind of "religious experience" as a condition of membership. In addition the sect frequently rejects an official clergy. The sect, in its relation to the larger culture in which it exists, prefers isolation, when possible, to compromise. This attitude, in its extreme form, leads to refusal of participation in government and to pacifism. The sect, therefore, may be characterized as separatist and semiascetic, but these traits do not appear in marked degree in some of the sects.

Recognizing that the sect-to-ecclesia phenomenon is a process, and that there are degrees of movement along the way, Becker points out that the *denomination* is a sect in an advanced stage of development. With the disappearance of the self-conscious fervor of the early sectarian phase, and the coming of the second and third generations the denomination, in defining the religious experience and organization, tends to make compromises. Age itself brings compromises. Any denomination is historically and doctrinally a sect in an advanced stage of development toward the ecclesia type. This, however, does not imply that the cycle must of necessity be completed, that is, every sect must finally become an ecclesia. It may imply that no sect remains simply a sect, because no religious group has ever been, or ever can be exempt from the natural and sociological history of an institution.

Becker introduces a fourth type, the *cult*. This type, while not important particularly in terms of the group under discussion here, has many representatives in contemporary American society. This is the religious situation in which the tendencies toward private, personal religion come to their fullest development. The structure of the cult is quite amorphous, and loose-textured. The ultimate goal is not the development of the organization itself, but the achievement of purely personal ecstatic experience. Thus, this type verges on the situation described by Troeltsch under the rubric of *mystics.* Emotional satisfaction is striven for here, and the emphasis is upon the needs of the ego. Curent examples of this type include Spiritualism, Unity, and Buchmanism. In one sense, the cult represents the extreme expression of the sect type. The cult develops the private, personal aspects of sectarian religious expression in an extreme form.

One final word concerning all the views set forth above must be added. The sect-to-church (or ecclesia) phenomenon is a *process.* The types are not rigidly divided off from each other. The religious situation should be viewed as a process in which new sects are being formed at any given moment of history, to meet needs unsatisfied by the contemporary religious organizations or groups. These sects, in turn, develop in response to their involvement with the extrareligious culture. If they grow and prosper, they move along the continuum from the sect end toward the church end, in the ways described above. If the sect does not do this it sooner or later disappears. The midpoint of this development might be called denomination.

In a highly significant treatment of sect and church, Liston Pope argues, "Though many other factors underlie its emergence, the sect arises as a schism from a parent ecclesiastical body, either a Church or a previous sect. It then becomes a distinct and independent type of religious organization but moves, if it survives, increasingly toward the Church type."[18] This movement toward the church type of religious organization, though it appears at first sight to be parallel to a movement of socio-economic class, is not a class movement, if by this we mean that changes in sect *depend upon* changes in the economic class, as a class.

Pope has carefully described the sect-to-church process in somewhat the following way. As a sect gains adherents, and thus appears to be increasingly successful, it begins to reach out for a greater influence in society, this "greater influence" being defined in terms of whatever interests the group most. What happens eventually is that the sect accommodates gradually to the surrounding culture. In this process, the group loses some of its adherents who are estranged from the culture. But, also, it attracts an increasing number of people who enjoy the cultural and economic privileges of the society.

In any sect, there are likely to be a few members who prosper economically. If and when this happens, these few either leave the group as their economic status improves or else they help to make over the group in keeping with their changing position. Thus, the position of a denomination with respect to how far it is along the scale from sect to church, tends to follow the economic fortunes of its more influential members. Further, the sect-becoming-church either raises its membership from childhood, finds new members from groups to which its approach appeals, or it declines in membership.

Pope is careful to point out that the sect is not always aware that what it is doing is striving to gain greater control over its cultural environment, and that in this striving it modifies its own religious character. This point is quite important, when we remember the tendency of sect members to deny that they are a sect. Yet the increasing contact with the larger society outside the religious group is forced upon the sect. For the sect cannot develop merely its religious aspect, paying no attention to anything else. Just as the sex impulse alone could not sustain the family as an institution, so the interest in religion cannot sustain, by itself, the religious institution. "The religious experience is not synonymous with life on the earth, and imperatives arising from mundane relations reshape perspectives and condition religious association as time goes on."[19]

As the new group grows, it begins to compare itself with other religious groups and to regard them as rivals. Finally, as rivalry increases, "each seeks to outdistance the others—no longer simply in religious possessions but in terms that the entire society accepts and can understand, which are, by definition, qualities that characterize a Church rather than a sect."[20]

One might, for example, mention the Christian Church in Plainville about which the men who solicited funds for the building said, "Let's build something that'll make that Methodist Church look like a woodshed."[21]

Pope, in setting forth the specific aspects of the movement from sect to church, suggests twenty-one points, each of which indicates a facet of the process.

This movement is:

1. From propertyless to property-owning membership.
2. From economic poverty to economic wealth, e.g., value of church property, minister's salary.
3. From the cultural periphery toward the cultural center of the community.
4. From *renunciation* or *indifference* toward the culture and social oranization to *affirmation* of it.
5. From personal religion to culture-centered religion.
6. From nonco-operation with other churches to co-operation.
7. From suspicion of rival sects to disdain toward all sects.
8. From a community excluding "unworthy members" to an institution embracing all who are socially compatible.
9. From an unspecialized, unprofessional ministry to a professional ministry.
10. From persecution to success and dominance psychology.
11. From voluntary, confessional bases of membership to ritual or social prerequisites only.
12. From principal concern with adult membership to equal concern for children.
13. From emphasis on evangelism to emphasis on religious education.
14. From stress on *future* in the next world to primary interest in *this* world.
15. From adherence to strict biblical standards to acceptance of general cultural standards.
16. From a high degree of congregational participation to delegation of responsibility to a few.

17. From fervor in worship to restraint.
18. From large number of religious services to regular services at stated intervals.
19. From "leadings of the Spirit" to fixed order of worship and administration.
20. From "folk hymns" to stately hymns of the liturgical tradition.
21. From emphasis on religion at home to delegation of responsibility to church officials.[22]

With the use of these characteristics it is possible to place a given religious group relatively in the scale from sect to church. The use of such a measuring rod is not, of course, exact in any quantitative sense, but it serves to emphasize that the sect-to-church phenomenon is a dynamic process, and that a given religious group may show some more sectlike traits and in other traits be more churchlike.

The most recent research on the sect-to-church process has indicated that the denomination is not the only alternative form which the religious movement may take, once it moves beyond the sect stage. J. Milton Yinger has suggested that a sect may, instead of developing into a denomination, become an *established sect*. He sees the need for postulating this type in order to account for certain facts of the current religious scene. For instance, the differences between the Methodists and Quakers in midtwentieth-century America are evident, yet both groups began as sectarian protests. An adequate theory must account for these differences. Such a theory is not provided by attempting to account for the differences in terms of the social mobility of the groups. Both Methodists and Quakers have moved up in socio-economic status.

Yinger advances the alternative hypothesis that the differences between two such groups must be accounted for in terms of the nature of the original sectarian protest which they represent. Here there is a crucial difference between the denomination and the established sect.

Those sects will tend to develop into denominations which, in the first instance, emphasized problems of individual anxiety and sin, those that are primarily efforts to reduce burdens of confusion and guilt. . . . (S)ects will tend to develop into established sects whose original concern was predominantly with the evils of society. . . . A sect will become a denomination instead of an established sect if the protest it represents can readily be absorbed into the dominant religious stream without a serious challenge to the secular social structure and without the necessity for a reorganization of the religious pattern.[23]

The established sect preserves more of the sense of isolation from the world, and stronger feelings of rejection of the values represented outside the group than does the denomination. This isolation and rejection tend to remain despite the changing socio-economic status of members of the group. The established sect represents a type of religious group which has not moved quite as far in the direction of the church type as has the denomination.

Harold Pfautz, in a further attempt to refine these concepts, has designated the *institutionalized sect* as an alternative type of religious group to the denomination and church, growing from the original sect or cult.[24] The institutionalized sect has become large enough that it cannot maintain the original intimacy of the sect, but because of the operation of a kind of selective recruitment it tends to be made up of people who think quite similar thoughts and take similar stands on the issues the group faces. The conflict with the larger society remains, but it has now become structured and institutionized, with emphasis on legal and ceremonial forms of conflict. In many respects, as compared with the sect, the leadership has become "official," even though there may be little evidence of specific training for this leadership. The directives concerning common values and conduct in the group continue to be specific and explicit. Certain things are taken as settled once and for all. Individuals who do not subscribe to these directives are not likely to remain with the group. Since it is more widely distributed in the society, and has a more complex structure than the sect, the institutionalized sect can more readily survive crises, although Pfautz points out that it may also be weakened in this phase by schisms.

Joachim Wach distinguishes three sociological types of religious movement: the *ecclesiastical body,* which is similar to the *church* type of Troeltsch, and the *ecclesia* of Becker; the *independent body,* which has most of the characteristics of the *denomination* (for instance, it is reserved toward, and critical of the state, but does not withdraw completely from the state); and lastly, the *sect,* the examples of which show it to be against the practices of the ecclesiastical bodies and the denominations, and to have a very strong sense of in-group feeling.[25]

The concepts of the sect, the denomination, and the church, as these have been developed by various sociologists, are now before us. In subsequent chapters, we shall make use of the basic documents of the movement known as Disciples of Christ to demonstrate the applicability of the sect-to-church concept to the history of this American religious movement. But before doing this we need to sketch the context of religion on the American frontier of the early nineteenth century, for Disciples of Christ are children of the frontier, and they have not entirely forgotten their ancestors, nor are they ashamed of them.

CHAPTER II

Religion on the American Frontier: Where Men Are Men and Salvation Is Free

W. E. Garrison's title for a history of Disciples of Christ is significant. He called it *Religion Follows the Frontier.* As Garrison himself says,

The significance of this body lies in the fact that it is a typical case of a group originating on the frontier, embodying in its first period the intellectual and cultural characteristics of the frontier, and gradually undergoing modifications of attitude, structure, and interests with the passing of the frontier stage, the developing economic, social, and cultural life of its environment, and the urbanization and sophistication of what had been a simple and rural society.[1]

The history of Disciples of Christ shows the evidences of the transformation from "sect" to "denomination." This change was due largely to what was happening in American society and culture. What has happened in the case of Disciples has also occurred with other groups, and to supply the context for the events in such a history is to tell again the familiar story of America's tumultuous history: of the growth of manufacturing and industry, which is the story of the change from Jefferson's America to the America of the Fords, Rockefellers, and J. P. Morgans; of the coming of railroads, the clearing of forests, the blanketing of prairies with farms, the rise of the cities. Disciples have never gained as great a following in the cities as have some other groups. They were nevertheless affected by all the changes which altered the total life.

One fact must be kept constantly in mind. Disciples of Christ were born on the frontier. A group which comes into being under such conditions never entirely outgrows its heritage. The ideals and attitudes of the frontier persist in many areas of American life besides church groups—politics for example—so this should not seem strange. Without seeing Disciples growing up in a frontier context it is impossible to understand them either adequately or correctly. The frontier, then, is the place where we must begin our study.

In 1893 Frederick Jackson Turner read a paper before the American Historical Society, on "The Significance of the Frontier." Since then it has been clear that America cannot be understood without considering that for many decades we had an open frontier. A number of historians have in recent years pointed out that Turner may have exaggerated the influence of the frontier on the course of American history. Yet when all the criticisms have been taken into account, the importance of the frontier for understanding much of American history remains. So the statement from Turner's paper which follows does not seem to overstate the case.

> Behind institutions, behind constitutional forms and modifications, lie the vital forces that call these organs into life and shape them to meet changing conditions. The peculiarity of American institutions is the fact that they have been compelled to adapt themselves to the changes of an expanding people—to the changes involved in crossing a continent, in winning a wilderness.[2]

Disciples of Christ may certainly be said to have adapted themselves to the changes of an expanding people—to a great extent at least) and they were part and parcel of the winning of the wilderness.

The frontier had an important effect upon the character of religious organization in the United States. We may then ask, what were some of the characteristics of this frontier which contributed to the rise of many sects? How did the evangelical groups win the West? To begin with, people on the frontier, even though many might be so inclined, did not have the opportunity to participate in church activities which they may have had in their former communities. Churches and preachers on the frontier were few. Life in this wild country made an occasional gathering to hear a traveling preacher more of a social affair than a religious activity. Indeed, many religious meetings could be classified with other occasions when the loneliness of the frontier was relieved, such as the cabin raising and the husking bee. Even weddings and funerals were the excuse for a "moral holiday," and any gathering became a kind of festivity.

Frontier life also had an effect upon the kind of preaching that could be done and the methods that could be followed in reaching the people. The frontiersman was more concerned with just staying alive than with living out his days in dignity. He was not much interested in intellectual excursions or theological subtleties. If he were to listen, the preacher would have to speak his language. What Turner quotes as a remark about the political ideals of the West applies also to religion.

> Said one of their rude petitions for statehood: "Some of our fellow-citizens may think we are not able to conduct our affairs and consult our interest; but if our society is rude, much wisdom is not necessary to supply our wants, and a fool can sometimes put on his clothes better than a wise man can do it for him."[3]

People on the frontier saturated both their religion and their politics with emotion. They may not have understood John Locke, and they certainly had never heard of Abelard, but they felt deeply about what religion they had, and about the democracy they had achieved. To be sure, in such a society there were many who sat in the seats of scoffers and even did some bragging about their irreligion. Not a few professed to be infidels, and some even swore they would keep the Sabbath day out of the West. But there was much genuine religious feeling on the frontier; it only awaited the coming of leaders who knew how to speak to the needs of the people living under these wild conditions.

Among the serious-minded of the new settlers were those who viewed the frivolity and boisterousness of frontier social gatherings with alarm. They recognized the need for a preoccupation with the hard task of getting a living in the wilderness, but they also wanted to continue the religious observances they had known in the East. The majority of the migrants who went west did not come from the denominations which by the last decades of the eighteenth century had achieved wealth and social position. Of the leading groups, it was the Presbyterians alone who had numerous members among the migrants. Many Baptists moved into Kentucky, Tennessee, and north of the Ohio River. Indeed, so many Baptists moved out of Virginia that Robert Semple called Kentucky "the cemetery of Virginia Baptist preachers."

The fact that the two most privileged religious groups, the Congregationalists and the Episcopalians, did not cultivate the fertile fields of the West was to have a great influence upon the future of religion in America. That these two groups had apparently ceased to be missionary-minded may be related to two facts: the decreasing influence of religion as a cultural force in colonial society, and the comfortable respectability which the people of these groups had achieved.

Be that as it may, the fact is that these more privileged groups gave the West to the more zealous Baptists and Methodists, and to some extent to the Presbyterians. There seems to be a general agreement among the writers who have dealt with this period that the best job of evangelizing the early frontier West was done by the Methodists. The Presbyterians made a great attempt to advance their church in the West. It would seem that they ought to have done much better than they did. After all, a great many of the pioneers who first crossed the Alleghenies were rugged, determined Scotch-Irish Presbyterians. Two features upon which the Presbyterian church continued to insist appear to have worked against its efforts to win converts on the frontier: its insistence upon an educated clergy, and the intellectualized preaching which resulted.

The Methodist circuit rider has become almost a legend in American history. This is no accident.

> This itinerant, riding horseback, letting his hair grow down to the shoulders in frontier fashion, using one-gallus suspenders, speaking the common language was one of the pioneers own kind. He was a natural democrat even though in a pulpit, a man of God with a message for every sinner. . . . No hardship was too severe. The worst weather the Ohio Valley man could witness was described by saying, "There's nobody out today but crows and Methodist preachers."[4]

The Methodist circuit rider, if he did nothing else, managed to reach the people because he was willing to go anywhere that they were, and did not wait for a meeting to be assembled. He went to people's homes and spoke to them wherever anyone would listen. The circuit rider, in effect, carried his church in his saddlebag.

The Presbyterians were handicapped in part in the rigidity of their creed and polity. This had something to do with the ultimate rise of Disciples of Christ. The Methodists, almost as if they breathed the frontier in with air, were young and enthusiastic. They emphasized doctrines and teachings that were attuned to the character of a free wilderness democracy. Free will, free grace, and individual responsibility—these went more harmoniously with the frontiersman's life than did Presbyterian predestination and election. A stiff, technical theology seemed out of place on the frontier; it was too different from the atmosphere of everyday life. Such an approach could not touch the hearts of the pioneers, who *felt* their religion.

After all, as Turner and many other writers have pointed out, many of the men who went West were men of boundless optimism. They felt that on the frontier their individual efforts would be sooner or later rewarded. If they were sinners, this was not an irrevocable condition, as the Methodists soon taught them. If conditions were hard, they would sooner or later get better. The attitudes bred on the frontier could not be confined within a rigid creed and intricate organization suited to older and more stable society.

American society was in frontier days, and is now, a mobile thing, constantly in flux. The ancient Greek philosopher Heraclitus, with his "everything is flux," would in certain respects have been at home in such a society. People were constantly picking up roots and moving to new places. Settled and stable institutions take time to develop, and it may be that the most important religious phenomenon on the early nineteenth century, revivalism, can be understood largely as a way of adapting religion to frontier conditions. Revivalism, like the rugged democracy of the wilderness, stressed the needs of the individual, and it meant that religion, without institutionalized methods and organization, could reach great numbers of people.

The Great Revival in the West cannot be understood without some reference to the low state of morality and religion just prior to its advent. The reports of immorality, gambling, and hard drinking in the West were not entirely exaggerated. William Warren Sweet observed that home-made whiskey was commonly served at social gatherings, and that church records on the frontier contain many accounts of church discipline on account of drunkenness. Those who wrote of life during the period of the last decade of the 1700's and the first decade of the 1800's mentioned such things frequently. Catherine Cleveland tells us,

> Many of the immigrants were men and women with no sense of moral responsibility. Criminals of all descriptions sought the new country where it was necessarily difficult to administer the law. Hard drinking and rough, degrading amusements formed the only recreation of the lower classes of society, and the lawless life of this element stamped many localities with a low moral tone.[5]

Furthermore, during the last years of the eighteenth century there had been an evident decline in church membership and religious interest. Apathy toward religion had set in, partly because there were no adequate facilities for its expression, and partly because the exigencies of life on the frontier had diverted men's minds to other, more pressing, things.

Freedom from family ties, church connections, and the influences and restraints of the community life of the Old World was an invitation to indulgences and loose ways of living. . . . By the end of the first third of the eighteenth century there were more unchurched people in the colonies in proportion to the population than was to be found anywhere in Christendom.[6]

This situation did not change as the years wore on and more people moved West.

This same condition has been described from another point of view by B. B. Tyler.

The moral and religious life of our fathers at the close of the eighteenth and beginning of the nineteenth centuries was very low. Unbelief in Jesus as the son of God, and in the Bible as a book of supernatural origin and divine character, and in what are esteemed by evangelical believers generally as the fundamental facts and truths of the Christian religion abounded. . . . The gospel was disregarded. . . .

It is said that in the year 1800 only one Congregational church in Boston remained loyal to the old faith. When the Rev. Dr. E. D. Griffin became pastor of the Park Street Church, in 1811, the current of thought and feeling against orthodoxy was so decided and intense that men went to hear him in disguise.[7]

What was true in the more settled areas was certainly more true on the frontier, where there was not an abundance of churches to remind people of the faith in which they had lost interest.

Conditions were ripe for revival. That seems apparent. This is largely an academic question, since a great revival did take place. Its main locus of operations was on the frontier. Many people may have lost interest in formal religious expression and organization, but the question, "What must I do to be saved?" was still very much a part of the intellectual or emotional capital of people living on the frontier. What was needed was some way to reach these people with an answer to this question which met their needs. This way was provided by the revival and its chief mechanism, the camp meeting.

Some of the religious leaders who went West were disturbed over the lack of interest in things spiritual which was everywhere apparent. The worldliness and increasing secularization of the people bothered them intensely. They began, therefore, to search for means to change this condition. The Great Revival was not, however, the result of carefully laid plans or a deliberate strategy; it came simply as the result of random, unplanned, spontaneous efforts of the preachers to break the shell of apathy and formal interest which prevented religion from being vital and real. Late in 1799 two brothers by the name of McGee—William, a Presbyterian, and John, a Methodist preacher—began having a series of special meetings in parts of Kentucky and Tennessee. Families, hearing of these meetings, started coming to them from what in those days was a great distance, and this meant that they had to camp there overnight. This apparently was the origin of the camp meeting.

The movement caught fire and began to spread over a wider area, with other preachers joining in conducting the meetings. Barton W. Stone, counted as one of the sources of the movement which later became Disciples of Christ, tells of his increasing interest in the excitement caused by the camp meetings. His reasons for this interest are significant.

> Things moved on quietly in my congregations and in the country generally. Apathy in religious society appeared everywhere to an alarming degree. . . . Having heard of the remarkable religious excitement in the south of Kentucky and Tennessee . . . I was very anxious to be among them, and early in the spring of 1801 went to the scene of a . . . prairie in Logan County, Kentucky. . . . With astonishment did I hear men, women, and children declaring the wonderful works of God and the glorious mysteries of the gospel. Their appeals were solemn, heart-penetrating, bold, and free.

The camp-meeting phenomenon was, to say the very least, a "remarkable religious excitement." The solid, refined citizens of a civilized society disapprove of such religious enthusiasm, because it often goes beyond the limits of decorum and polite forms. It is nevertheless possible for a whole community to be gripped by a wave of religious emotion. Such an occurrence is much less probable in an old and settled community, except perhaps among the disinherited, but in the rude environment of the frontier a flood of emotionalism is not at all unusual. Indeed,

> The very atmosphere of life in the wilderness . . ., the consciousness of danger, seen or unseen, the awful sense of human weakness in the presence of the mighty power that seemed to brood over the forest, rendered the mind susceptible to impressions, especially when ideas were presented with an enthusiasm that riveted the attention. An innate craving for excitement drew the people to the place that promised variety after the monotonous round of daily duty.[8]

The story of what actually went on in the Kentucky revival of about 1800, with which the names of Logan County and Cane Ridge are prominently associated, is one of the most fascinating in American history. It should not be thought, however, that such movements are unusual or peculiar to the Kentucky frontier. Cleveland mentions the fact that demoniacal possession, the witchcraft delusion and other periods of religious excitement are similar to this Great Revival. Davenport's study of "primitive traits in religious revivals" discusses the same phenomena in connection with a number of religious movements, including the Ghost Dance of the North American Indians.

What did go on at these meetings seems almost unbelievable, but the records establishing the facts appear to be incontrovertible. What Barton W. Stone saw at the Cane Ridge is typical of many reports.

> Many, very many, fell, . . . and continued for hours together in an apparently breathless and motionless state, sometimes for a few moments reviving and exhibiting symptoms of life by a deep groan or a piercing shriek or by a prayer for mercy most fervently uttered. After lying thus for hours . . . they would rise, shouting deliverance.

What was called the "bodily exercise" was to become a common event at these gatherings. It included falling to the ground, barking, dancing, and jerking.

What we have here is a real social contagion, almost irresistible in its effect. This is evidenced by the number of reports telling of persons who considered themselves above these extravagances and who came to the meetings to scoff and to ridicule, only to catch the "disease" themselves. One such story is this.

An intelligent deist[9] in the neighborhood of Cane Ridge . . . said to Mr. Stone, "I always thought before you were an honest man; but now I am convinced you are deceiving the people." Mr. Stone reported, "I viewed him with pity and mildly spoke a few words to him. Immediately he fell as a dead man, and rose no more until he confessed the Savior."[10]

Some may doubt Stone's power to work a miraculous conversion, but there is no reason to doubt the facts on which the story is based.

The Great Revival is in many respects a shocking and disgraceful chapter in our history. But this is not by any means the whole story. Granting all the worst that can be said about such mass contagion and irrational behavior, it remains true that the revival stimulated the religious life of the country and certainly had a part to play in the development of the West. No one knows, of course, the exact numbers of the people who took part in the bodily exercises and other regrettable happenings. Certainly, thousands of persons were deeply moved, and many were motivated to give religion a more prominent place in their lives. Not a few people could date their conversion from some revival meeting or other. Certainly the Great Revival put an end, at least for the moment, to the religious apathy which had overtaken the country.

One cannot overlook the fact that many persons who were seized by the contagion of the moment did not effect a permanent change in their lives, and probably many persons became disgusted and were from that time on revulsed by *any* religious emphasis. Yet the moral tone of many communities was undoubtedly raised, because people were urged to give time and thought to living according to "righteousness and godliness." B. B. Tyler's estimate is obviously too sweeping, and it claims much too much, but there is some truth in what he says

The permanent effects, from every point of view, were extensive, abiding, and in the highest degree salutary. The low plane of morals previously occupied by the people was abandoned. Infidelity received a permanent check. A distinctly religious phase of life was entered upon by entire communities. In all the churches formalism gave way to spiritual life and fervor.[11]

A serious controversy, one which was to have a direct bearing upon the origin of Disciples of Christ, developed in the Presbyterian church over the revival phenomena. The battle was so furious that it soon split the group into revivalists and antirevivalists. Those who were against the meetings wanted to maintain the established and more dignified forms of worship, and they were shocked at these rowdy meetings. Futhermore, they claimed, the revivalists' views are really subversive of ecclesiastical authority. They uphold for each convert an inner light of the spirit which can interpret the Scripture without benefit of any official guidance. This is a common left-wing, sectarian, Protestant view, which keeps cropping up whenever people are restless and dissatisfied with the old ways.

The so-called "regular" Presbyterians approved a mild and refined type of revivalism. They worked together with the Congregationalists under a "Plan of Union." What they wanted was a revival in which there was "no wildness and extravagance," where "the word of God distils upon the mind like gentle rain, and the Holy Spirit comes down like dew, diffusing a blessed influence all around."[12] This pale, Milquetoast version of the revival made little impression; it smacked too much of Calvinistic election and the smug aristocracy of the settled areas. The Great Revival was in part effective because it offered salvation to one and all.

"We urged upon the sinner to believe *now,* and receive salvation," said Barton W. Stone, speaking of the preaching emphasis in the revival meetings.

No previous qualification was required, or necessary, in order to believe in Jesus, and come to him—that if they were sinners, this was their divine warrant to believe in him and to come to him for salvation. . . . When we first began to preach these things, the people appeared as just awakened from the sleep of ages—they seemed to see for the first time that they were responsible beings, and that a refusal to use the means appointed, was a damning sin.[13]

In this context and in the emotional excitement of the revival the characteristic doctrines of Calvinism were almost ignored. Salvation was offered freely and without reservations. This was a development with important social significance. One may argue that such preaching emphasis was both cause and result of frontier religious conditions.

With such an atmosphere of freedom and simplicity, it is not surprising that new movements of various kinds should begin to spring up. What is strange, however, is that a great many of the leaders of these movements came to the common conviction that they knew what was wrong with the church, why it was so divided, and what simple steps should be taken to remedy the situation. Coming at the problem independently, a group of frontier religious leaders, whom W. E. Garrison calls "seekers for the pure and simple gospel" reached the conclusion that Protestantism was divided and ineffective because it had allowed speculative opinions to divert people from "plain Bible teaching." What is needed, they said, is to go back to the Bible and simply follow the divine patterns and commands given there, ruling out any and all "human opinions" as tests of faith or fellowship. The names usually associated with this movement are those of Elias Smith, Abner Jones, James O'Kelly, Rice Haggard, William Kincaide, Barton W. Stone, and Thomas and Alexander Campbell. These men were not all agreed upon the detailed purposes and methods of the proposed return to the Bible. Yet their general aims were similar. Most, if not all, of these names are unfamiliar. With the exception of the last three they are not especially important for our purposes. It is sufficient to note that it was in this context that Disciples of Christ began their existence.

Disciples, perhaps in a flush of self-consciousness, claimed to be a part of the Reformation, which had begun several centuries before. Isaac Errett, claiming a genuine place for Disciples in the heritage of the reformers, said,

> At one and another trumpet call of reformation, multitudes came forth from Babylon. . . . We inherit the blessed fruits of their labors. . . . As we embrace the chains they wore and take up the ashes from the altar-fires of spiritual freedom, we ask not whether these lofty heroes of the church militant, to whom we owe *our* heritage of spiritual freedom, may commune with us—but rather, if we are at all worthy to commune with them! . . . *Our reformation movement is the legitimate offspring of theirs.*[14]

This may perhaps be claiming too much, but it at least may be argued that the Disciples movement was the leftwing of the Reformation translated into American, and specifically frontier, language.

CHAPTER III

The New Reformation and the Sectarian Critique of the World

Disciples of Christ, as a religious movement, have undergone a transformation from sect toward denomination. This could have been predicted, had the tools of sociological analysis been then available. This is apparent, both from the "inner logic" of the group's existence, and from the influence of social environment upon any institution. Beginning with a certain set of presuppositions, Disciples of Christ involved themselves, as do all incipient institutions, in the making of a "system"; the more definite this system became, the more machinery was required to propagate and perpetuate it, and the more rigid became the free and simple principles of the founders. Here is one phase of the movement from sect to denomination.

The other phase of this development, the influence of the environment, refers to the reactions of the group to the social, economic, and intellectual changes accompanying the passing of the frontier. Both of these processes are important in the history of Disciples of Christ. But they are really a part of the "natural history" of an institution. These two phases, the inner and the outer, interact to effect the movement from sect to denomination, and the interaction involved is reciprocal.

In the year 1807 Thomas Campbell, a Presbyterian minister from Ahorey, in county Armaugh, Ireland, did what so many of the Scotch-Irish did at this time: he came to America. Shortly after his arrival he presented his papers to the Seceder Presbyterian Synod at Philadelphia, and was thereupon assigned as pastor in the presbytery of Chartiers, in Western Pennsylvania, with headquarters at Washington. Before long, he initiated a chain of events that was to provide another main source of the Disciples movement. The occasion was a trip which Thomas Campbell took through a sparsely populated section north of Pittsburgh, during the course of which he was to administer sacraments to the small groups of Presbyterians settled in the area.

Many persons, he discovered, were isolated from any church and were deprived of the ministrations of the Christian faith in any form. In one of his precommunion sermons, Thomas Campbell deplored the "party divisions" among the churches, which left so many people uncared for, and invited all those present to partake of the sacraments if they felt *they* were prepared. Such loose dealing with the sacrament of the Lord's Supper was too much for these strait-laced Seceder Presbyterians. When the word got back to the Synod, charges were brought against Campbell because, it was alleged, he "failed to inculcate strict adherence to the Church standard and usages, and had expressed his disapproval of some things in such standard and of the uses made of them."

Campbell was, to be sure, released from censure on a technicality, but things were never the same between him and the Synod. He felt himself to be a marked man, and lived under a cloud of suspicion and distrust. Such feelings could have only one result, and it was not long before he formally rejected the Synod's authority, and severed all connection with it. This meant that he gave up his right to preach as Thomas Campbell, Presbyterian minister; but nothing, in the free frontier situation, could stop him from giving voice to his views as Thomas Campbell, private citizen and earnest Christian. So, where he was not permitted to preach in churches, he preached in homes, inviting all who would to return to the Bible as the only rule of faith, and to unite in a simple Christian fellowship, without regard to any group with which they were affiliated.

A few persons were attracted to this plea for the union of all Christians, and to Thomas Campbell personally. A meeting was held at the house of one Abraham Altars, between Mt. Pleasant and Washington, Pennsylvania, the purpose of which was declared to be "To confer about the existing state of things and to give, if possible, more definiteness to the movement in which they had thus far been cooperating without any formal organization or definite arrangement." In the phrase, "to give more definiteness to the movement" one sees the recognition that a new group was in process of formation, which sociologically considered was a new sect. Here it was that Thomas Campbell proposed his now famous dictum, "Where the Scriptures speak, we speak; where the Scriptures are silent, we are silent" as the rule of faith and church organization.

When this dictum was proposed, it is reported that the local postmaster, one Andrew Munro, said, "Mr. Campbell, if we adopt that as a rule of faith, then there is an end of infant baptism." Thomas Acheson burst into tears, exclaiming, "I hope I never see the day when my heart will renounce that blessed saying of Scripture, 'Suffer the little children to come unto me.' " James Foster, perhaps more truthful than tactful at such a moment, replied, "Mr. Acheson, I would remark that in the portion of Scripture you have quoted there is no reference to infant baptism." In any event, the principle was adopted as the sense of the meeting.

Soon thereafter it was voted to form a group to be known as the Christian Association of Washington. These, in brief, are the events leading to the reading of Thomas Campbell's *Declaration and Address,* now thought of as the Magna Charta of the movement. "The church," said Mr. Campbell, "is essentially, intentionally, and constitutionally one." But the sad truth is that there is bitter strife among the warring factions in Christendom. What is the remedy for this situation? This is to be found, Mr. Campbell tells us, in the promoting of a "simple, evangelical Christianity, free from all mixture of human opinions and inventions of men. . . . Nothing ought to be inculcated upon Christians as articles of faith; nor required of them as terms of communion, but what is expressly taught and enjoined upon them in the word of God. . . . By simply returning to the original standard of Christianity, the professions and practice of the primitive Church . . . is the only possible way that we can perceive to get rid of those evils."

The significance of this document from the point of a cultural understanding of Disciples is that it is a symbol of the almost inevitable events that were to follow. The movement was to start no new church; it was simply interested in inviting all Christians to unite in restoring their religion to its pure state so that all could come together without being interfered with by "human opinions." Yet almost before the "restoration" got well under way, in a postscript to the Declaration, the matter of a Christian catechism, which was to exhibit that "complete system of faith and duty contained in the sacred oracles, respecting doctrine, worship, discipline, and government of the church" was mentioned. One may argue that this is what Luther and Calvin, and who knows how many others, had been trying to do. One can rejoice in noting that the proposed catechism was never written; but this does not diminish the importance of the fact that it was even suggested.

Actually, though the catechism was not forthcoming, the members of the new group were left with a vital problem—a problem which always tends to make a sect into a denomination. In any organization it is necessary to define objectives, to articulate purposes. In this case the objective was to return to a simple Christianity, based upon the Scriptures, which would unite the divided factions in the church. That sounds plain, and it is easily understood. But that is because it says nothing—at least nothing very specific. Just what is a simple Christianity based upon the Scriptures? Unless we can agree on this we shall not know where we are going. We have to decide what the will of Christ is before we can follow it; and the matter cannot be left entirely to individuals, or there will be no common basis for group experience. Herein are planted the seeds of a new religious denomination.

That the Christian Association was really a new sect, though it believed itself to be simply a movement to purify the church, is shown by the results of Thomas Campbell's efforts to have the group received into the Presbyterian church. The Synod listened to what Campbell had to say, and then decided that groups like the Christian Association were "destructive of the whole interest of religion by *promoting divisions instead of union,* by degrading ministerial character, by providing free admission to any errors in doctrine and to any corruptions in discipline . . ." It is a fact of some sociological significance that a group which claimed not to be a new sect is believed unmistakably to be one by other groups. The Presbyterians thought that the Campbell group was not needed for a return to a faith and practice based on the Bible; what did Campbell think the Presbyterians had?

The Christian Association, with its members not in good standing in the churches to which they did belong, and with the refusal of the Presbyterians to accept them, became what the rest of its immediate world said it was—a separate church (sociologically speaking, a sect). "They had begun," says W. E. Garrison,

> with the intention of being a leavening influence in the existing churches. They were now committed to a principle of proceeding to "reformation without tarrying for any."[1]

The Valley of Brush Run was selected as the site for the new church—the harbinger, as it believed, of the new reformation—and on June 16, 1811, the first services were held. Already the group had moved beyond the situation referred to in the *Declaration and Address.* "This society by no means considers itself a church, nor does it at all assume to itself the powers peculiar to such a society." Whatever this society considered itself, it was taking on a certain structure, and certain powers, peculiar to religious groupings.

Thomas Campbell was not alone in the leadership of this new movement; his son, Alexander, who had arrived in America only a few weeks after the printing of the *Declaration and Address,* soon came to the fore as the one who was to carry on the fight. It was the ordination of Alexander Campbell—an obvious act of defiance of the ecclesiastical authorities—by the Christian Association which further underlined the realization of the new group that it had a separate and distinct existence. Things went even further in this direction, when the birth of Alexander Campbell's first child in March, 1812, raised the very practical question as to the validity of infant baptism. In the social milieu of the period and the locality the question was of the utmost importance.

To go into the reasons behind the decision that infant baptism and sprinkling are not permissible, because not scriptural (in the opinion of the Campbell group), and the steps leading to the adoption of adult immersion as the correct and biblical form of baptism is beyond the limits of this present inquiry. Suffice it to say that such a decision was reached, and immersion has been from that time on regarded by all orthodox Disciples as the desired, if not absolutely essential, form of baptism. The decision was not without social significance, since the adoption of that view was all that was needed to make the existing separation from the Presbyterians final and absolute. Already there was in this community a strained relationship between the Presbyterians and the Baptists on this very point, and the open acceptance of immersion drove the Christian Association into the arms of the Baptists.

After a preliminary period of sounding out the situation, the Brush Run Church made application to the Redstone Association of the Baptist Church, and was admitted into this body in the fall of 1813. This event, too, was to have its effects upon the developing character of the group later to be called "Disciples of Christ." The Brush Run Church was searching for relationships and methods of procedure that would give increasing stability and prestige to its efforts. This is evidence of cultural growing pains. To advocate the reform and purification of the church is a strenuous undertaking at best, but to do this from the outside is even more difficult. This is not to say that the new group was happy or satisfied in its relationship with the Baptists. But being in an already established church enabled the Campbells to mobilize forces.

During the period of union with the Baptists, the development of the principles dealing with the "restoration of the ancient order" proceeded apace. At the same time, certain of the traits which mark the sectarian group in its earliest stages were much in evidence. Both the restoration of the ancient order and the sectarian characteristics were involved in the separation from the Baptists, which occurred several years later. Here also one can see the evidence of the growing sense of separateness which was the result of the refusal of the established churches to accept the restoration.

This increasing group consciousness is most clearly revealed in the years covered by the publication of Alexander Campbell's magazine, *The Christian Baptist.* This publication, issued during the years between 1823 and 1830, is a veritable gold mine for the discovery of the evidence of sectarian traits in the early history of a religious movement. Motivated by the passionate desire to see religion returned to its simple and pure state, Alexander Campbell turned a sharp pen and an angry wit upon the established churches. Almost immediately, he began his exposé of pride, worldliness, and paganism. Much of this material was contained in his running "serial" on the "Restoration of the Ancient Order," but some of the most revealing parts of his polemic are to be found in certain of the anecdotes appearing from time to time.

The journalistic efforts of Mr. Campbell were not without influence. They were in part an expression of the cultural milieu of religion in America at the time. This is shown by the amount of controversy which his writing evoked. At the very end of publication of *The Christian Baptist,* Campbell was able to say,

No person was ever more misrepresented, or more diversely and incongruously characterized than the humble editor of the Christian Baptist. . . There is no danger you can apprehend from me, if you have scripture or reason on your side. I will not hurt a hair upon your head, nor endanger a penny in your pocket, if you have reasons an ounce weight—if you have a "Thus says the Lord" for it. . . . I have vowed to serve the King to the end of the war, or as long as he gives me a post in the Army of the Faith.[2]

Alexander Campbell was called, it is true, almost every name in the religious universe of discourse; he was accused of holding any and every view which could possibly discredit him with anybody. The storm of opposition which greeted him was the result both of fear of what a new group might do to upset existing patterns and of Mr. Campbell's flair for "exaggeration and bitterness." "His own friends warned him of the unwisdom of such immoderation. His hand was against everything; and every man's hand was soon against him. His spirit of iconoclasm led him to demolish very many useful and indispensable customs of organized Christianity."[3]

One of Campbell's favorite whipping boys was the clergy, whom he called variously "hireling priests," "scrap doctors," and "textuary divines." In his castigations of the clergy, by which he meant the ministers of the established Protestant denominations as well as Roman Catholic priests, Campbell left us conclusive evidence of the early sectarian traits of his restoration movement. The restoration was, he believed, based upon principles which were easily understood by plain people, and no learned preachers were needed to explain them. An appeal in this vein certainly would be attractive to the frontier mind, which had no patience with hairsplitting done by educated divines who knew Greek and Hebrew but did not know how to make religion live "in the heart."

"We conceive it would be much easier," Campbell said, to prove from the bible and from reason that in five thousand carpenters, masons, tailors, farmers, there is a larger proportion, in each, of members of the kingdom of God, than in the same number of regularly educated ministers. . . . . Thousands of ignorant, unlettered men, not fettered by the rules of grammar, not circumscribed by the restraints of reason . . . are nevertheless both fluent . . . and eloquent speakers.[4]

Disciples were later, like other groups which outgrew the sectarian stage, to see the value and desirability of an educated ministry; but in the early period when, under frontier conditions, neither the inclination nor money for such an interest in education was forthcoming, the emphasis upon the accessibility of everyone, including the ignorant and untrained, to spiritual understanding, was in tune with the times.

Another sectarian trait of which Alexander Campbell made much is the disdain for titles. Since education and training do not count for anything in the true kingdom of God, the titles used to set apart the ministry should be abandoned. Who do these clergyman think they are, anyway? Besides, the use of such titles is unscriptural.

Some of the populars sneer at the term *bishop,* as if the Spirit of God had not chosen it to designate the only legitimate "officer" in a christian congregation, who is, from office, to teach and rule. They love *Rabbi, Rabbi,* or *Reverend* and *Right Reverend,* too well to lay them aside, or to exchange these haughty titles for the apostolic and humble name of overseer or bishop.[5]

There are no "reverends" in the kingdom, but there are bishops, provided you spell the word with a small "b," and provided also that you use the word in much the same way you would use the word "farmer" or "merchant."

Aside from the revealing of sectarian emphases in early Disciple history, one can see that there is a real point—a point which transcends the sectarian level—in Campbell's attack upon the clergy for "putting on airs." This may be indicated by an anecdote he published with obvious approval.

An English country parson was bragging in a large company of the success he had had in reforming his parishioners, on which his labors, he said, had produced a wonderful change for the better. Being asked in what respect, he replied, that when he came first among them they were a set of unmannerly clowns who paid him no deference. . . . ; did not so much as pull off their hat when they spoke to him, but bawled out as roughly and familiarly as though he were their equal; whereas now they never presumed to address him but cap in hand, and in a submissive voice, made him their best bow when they were at ten yards distance, and styled him *Your Reverence* at every word. A Quaker who heard the whole patiently made answer—"And so, friend, the upshot of this reformation, of which thee hast so much carnal glorying, is, that thee hast taught thy people to worship thyself."[6]

Campbell must have sensed, subconsciously at least, that such a story would appeal to many people who had become conscious of the class structure, which even at this time already existed in American society.

Mr. Campbell's ability at satire, and his realization of the sort of appeal which would influence people under the conditions of the early 1800's is shown in a series of paragraphs bearing the title of "The Third Epistle of Peter," supposed to have been discovered in an ancient manuscript, but obviously a clever attack upon the worldliness and secularization of the clergy and the churches. It was, he said, a looking glass for the clergy. This piece is more or less of a summary of many of the points in the sectarian attack upon the established order. "The Third Epistle of Peter" is really a catalogue of the "vices" of which the restoration movement accused the churches, and it demonstrates that the sectarian mind often appeals to things other than the Bible to support its position.

Here beginneth the Third Epistle of Peter.

Be you not called as men are called, but be you called Pope, Archbishop, Archdeacon, or Divine, or Reverend, and Right Reverend, or some like holy name; so you show forth your honor and your calling.

And let your dwelling places be houses of splendor and edifices of cost; and let your door be decked with plates of brass, and let your names, even your reverend titles be graven thereon; so shall it be a sign. . . .

Let the houses in which you preach be called churches, and let them be built in manner of great ornament without, and adorned with much cost within; with rich pillars and paints, and with fine altars and pedestals, and urns of precious stones, and cloths and velvet of scarlet, and vessels of silver. . . .

And let the houses be divided into seats for the congregation, and let every man know his own seat; and let the first seats in front of the altar be for the rich that pay by thousands. . . And let the poor man sit behind the door. . . .

If the houses of players and vain people who deal in idle sayings and shows of mockery, be rich and gorgeous, how much more so should be the houses that are dedicated to him "that is meek and lowly of spirit."[7]

The love of money is, as the saying goes, the root of all evil. Mr. Campbell and his followers thought so, which is an indication that they probably had very little. People who start new religious movements are not usually distinguished by their wealth; it is casting no aspersions then, to point out that it is difficult for a group without money not to emphasize and underline the assertion that true religion does not depend upon money or position. With the truth of this assertion we are not at the moment concerned. The important point is that things not available to the group because of their lack of resources tend to be regarded either as unnecessary or as obvious vices. The Campbell group, again revealing the sectarian nature of its cultural orientation, approved, one is certain, the statements of Alexander Campbell's magazine on the centrality of money in the degradation of the churches.

Money is of vital consequence in the kingdom of the clergy *wrote Mr. Campbell.* Without it a clergyman could not be made, nor a congregation supplied with a "faithful pastor." O Mammon, you wonder-working God! . . .

A wealthy and a polite congregation sits very uneasy under the pious efforts of a homespun, coarse, and awkward mechanic. His sing-song monotony, and sawing gesticulation, animated by the zeal of Elijah freezes the genial current of their souls. It will not do. . . To the west he goes (taking, one supposes, his pure and undefiled simple religion with him!). In the wilderness he is like John the Baptist. His disgusting elocution, his awkward figure, and his frightful gestures, are all unsullied sanctity, unfeigned devotion. The rural saint is full of his praise. . . . The modern clergy say they do not preach for money. Very well; let the people pay them none, and they will have as much of their preaching still.[8]

The polemic against the evil which money was doing in the churches was obviously a part of a general program of convincing people that pure and simple religion needed to be restored, and that the restoration could be accomplished by adopting the Campbell principles. The evil of money is, after all, a part of the spirit of the times.

The spirit of the present order of things is too much akin to the spirit of this world. It looks with a countenance beaming too much complacency on the pride and vanity, on the tinsel and show, on the equipage and style, on the avarice and ambition, on the guile and hypocrisy of this world. Its supreme petition is not "Lord, what will you have me do?" but "O you sons of religious fashion! you leaders of religious taste! you synods and councils! you creeds and systems! you mitred heads and patented divines! and you O Mammon! tell us plainly, tell us fully, what you would have us to do to gain your admiration, and if possible too, to save our souls." . . . This appears to be the leading and triumphant spirit of the present order of things.[9]

Here is reason enough why, in Alexander Campbell's opinion, a new reformation—nay, a restoration—of true faith is required. That true faith is once and for all supplied in the Scriptures, and to these we must go to begin our restoration of the ancient order.

The unity of the church and the purity of religion can be established only on the basis of the Scriptures. In the Scriptures, God made his plans evident; he set down a blueprint for the organization of that divine institution, the church. A unity founded on anything less than the plan of God, as found in the Bible, is not to be countenanced. This was the burden of Alexander Campbell's plea.

Had the founder of the christian faith been defective in wisdom or benevolence, then his authority, his testimony, and his commandments, might be canvassed with as little ceremony as the discoveries and maxims of our compeers and contemporaries; then his religion might be improved, or reformed, or better adapted to existing circumstances. But as all christians admit that he foresaw and anticipated all the events and revolutions in human history, and that the present state of things was as present to his mind as the circumstances that encompassed him in Judea . . . it follows . . . that the institution of which he is the author and founder, can never be improved or reformed.[10]

But it can be restored!

The churches should get together, thought Alexander Campbell and his group. Their being apart is sinful and unnecessary. But they have to unite on the right basis! No merely human creed or statement of opinion will do. The new group thought of the statements of faith or belief issued by the existing churches as "human opinion" and not the divine pattern. This is of some significance in indicating a growing group-consciousness. Indeed, Campbell went so far as to say that

Should the Christian community be united upon the Westminster, or Methodistic, or Baptist, or any human creed, then the plan of heaven is defeated, the apostles disgraced, the Saviour's prayer unanswered, and the whole order of heaven frustrated, and the throne of the universe subverted. He that advocates the necessity of creeds of human contrivance to the unity of the church unconsciously impeaches the wisdom of God.[11]

Evidently Mr. Campbell did not believe that his own reading of the Scriptures amounted to a "human opinion." To the objective observer, it appears that the Campbell group, being *sociologically* a sect, omitted to recognize that other groups, too, thought their teachings to be only an exact translation of biblical requirements.

To the sectarian mind, what other groups think, if it differs from the distinctive teaching of the in-group, can be the result only of ignorance or downright sinfulness. When the outside world calls the sect to account for not being faithful to its own stated objectives, the reaction is the formulation of a sincere, but pathetic, casuistry. Gratuitous distinctions are drawn, designed (unconsciously, to be sure) to let in the beliefs and practices that the group wants to maintain, and to exclude (strictly on the basis of reason, of course!) the beliefs and practices which it desires to ignore or omit. Alexander Campbell became involved in this process when, defending the new group against the charge that they had deliberately omitted certain obvious commands of Scripture, he drew what looks suspiciously like a hairsplitting distinction between Jewish and Christian "times" and between what is essential to worship and what is not.

In December, 1825, a reader of the *Christian Baptist* sent Campbell a letter in which he stated,

> I was astonished, finding you so great an advocate for primitive christianity, to hear you say whatsoever the apostles commanded constituted the practice of the first christians, and yet not notice the plain commandment of washing feet, and that of the kiss of charity . . ., and upon this ground contend[ing] for weekly communion and yet not stating that the night was the time, yea, the only time, according to Christ's institution and the practice of the apostles to observe this ordinance.[12]

Alexander Campbell's answer demonstrates how the leader of a movement attempts to keep the situation, of which his leadership is an expression, from getting out of hand, or from going beyond the bounds of what common sense could seem to dictate. He must have sensed that any principle, if carried to its logical extremity, can be made to look ridiculous. This, of course, would be unfortunate for the new group's future. As to the business about the observance of communion at the same time of day at which the disciples had observed it, Mr. Campbell said, "We might as well argue that, because Paul immersed the jailor at the dead hour of night every person should be immersed at the same hour. . . . The same sort of logic would oblige us to observe it [the Supper] only the last night of our lives . . . and to have no more than a dozen fellow participants."[13] It would be of no avail to point out to Mr. Campbell that his own reasoning is probably a *non sequitor;* the significance of his answer lies beyond the particular points in the argument. Campbell proceeds to dispose of the foot-washing problem in much the same vein, arguing rather tortuously that foot-washing is not a religious observance, and therefore need not be followed in the restoration of the primitive church.

The real significance of such arguments was hinted at by Mr. Campbell himself in another connection entirely. Referring to other religious leaders—obviously not to himself—he pointed out that when one wishes to defend his view by an appeal to the Scriptures, he quotes only passages which bear out his own conclusions, and is strangely silent about other passages which would not help him.

> Not one of them will quote with equal pleasure or readiness every thing said on the subject. . . . Now, suppose that all these would abandon every word and sentence not found in the bible . . . and without explanation, limitation, or enlargement quote . . . and apply on every suitable occasion every word and sentence found in the volume . . . how long would divisions . . . exist?[14]

The sociologist's answer to this question would have to be, Longer than you realized, Mr. Campbell, because the divisions are not fundamentally based upon this refusal to quote from the whole Bible. This is, among other things, a symptom of the "social sources of denominationalism" and a part of the natural history of a religious situation.

Actually the trouble was not that all the religious leaders, except Campbell, failed to give the complete scriptural picture of the way the church should be set up, and the way it should conduct its ordinances, but rather that the particular arrangements they did support had become vested interests, with which both their own personalities and the cultural orientation of their movements had become associated. Just as no entrenched economic class ever gives up its privileges voluntarily, so no established religious group gives up its position (either social or religious) without a struggle. The Campbell group already showed signs of being involved with an "established orthodoxy" itself, a factor which was to become even more significant as the years went by.

Next to the worldliness of the clergy and the disaffection of the churches in the matter of the ancient order, Mr. Campbell's favorite subject was the unwarranted claim to authority on the part of church associations and societies. The objections to such associations, based upon the grounds to be noted in a moment, can be interpreted in the light of frontier individualism. No matter what biblical, or other arguments might be urged, behind the objections to official church societies was always the frontier attitude—every man for himself! The Westerner was always jealous of his political rights and suspicious of any attempt to interfere with his freedom; and such a feeling inevitably spilled over into other areas of his life.

> I have no objection to congregations meeting in hundreds at stated times, to sing God's praise, and to unite their prayers and exhortations for the social good. But whenever they form a quorum, and call for the business of the churches, they are a popish calf, or muley, or a hornless stag, or something akin to the old grand Beast with seven heads and ten horns.[15]

He had stated earlier that an individual church or congregation of Christ's disciples is the only recognized organization in the New Testament. There can be little question that Campbell thought his study of the New Testament supported this view, but that the question was raised at all is of much more importance than are the precise grounds for the conclusions. The people to whom Campbell and other antisociety preachers appealed wanted no interference in their affairs, and believed themselves perfectly competent to handle their own problems, religious or any other kind, provided they were not either dictated to or exploited. One suspects that both dictation and exploitation were feared if any society beyond the local church was allowed to have any say in things.

Alexander Campbell spoke not only for himself, but for much opinion in the western part of America in the first decades of the nineteenth century, when he stated that

> Whether such an alliance of the priests and nobles of the kirk be called a session, a presbytery, a synod, a general assembly, a convention, a conference, an association, or annual meeting, its tendency and result are the same. Whenever and wherever such a meeting either legislates, decrees, rules, directs, or controls, or assumes the character of a representative body in religious concerns, it essentially becomes the man of sin and the son of perdition.[16]

So prevalent was the attitude just expressed that certain leaders, among them Alexander Campbell, opposed even societies to send missionaries to convert the heathen. Later, of course, he reversed his position and supported the organization of missionary societies, thus illustrating the effect of social change upon earlier attitudes.

The arguments of the antimissions agitators may be summarized under four main heads. To begin with, and in line with what we have already said, boards and societies, because they involve a centralization of authority, are subversive of the Baptist principle of democracy in church polity. John Taylor spoke of the "mighty Convention" as being like the operations of Tetzel during the period when "the Pope of Rome and the Mother of Harlots were at their zenith." The money basis of the missionary enterprise was a second ground for objections, and the objectors lost no time in comparing the collection of missionary money to the selling of indulgences. Alexander Campbell spoke of Mrs. Judson, wife of a Baptist missionary, as follows: "The visiting dress of this self-denying female missionary could not be valued at less than twelve thousand dollars."

This money-basis objection was considered important because it was believed that money collections meant an alliance with things worldly. Campbell reports a meeting of the Goshen Association, where the propriety of general associations was questioned. One Brother Higgason, it was reported, carried his point with ease when he showed that "money was a bond of union of that association, and . . . it was an unlawful amalgamation of the world and the church."[17] The church and the world must not co-operate, even to do the Lord's work! Later, the Disciples' group was to change its mind about this, as have so many other religious groups which wanted to gain and keep a degree of prestige and allegiance in the eyes of the world. Most Disciples today would, I believe, recognize both the irony and the practicality of the statement, "The *Lord* loveth a cheerful giver, but *we* cannot afford to be so particular."

The third source of objection to missionary societies was a certain jealousy of the educated and salaried preachers they sent out. As we have indicated, the frontier and hinterland churches did not think they needed an educated minister; and what was one to think of a minister who accepted money for preaching? A frontier preacher when he was asked to state his objections replied, "Well, if you must know, Brother Moderator, you know the big trees in the woods overshadow the little ones; and these missionaries will all be great men, and the people will go to hear them preach, and we shall be put down. That's the objection."[18] Besides, we can do better without these dandies! "These poor and ignorant preachers, that never saw a college wall, would, in one year, cut and slash down more stubborn sinners with John Bunyan's Jerusalem blade, than a score of these nice fencers, who wear only a silver-handled dirk and a pocket-pistol."[19]

The major objection, however, was that missionary societies are not authorized in the Bible. Did the men who spread Christianity throughout the world in Paul's day get a seminary education before undertaking their tasks? Of course not. It is unholy and unnecessary to educate a man to do what God calls him to do. Alexander Campbell, again showing his gift for satire, pictured Paul and Barnabas before a missionary society.

"On Wednesday, the 11th of June, A. D. 44, the Rev. Saulus Paulus and the Rev. Joses Barnabas were set apart as missionaries to the Gentiles. . .

"Mr. Paulus is a young man, and a native of the city of Tarsus; he received his classical and theological education in the theological seminary at Jerusalem. He appeared before the committee a man of good sense, of ardent piety, and understandingly led by the spirit of God to the work."[20]

Campbell had taken this idea from a newspaper item telling of a new missionary being sent out.

Later, when Campbell reversed his position, and supported missionary societies, his opponents were to throw at him some of his own diatribes on the subject. But by this time Campbell had found arguments to support his new position, and its inconsistency with his former view was not particularly disturbing to him. In the interests of accuracy, it should be pointed out that Alexander Campbell was not opposed to *missions* so much as to *societies.* From the standpoint of the cultural understanding of his group the objection to societies seems to be more significant, in any case.

Enough evidence has been presented to show that the Campbell group—later Disciples of Christ—exhibited many of the traits associated with the sectarian phase in a religious organization's history. It can readily be understood that in such an atmosphere of developing group-consciousness, of hostility toward those who differed, it would not be long before a form of self-conscious ethnocentrism would show itself. This too reveals itself in the pages of Campbell's *Christian Baptist,* and it helps to explain why the new group was not long to remain with the Baptists.

The word had apparently been passed around that Campbell would not be allowed to expound his "pernicious views" in Frankfort, Kentucky. This, said Mr. Campbell,

is as ridiculous as a motion that was made some few days ago by a foster child of celebrated *Rake* respecting myself; "I move," said he, "that this congregation declare *non-fellowship* with Alexander Campbell." And the poignancy of the wit was, that Alexander Campbell rarely travels to the mountains of Pennsylvania, and never asked the mover for any sort of fellowship. . . . I view such a motion pretty much in the same light as I would the motion of a musselman who would have it decreed in a mosque that I should never be the Dey of Algiers.[21]

Campbell's movement was growing and beginning to feel its strength; he was not, therefore, in the mood to be apologetic or diplomatic in his utterances.

The sectarian atmosphere of controversy and "persecution" was not wanting, either. A correspondent from Kentucky wrote to Campbell, asking him what "Campbellism" is. "It is," Mr. Campbell told him,

a nickname of reproach invented and adopted by those whose views, feelings, and desires are all sectarian; who cannot conceive of christianity in any other light than an *ism*. These *isms* are now the real reproaches of those who adopt them. . . . They who bestow such names are actuated either by a spirit of foolish jesting, or that vengeful spirit which would sacrifice the life as well as the reputation of those who deprive them of the means of self-aggrandizement at the expense of the intelligence, liberty, and true happiness of mankind. . . . I have always disclaimed everything sectarian; and if the people of the different sects slander me or any of those who prefer the scriptures to any human creed, and the kingdom of Jesus the Messiah to any sect . . . they answer to him who judges righteously.[22]

Alexander Campbell and his group, in other words, are on the side of righteousness; all others who oppose their views, are living in outer darkness. *They* are, that is, sectarians.

Here we note the use of the word "sect" in the nonsociological, nonobjective sense. Candor requires the admission that, seen from the other side of the fence, the situation in which Disciples of Christ were involved looked entirely different. A Mr. McConnico from Tennessee reported to his church that

Campbellism has carried away many whom I thought firm. These wandering stars and clouds without water, ever learning and never able to come to the knowledge of the truth, make proselytes much more the children of the devil than they did before. O Lord! hear the cries and see the tears of the Baptists; for Alexander hath done them much harm. The Lord reward him according to his works. . . . See them dividing churches and spreading discord, and constituting churches out of excommunicated members. Such shuffling—such lying—such slandering—such evil speaking—such dissembling—such downright hypocrisy—all under the false name of Reformation.[23]

With this background in mind, the separation of the Campbell group from the Baptists was only a matter of time. We do not propose to enter into the argument over the theological and religious issues involved in this separation, nor to trace in detail the historic events leading up to it. The points at issue were the "design of Baptism," the proper way to observe the Lord's Supper, the old and new covenants, the ordination of ministers, and the question of faith and regeneration. The reader is referred to the standard histories of Disciples of Christ and the Baptists for a discussion of these points. These issues furnished the "occasion" for a separation which, viewed in terms of the sociology of the sect, was bound to take place, given the conditions or religion in this frontier setting.

CHAPTER IV

Discomfort in Zion:
the Separation from the Baptists

The movement which was to be known as "Disciples of Christ" had within itself the elements of a kind of dialectic. Two motives and social principles were really implicit in the existence of the group from the very beginning. One of these, as we have seen, was the passionate desire to have the churches united on the basis of loyalty to Christ. The other was the defense of a particular set of ordinances, a distinctive interpretation of the "plan of salvation," believed to be clearly delineated in the New Testament. These motives were the foci of a dialectic, which even today explains much of what goes on in the church of Disciples of Christ, both on the doctrinal level and in terms of the social process. It was in the years from 1827 to 1865 that this dialectic became clearly apparent, and showed definite signs of development—all of which was, as we shall see, to throw considerable light on the way in which a sect becomes a denomination.

An extensive research in the most important source material of Disciples discloses conclusive evidence of three distinct manifestations of the sect-to-denomination phenomenon. Each of these stems either directly or indirectly from the aforementioned dialectic—unity versus restoration. The first of these manifestations is the development of a consciousness of group "apartness" or sense of difference from other groups. This, as we indicated in the introductory chapter, was the particular aspect of the sect phenomenon stressed by Park. The second manifestation of the sectarian sequence is the development of a recognition of the need for organization and consolidation of efforts, which was to modify, if not to erase, the earlier objections to organizations and fear of authority. The third item in the list of sectarian traits is a conscious and determined campaign against "worldliness" and paganism, both in the church and outside it, mentioned by Elmer T. Clark as a prominent note among the sects. These manifestations of the sect nature of the group were present in the movement of Disciples. This much can be documented beyond any question.

When we left the Campbell movement in the previous chapter, it was about to separate from the Baptists. It is a question for argument as to whether the Campbellites were "thrown out" of the Baptist church, or whether they simply left the fold. One suspects that the answer would depend upon the point of view. But since this is really part of the development of group-consciousness among the group known as Disciples, we shall leave the issue to be sharpened as the account proceeds. The fact to be noted at this point is the fact that the Disciples did split from the Baptists.

Needless to say, this separation was not accomplished at one stroke or by any one act.

> The unity or division of a group which has no authoritative general organization depends upon a multitude of local conditions, the spirit of many individuals, and the attitude of many congregations. It is not a matter that is determined by the action of a central administrative body, or by a resolution passed by a convention. It is accomplished by the breach of actual fellowship in the body which is about to suffer fracture, and by the development of a group consciousness on the part of the fraction which is about to be separated.[1]

By the end of 1830, this process of "fracturing" was pretty well completed, though some individuals with Disciples sympathies still lingered in Baptist churches. Those who yet remained with the Baptists were expelled as soon as discovered[2] so that by 1833 there could be absolutely no doubt in anyone's mind that a definite separation had occurred.

Even before this time, the followers of Campbell were, in the eyes of many, already a distinct group. This is significant in terms of the developing group consciousness. Campbell's group was known to many as "Campbellites" though Alexander Campbell himself strongly repudiated the term. "We wish all the friends of the ancient order," he said, "to remember that our motto is, and we hope ever will be, to call no man master or father in the things pertaining to the kingdom of our Lord."[3] More than this, when Campbell quoted a question sent to a Baptist association about what Campbellism is, he reported that the association said it did not know. But even though a Kentucky Baptist Association could aver that it did not know what Campbellism is, the significant thing is that the use of the term, of itself, showed that there was something here definite enough to require a particular name. Whether anybody in official capacity would admit it or not, it was generally known that some Baptists were not really Baptists at all.

Alexander Campbell was perfectly sincere, when in his *Christian Baptist* for February 6, 1826, he said,

> I have no idea of adding to the catalogue of new sects. This game has been played too long. I labor to see sectarianism abolished, and all Christians . . . united. . . . In one thing, perhaps, they [the Baptists] may appear in time to come, proudly singular, and pre-eminently distinguished. Mark it well. Their historian, in the year 1900, may say, "We are the only people who would tolerate . . . any person to continue as a Reformer or Restorer amongst us."

But alas, Campbell did not reckon with "the social sources of denominationalism!"

Yet, if this dream about the Baptists was not, as Campbell later realized, to come true, there were other problems and developments on the hither side of the separation which were to occupy the attention of the new church. Here, the manifestations of the sect-to-denomination phenomenon became important. The development of a consciousness of a common group life, and the process of arranging mechanisms and organizational procedures through which that common life may be adequately and effectively expressed, constitute an interesting and exciting chapter in the history of the Disciples; it is a chapter which, one presumes, could be duplicated in the history of any sect. But that the Disciples did follow the patterns laid down in our first chapter remains to be shown.

There are, as W. E. Garrison has suggested, two sides to this process of a developing group consciousness—the growth of a body of practices, ideas, habits, phrases, and leaders, and the sense of a keen feeling of differentness. Both of these aspects are amply and copiously illustrated in the source material on Disciples. If we date the separate existence of the Campbell movement from the dissolution of the Mahoning Baptist Association at Austintown, Ohio, in August, 1830 (which is sometimes used as the symbol of the separation process), it is possible to say that by the end of the first decade of distinct existence the Disciples had developed an unmistakable in-group feeling.

Alexander Campbell began his new publication, *The Millennial Harbinger,* on this note. What the new movement desired to do was to disinter the remains of the gospel and restore it to its former purity. "We expect," he wrote in the introduction to the first volume,

> no new revelation of the Spirit, no other than the same gospel and the same religion, only that it shall be disinterred from the rubbish of the dark ages, and made to assume its former simplicity, sublimity, and majesty. . . .
>
> If all who love the Lord and the salvation of men would unite their energies and bury the tomahawk of party conflicts, no seer

could predict how rapid would be the march and how extensive the triumphs of the gospel.[4]

But the tomahawks were sharpened rather than buried; the Campbell group's offer of peace to all and unity in Christ was not received with open arms at all.

The rest of Christendom did not regard what the followers of Campbell were doing as any particular contribution to the progress of religion. This was looked upon by the Campbell group in various lights, ranging from ignorance and misunderstanding to selfishness and downright sinfulness. The criticisms which others made of the new movement were obviously taken to heart; how else can one explain the fact that so many of them were reprinted and either answered or commented upon in Campbell's magazine, *The Millennial Harbinger?*

This was carried so far that even a most engaging, if vindictive, set of verses about the Campbell movement was in part reproduced. These verses are symptomatic of the fact that the Campbell group was making an impression upon the religious world of the day; and they illustrate how social processes and ideologies become embedded in the folklore. It is known that they were being circulated by ministers who opposed Campbell's efforts at "restoration."

All *sects* are wrong, he's often said,
They should be number'd with the dead;
Confessions, creeds, serve to divide;
They must, they shall, be thrown aside.
I little care what men believe,
Provided they *my faith* receive,
And come to me, with me unite,
And think my views and plans are right,
And *swear allegiance to the water*—
As for the rest, 'tis little matter;
Whate'er they think, whate'er they do,
Can naught avail; they're subjects true.

. . . .

Though your sins be black as jet,
Never mind to mourn and fret—

Come to me, no longer dream,
I will plunge you in the stream,
Up you'll come in garments white,
Holy as a saint of light,
Come to me, each son and daughter
Here's the "gospel in the water."
O ye blinded generation
Won't you have this *cheap* salvation?[5]

Only a small portion of the verses has been quoted; they were said to have gone on for page after page, and one suspects that as the verses traveled around new lines were added.

The struggle for the "ancient gospel" was so fierce that the language of battle and warfare was often used. "There are no winter quarters in the good fight of faith," Mr. Campbell told his readers in 1834.

Neither is there a truce nor an armistice in the war between truth and error. . . .In our part of the camp, and along the lines of the antagonist armies, in our continent, the belligerents are still active. As respects the faith formerly delivered to the saints, the allied sects, like the ancient Philistines, are still sounding new defiances against the armies of the God of Israel.[6]

Along with this militancy went other aspects which show how the group consciousness of Disciples was increasing. There was, for example, the attempt to claim a vistory on the ideological front by linking the Disciple movement with the triumph of righteousness over evil, to show that since truth always wins in the end, the other groups will have to give in eventually. The universe is on our side, it was implied, so it will be only a question of time until our views win out.

"By some strange fatality," wrote Mr. Campbell,

the opposers of reform have always defeated themselves. It is true they formerly succeeded in keeping a part of their kingdom from an apostacy from error. . . . In this way their gain was the loss and ruin of their own posterity. . . . In every war against the New Testament the loss is loss, the gain is loss, and every victory is a defeat. Thus error always defeats itself.[7]

Still further, the future was to belong to Disciples. The sectarians, it was asserted, by their methods and by their stubborn insistence upon their errors, are really bringing about their own downfall. Movements based upon errors are bound, in the end, to fall apart of their own inner decadence.

The dull monotony of sectarian tenets, added to the unchristian temper and demeanor of their proclaimers and advocates, are never likely to have a strong hold on the affections of the rising generation. The ignorance of the Christian and Jewish Scriptures, which abounds among those imbued with the spirits of the sectarian institutions, eminently disqualify the indoctrinated to hear or judge for themselves on the great questions which now agitate.[8]

What Disciples thought about the question of who, in the case of separation from the Baptists, was the schismatic, is not difficult to guess. As early as 1837 the claim that it was the Baptists who were at fault was openly asserted. "The Baptists ought never to have become schismatical and forced divisions, but ought rather to have tolerated reform and met us with the liberality and cordiality which we have always shown to them."[9] This claim is significant, if only for the fact that it was to be repeated often. It is not our purpose here to evaluate the claims made by either side, but only to show the sectarian atmosphere within which the new movement was devoloping.

That the Disciples were developing a set of in-group "rationalizations," and a body of peculiar doctrines, is convincingly demonstrated by the fact that Campbell himself felt called upon to discuss the scriptural basis for ingroup feeling, though of course he did not call it that. "Is not Paul your model of a catholic spirit and of true charity?" he asked.

And his motto was, "Let every man be accursed who does not preach the same gospel as I do." . . . The better we understand and the more highly we appreciate the gospel which Paul preached, we become the more jealous of its purity, and the less favorable our opinions of those who would change a word or a letter of it. As men recede from the original gospel they grow in the world's esteem and in charity for the world; and as they approach to it their charity will be less catholic, but more scriptural.[10]

This might well be taken as a "creed" for those in the Disciples movement who have followed the "restoration" aspects of the dialectic.

Not all groups on the religious scene were opposed to Disciples, or rather, more accurately at this time, the followers of Campbell. It will be remembered that in an earlier chapter we discussed the participation of Barton W. Stone in the religious movements which had swept across the frontier, and mentioned that here was one of the sources of Disciples of Christ. During the first decade of the Campbell movement freedom from the Baptists, a union of the followers of Barton W. Stone and those of Alexander Campbell was effected. In 1824 Campbell met Stone while touring the state of Kentucky, and even at this early date they saw the similarity of their programs for the advancement of the primitive gospel.

In 1828 a correspondent wrote to Barton W. Stone's *Christian Messenger* asking why the two groups did not unite. Stone replied, "If there is a difference between us we do not know it. We have nothing in us to prevent a union; and if they have nothing in them in opposition to it, we are in spirit one. May God strengthen the cords of Christian union." There were certain slight differences between the two groups, but they were not serious enough to prevent the merger from being successful. Again, as in the case of the separation from the Baptists, the operation could be carried out only by informal actions on the local level. The co-operation of the two groups was to be very important in the numerical expansion of the Disciples movement, though a large minority of Stone's group refused to come into the scheme.

In both of the groups which united there was a decided sentiment for the use of biblical names, rather than unscriptural or "sectarian" nomenclature. Stone's party preferred the name "Christian" for the church, quoting a passage in Acts 11:26, "The disciples were called Christians first in Antioch";

while Campbell liked the term "Disciples" better, arguing that it was just as scriptural and more distinctive. Both of these names are deeply embedded in the lore of the movement. The question of the correct name for the group still elicits considerable discussion in some quarters. The official change of the name of the group from Disciples of Christ to Christian Church seems to have come about largely for pragmatic reasons. One still hears both names freely used. The discussion may even become somewhat emotional when it hinges upon such matters as whether the word Disciples is to be spelled with a small or a capital "d." Some of this concern over the name of the movement appears to have its source in the fact that one part of the group traces its roots back to Barton W. Stone, and another to the Campbells.

Disciples developed an increasing sense of their apartness or difference from the rest of the religious world. One does not exactly find this surprising. Tertullian once remarked that the blood of the martyrs is the seed of the church; and while there was no blood shed in the controversy of Disciples with their opponents, the principle behind Tertullian's statement is not without point here. It seems to be an established social principle that a rising group often thrives when it is opposed or persecuted, and the principle certainly was in operation so far as Disciples are concerned. Those who opposed Campbell and his followers gave them ample opportunity to develop a feeling of martyrdom.

There were, for example, statements like this. " 'If this *papas supremus* of the *Reformers* be right, why was not Simon Magus a christian?' 'Mr. Campbell, I can neither attend to you, nor any of your *understrappers.*' 'Do you know, sir, there is a heavy rod in soak for you?' . . . 'How vile and relentless must be the heart of him, who, sheltered under the apparent sanctity of his ministerial cloth, will, without remorse or scruple, deliberately and with malice aforethought, thrust his envenomed poinard of detraction into the vitals of the fairest reputations.' 'Who but Alexander Campbell and his reckless followers would do it?' "[11] Campbell had collected such statements from various sources, and he was sensitive to the things people said about his movement—not, one might add, without reason.

The atmosphere of acrimonious controversy and vituperative dialectic is conducive to the development of hostility toward those who differ. It is, one may say, both cause and result of this in-group feeling. When his opponents became what Mr. Campbell considered as too nasty, he was supremely capable of returning the compliment, and one may assume that he spoke the sentiments of many of the group of Disciples when he did so. Replying to the letter of a certain Mr. Waterman, who had accused him (and, by implication, his followers) of uncharitableness, Campbell said,

> I expected from a minister of so much reputation for good sense and sound logic, something more manly, sensible, and edifying . . . than this cheap, common-place, canting sort of exegesis of sectarian charity. . . .
>
> What has my charity to do with the truth or falsehood of my views of religous faith or practice? Are we to decide upon the weight of a man's person by the color of his hair, or on the strength of his logic by his taste for music? Is a man a grammarian because he loves oysters, or a rhetorician because he is lenient to the faults of his wife? . . .
>
> . . . Ridicule is not the test of truth, else Voltaire and Bolingbrooke would have laughed the gospel out of the world before we came upon the stage.[12]

This was the age of flamboyant rhetoric, which is not without its charms, though it may show that the participants were inclined to take themselves a bit too seriously. Even so, it may be evidence that people in the America of this period took their religious beliefs and practices with great seriousness.

Campbell and his followers were not reluctant or reticent in their willingness to compare themselves with the reformers and prophets of other ages. Indeed, this comparison was often urged as grounds for rejecting the charge that the Disciples were a new sect, hindering rather than helping the cause of true religion. A Mr. Jennings had charged Campbell with being a "factionist" but Campbell was ready with his answer.

His [Mr. Jennings] remarks reminded me of the charges against Luther for rending the seamless coat of Christ and for destroying the integrity of the Holy Apostolic Church. . . . In one sense of the word party, or sect, the kingdom of Jesus would be a sect or party so long as there were Jews, Mahomedans, or Pagans on earth. In this sense only could our views be denominated sectarian.[13]

Disciples made progress in terms of numbers and increasing prestige. Against a background of fierce competition to gain a hearing, they were able to hold the positions which they had taken in the struggle. It was only natural that with this growth should go a feeling that divine favor smiled upon their efforts, or that, if it did not at the moment, time would remedy the condition. Letters from many parts of the advancing frontier, and from some older areas too, began to pour in to Campbell's editorial office; all told the same story—it was a hard fight but the battle for the restoration of the ancient gospel will be won. A letter from Ramsey's Creek, Missouri, stated:

The sects have commenced persecution, and are rallying their forces for a crusade against us. May the Lord help us to brook sternly all opposition and sustain the best of all causes! . . . People are beginning to read for themselves; light is elicited, priestcraft is losing its charms, and of course sectarianism and infidelity must recede. It is not my opinion that the sects will possess themselves of the great valley of the Mississippi, for which they have been striving.[14]

Disciples were able to use even the complaints of other groups against them as ammunition in the fight. Mr. Campbell, replying to a Mr. Brantly, who had objected that Disciples were disrupting the religious world, said, " 'You object that we are the turners of the religious world upside down. "Many" (you say) "of the Baptist churches in Virginia, Kentucky, and Ohio, have been infested and distracted with the spirit of innovation attendant upon the efforts of these professed restorers of the ancient gospel." Blessed be the Lord of hosts for this voice of triumph from the lips of an enemy. . . . Infested and distracted with what? The ancient gospel. . . . Just as it ought to be. . . .' "[15] Obviously, the rest of the religious world did not share the Disciples' high opinion of the salutory power of the medicine which they proposed to inject into the patient. The other groups appear not only to have been convinced that the medicine would not work, but also that the patient was not sick.

The charge that the other groups were unfairly misrepresenting the beliefs and purposes of the new movement was frequently made. One has reason to suspect that this is important not merely for suggesting the rich soil which was provided for the nurture of the in-group hostility, but also in suggesting that the doctrinal issues were not nearly so significant in provoking opposition as was the fact that a new group was attempting to disrupt the *status quo* in the religious situation. People have a habit of not wanting to be reformed, and they resent even the suggestion that reform might be in order. It is not surprising that Absalom Rice would write from Callaway County, Missouri, in December, 1836,

> The sects seem to take pleasure in misrepresenting us and throwing every odium on us in their power, but generally dressed in some fictitious garb. Whether you visit a Methodist camp-meeting, a Presbyterian collection, or Baptist association, your ears are stunned with the war-trumpet and the marshalling of the troops, and the exhortations of the recruiting officers, forming one grand crusade . . . against "Campbellism"; while they are raising phantoms and fighting ghosts and hobgoblins that exist only in their own imaginations.[16]

We have suggested that there is implicit in the development of Disciples a dialectic between the *unity* emphasis and the *restoration* emphasis. This is clearly demonstrated by the events and evidence of the first decade of the independence of Disciples of Christ from other groups. Both sides of the dialectic could operate at the same time, though not without some results that were definitely schizoid in effect. This is shown in the early attempts to maintain the principle of adhering to the New Testament pattern and yet allow for the necessary adaptations to circumstances that were bound to come.

Alexander Campbell, discussing the suggestion that one could have communion and fellowship on a Christian basis with unbaptized persons, because nothing could be cited in scripture which forbids it, said that whether an explicit command forbidding the practice could be found was not the point. "The question is," he argued, "By what authority, command or precept, does he commune at the Lord's table with unbaptized persons? It is not enough to say there is no command against it. Is there no command for it? . . . Whatever is not commanded by the Lord is human."[17] By this he could have meant only that he was not so sure it was a good idea to have anything to do, in a religious way, with persons who are not of correct beliefs.

Yet see what happens when six years later (1836) in an entirely different context Campbell was able to assert the exactly opposite principle. In 1830 he had said, "What we do must be expressly commanded!" Now, in what follows he says, "Liberty is permitted in what is not revealed!"

> For while nothing can be required for which there is no divine warrant, and nothing will be tolerated which is opposed to the laws and teachings of Christ and the Apostles, the greatest liberty of opinion is permitted as it respects everything which is not revealed. Of this kind are the order of the exercises of public worship, the manner in which the commemorative institutions are to be attended to, the kind of building which the church is to occupy; and in the same class are found the various ways and means by which the gospel is to be spread abroad.[18]

This was to be an important idea when Disciples began to demand more adequate material embodiments of their strength and more efficient organizational procedures. Yet the "liberty is permitted" principle is radically contradictory when compared to the "must be expressly commanded" principle. It is difficult to see them coming out of the same movement, unless we are allowed to conclude that social change had made the older principle unsatisfactory, or that, because time makes ancient good uncouth, new occasions teach new duties.

The temptation to suggest that the two opposing principles were invoked at different times, depending upon whether the proposed practice or belief was something that the new movement feared or something it wanted to encourage, and without any particular sense of inconsistency, is a difficult one to resist. Consistency, after all, is the hobgoblin of little minds, and the intellect can be made to do strange tricks if vital interests in which our personalities are involved are at stake. During this early period, Disciples were careful to protect the distinct principles upon which the new group had been built, but it is amazing how careful they were (unconsciously, to be sure) to leave the door open for any changes that would be necessary later.

Alexander Campbell was even fond of the word "innovations," though when he used it, he referred to the assertion that his own movement constituted an innovation when compared with what he called the "sects."

> Innovations must be made—reform must, of necessity, take place—great changes must be introduced. . . .
>
> Why, then, are so many ministers and churches afraid of innovations? Are ministers afraid they shall lose their livings? Are they afraid they shall become unpopular? . . . Why are the churches so much afraid. . . . Are they afraid they shall be obliged to dissolve their partnership with the world. . . . to lay aside their gay equipage, their gewgaws, and all their extravagances in dress and other things?[19]

Had Mr. Campbell been around at the time, later history would have given him an answer to the questions. How right you are, Mr. Campbell—on both counts! Innovations, indeed, must be made, and people will be afraid of them, including some of your own religious descendants. But, then, how could you have known that thirty-five years later your own words about the necessity of innovations might be used to justify changing some things which you believed to be fixed and inviolable?

Disciples may have unconsciously realized what future needs might be. As early as 1834 a door, through which one might drive a truck, was left open for later developments. The allegiance to restoring the New Testament pattern was not given up. It was simply discovered that if one looked long and hard, he could find scriptural authority for whatever circumstances might require. "There is a way," wrote Campbell,

> of searching the scriptures for authority for certain matters, and we may be sure we shall never find it. If anyone was to seek authority for building a house to meet in, or for printing, translating, and publishing the Bible . . . he would never find it, if he expect to find it in the form of the ten commandments, or in the way that Moses reared the tabernacle. . . . There is, however, authority in the New Testament . . . for every thing necessary to the comfort and edification of the church and the conversion of the whole world.[20]

The phrase "everything necessary to the edification of the church" is of such an omnibus character that it could conceivably include everything that the church has ever done. And this in a church that is supposed to be legalistic and rigid about restoring the primitive church!

One sees also in this early period of the independent existence of Disciples the sectarian emphasis upon the condemnation of "worldliness." This, too, has been given to posterity in the form of a set of verses, again indicating that it had reached the folklore stage. Based on the old idea that pork is forbidden, but Mahomet did not say which piece of the animal, the verses, brought up to date, show how by a subtle process worldliness overtakes the believer.

> Renounce the world, the preacher cries;
> We do, the multitude replies.
> While one as innocent regards
> A snug and friendly game of cards;
> And one, whatever you may say,
> Can see no evil in a play;
> Some love a concert or a race;
> And others shooting, and the chase;

E'en dames, their fortunes to enhance,
Will have their children learn to dance,
And ape the fashions late from France.
Revil'd and lov'd, renounc'd and follow'd,
Thus, bit by bit, the world is swallow'd;
Each thinks his neighbor makes too free,
Yet likes a slice as well as he;
With sophistry their sauce they sweeten,
Till quite from tail to snout 'tis eaten.[21]

As early as 1834 the spirit of the world described in the foregoing verse had apparently entered the churches to a considerable degree. Alexander Campbell discerned the fact that already the class lines were beginning to be sharpened, and that these lines were reflected in the church.

The spirit of the world has invaded the church. The love of the world triumphs over the love of God. The fashions of the world have supplanted the manners and customs of Christians. . . . The whole order of Christian worship is fashioned to the caprice of the rich and influential, whom it would allure into the ranks of its profession by a compromise of all its heavenly attributes for the fascinations of rank and fortune. . . . Every thing to suit the whim of carnality. . . .

"Cut your sermon down to thirty minutes, rather than tire or jade *a respectable gentleman,*" says an exhorter in the *Religious Herald*. . . "Give the country folks one hour at most, but the town's folks never more than forty-five minutes."[22]

Disciples had, at this time, one must presume, very few "respectable gentlemen" of rank and fortune, who might be offended by a tedious sermon.

Even earlier than 1834 Campbell realized how pervasive was the influence of the surrounding culture. Visiting a large city in the Ohio Valley region, he observed that churches there were being built on the same principle as bridges and turnpikes, with stock being taken by capitalists and pew rents supplying a dividend to them. So at last it has come to this! "The rich are now to have the gospel preached to them in houses owned by the rulers of the darkness of this world. Satan . . . will soon reform, seeing he now builds meeting houses for the proclamation of the gospel."[23] The Devil, already well known for his ability to quote scripture, also builds churches.

Wesley, as noted earlier, perceived the connection between the virtues inculcated by evangelical religion and the rise of its adherents in the socio-economic scale. He was aware, also, that as people increased the pace of their upward mobility, and as increased wealth allowed them greater cultural advantages, their religion tended to be less important to them, except as a symbol of respectability. Alexander Campbell saw this process at work also, and he was not slow to observe that the older denominations were prospering, but they were also losing their "purity, piety, and moral soundness."

> The Presbyterian, Methodist, and Baptist communities have for some twenty-five years past grown very fast. They have enjoyed what the great mass of society calls great prosperity. But highly superficial must be his knowledge of church history, who does not know that the most rapid growth and outward prosperity of a religious society are no evidence of purity, piety, or moral soundness. . . . It often happens that the purity and the piety of a denomination decline in the exact ratio of its increase in favor with the people and the number of its proselytes. . . . Those will be found most corrupt who have the most wealth, the most colleges, the most splendid temples, cathedrals, synagogues, and altars, and the most learned, eloquent, and powerful public advocates. . . . *Yet wealth, and colleges, and meeting-houses, and learning, and eloquence, and popularity are all good, desirable, and useful, when not abused.* But it is almost as impossible for Christians not to abuse these, as it is for children to sport with flint and steel. . . . without detriment.[24]

This long quotation is a concise statement of a very important principle. No law which states that the loss of religion in individuals and churches is directly proportional to the increase in wealth involved can be established. Social change, rising standards of culture and education, increasing wealth and social position do, however, alter the nature of the effect of religion upon the people concerned. This may be taken as absolutely certain. The sectarian emphasis in the foregoing statement of this idea is contained in the assertion that the things spoken of as retarding the purity and piety of religion are yet "good, desirable, and useful, when not abused." In effect, then, the Disciples did not have things yet, but would take them if and when they came. We will risk the dangers involved, and trust that no spark will fly from our flint and steel.

Other items in the catalogue of worldly pleasures did not escape the attention of the early Disciples' movement. "Can any man, consistently with his profession of a Christian, own or keep what is vulgarly termed in the West a 'Doggery'—a grocery of ardent spirits and wines, which he vends . . . to gratify, and minister to, the beastly appetite of the drunkard and dissipated?" wrote a questioner to the *Millennial Harbinger*. This was obviously a loaded question. One can be sure that the questioner received the answer he expected. "I cannot understand," Mr. Campbell replied, "how any person, enlightened in the New Testament, could voluntarily, and with a pure conscience, stand in such a 'Doggery' . . . for one hour, much less officiate as a waiter from day to day on those miserable sinners who resort thither to drink down curses upon themselves."[25]

Along with liquor, dancing also was placed on the social index. The Bible may say, as it does in Ecclesiastes 3:4, that there is "a time to weep, and a time to laugh; a time to mourn, and a time to dance"; but if it did say this, the good Book had in mind a religious act and not the perverted and pagan form of it indulged in by the worldly of the middle 1800's. "No instances," averred the *Cross and Baptist Journal,* which Campbell had reprinted on this point, "of dancing are found upon record in the Bible, in which the two sexes united in the exercise, either as an act of worship or amusement . . . except that of the 'vain fellows,' devoid of shame."[26] This, one may suppose, settled the question, at least for Campbell and his group. A Christian could not indulge in social dancing, and that was that!

While in most social and economic questions Disciples in general held that they were matters of opinion, that is, they were not mentioned as such in Scripture and so could not be made terms of religious fellowship, certainly Disciples reflected the prejudices of a predominantly agrarian society against the speculator. The speculator, according to Alexander Campbell, is an immoral person.

He deals in the necessaries or comforts of life, and does no more than deal in them. He carries them to no place, he puts no improvement on them, increases them in no way. His whole employment, address, and art is simply to raise the price . . . to consult no one's interest but his own. . . .

This calling, in all its branches, is but sheer selfishness at work to enrich itself on the labors of others . . . and is wholly incompatible with the genius of Christian mortality.[27]

Not only speculators are in danger of selfishness and worldliness. Even preachers—perish forbid!—are susceptible, especially under the spell of southern skies and, more particularly, of beautiful ladies.

A southern sky, or soil, or society, or something . . . is most prostrating to the moral constitution of preachers. . . . Young preachers are apt to fall in love with southern ladies; whose general amiability and numerous attractions, especially when rich, soon subdue their too susceptible hearts into the delicious allegiance of the matrimonial covenant. . . . The preacher soon finds an opiate for his conscience, and a quietus for his active benevolence.[28]

This most interesting phenomenon was observed by Mr. Campbell on a tour of the South. Since all pretty girls, with wealth, do not live in the South, one suspects that he might have observed the same dangerous elements in operation north of the Mason-Dixon line.

Both the increasing sense of group solidarity, and the sectarian critique of worldliness, then, found expression in the early stages of the independent existence of Disciples of Christ. But this was not all. The growing sense of the need for organization and more efficient methods also was manifested even at this early period. This, too, as we have suggested, is a part of the sect-to-denomination development. As early as 1830 Alexander

Campbell, speaking in terms of the newly felt needs, affirmed the proposition that while the root of evil is, to be sure, money, it is very necessary in the task of spreading the gospel and so may legitimately be solicited. "Although we are opposed to the whole monied scheme of converting the world, and to the hireling systems of the clergy, . . . yet it is not true that the New Testament furnishes no authority for calling upon the citizens of Christ's kingdom for aid in promulgating the glad tidings, or in teaching the christian religion. Paul received such aid and *commanded* it."[29] The need for money was evident, so the way for its collection and use in the cause was evidently being prepared on the ideological front.

Yet Campbell's earlier teaching had made an impression even when Campbell himself recognized the new needs. The obvious conclusion is that the scriptural authority for the appeal for money for organizing missionary activities, if it existed at all, was there to be had all the time. Campbell and his followers, being occupied with other issues and not experiencing a felt need for it, had ignored that authority until the occasion for its use arose. In the same year in which Campbell had asserted the legitimacy of appealing for funds, a correspondent wrote to him with an appeal based squarely on Campbell's own earlier condemnations of such practices. "Let the Church of Jesus come up out of Babylon; let her shake herself from the dust; let her wash herself and put on her beautiful garments; let her cast out of her bosom all the money lovers, . . . proud and high-minded, and their households; then she will shine forth like the sun. Then will she not need the money of the wicked to pay her ministers; and, if offered will refuse it."[30]

Some of his group were engaged in reminding Alexander Campbell of things he had said on earlier occasions. Campbell himself was addressing his attention to the weighty question of what Disciples of Christ ought to do about co-operating, one church with another. Indeed, Disciples had scarcely become a distinct group when they began to feel a necessity for some kind of machinery of co-operation. As we pointed out earlier, there was in the background of the group a strong fear of associations and conferences which went, in their purposes and activities, beyond the local congregation. Campbell himself had much to say in the *Christian Baptist* on this point.

Yet in 1835 we find him saying, in a statement which shows how the Disciples were already growing out of the sectarian stage,

> That christians should do nothing for the conversion of the world beyond the immediate influence of their personal behavior, must spring from a morbid sensibility, from a sort of mental or moral dyspepsia, of which they ought to be cured if possible. . . .
>
> Co-operation among christian churches in all the affairs of the common salvation . . . is the very essence of the christian institution. . . .
>
> There is too much squeamishness about the *manner* of co-operation.[31]

This is to say that the need for co-operation is, or should be, evident to everyone, and this means organization. Campbell, speaking for the needs of the future, was saying, "This job must be done, and we ought not waste time arguing about whether we can legitimately co-operate." It is apparent that this represents a significant change in attitude away from earlier sectarian views.

The agitation for education among Disciples of Christ also began during this first decade of independence. In 1831 Alexander Campbell, still mindful of his earlier sentiments on the subject, could put ink to paper with a scathing reminder that education was not necessary for the man who wants to be a Christian saint. "The saints," he said,

> have derived their qualifications to perform their Master's service, not from poring, for years, over the profane remains of heathen historians, divines, priests, and moralists . . . not from . . . the unintelligible wranglings of contentious and contending Doctors of human divinity . . . not from theological seminaries, those prolific, filthy, hotbeds of sophistry, error, prejudice, nonsense, and factions . . . but from the unadulterated oracles of the God of truth.[32]

Five years later Campbell published, with obvious approval, a letter in which the agitation for education among the groups was quite evident.

> The establishment of a college, or colleges, is not hereby recommended for the purpose of educating persons in the principles of scholastic theology, and thus preparing them to act as clergymen; for in the popular import of the term, we have no clergy,

the letter began.

> Yet it is necessary that persons employed in teaching must, and ought to know, more than those whom they teach. . . . We . . . should not be behind hand in devising ways and means by which our posterity may all enjoy the benefits of an early education, that they may both be able better to investigate the sacred writings, and to understand the genius of the christian religion.[33]

This points to the principle mentioned by H. Richard Niebuhr, that the demand for education among religious groups was often tied to the desire to have the younger generation adequately trained in the principles and teachings of their faith. It is significant that the need for such education is recognized at all, in view of the earlier attitudes. This, too, is clear evidence of the effect of social and cultural change.

A significant number of references to the matter of whether preachers should be paid are also to be noted during this period. In 1831 Campbell had taken the position that we can consider paying our preachers and evangelists, but he was careful to add that no recognition of the clergy as "spiritual fathers" was to go with the pay. Preachers perform a useful service in preaching the gospel and converting the world, and they may rightfully be sustained in this work, but we need no official clergy to be our mediators of faith or salvation.[34] Here was the old fear of raising up a priesthood in the church as distinct from the ordinary members, but it is nevertheless evidence of changed conditions when one contrasts this attitude with the early castigations of the hireling priests and clergy.

By 1835 the problem of recruiting a sufficient ministry and providing for their support had become so acute that a definite stand favoring the support of the clergy had to be taken.

> The hireling is one who works for wages merely; but every one who receives wages is not a hireling. Were that the truth, then Paul himself was a hireling; for he says, "*I received wages* of other churches to do you service." There is priestcraft, and in opposing that, shall we establish laycraft? And indeed, when I see men sent out by congregations to republish the gospel, and impoverished by their labors so as to become objects of sympathy, if not positive charity—then I think it is time to watch against laycraft.[35]

The attitude expressed here by Alexander Campbell was to change even more decidedly in favor of the view that preachers could legitimately be paid. If men were to devote their full time to the spread of the restoration movement, they would have to be sustained by the churches.

Enough has been said to show that during the first decade of their separate existence Disciples of Christ manifested at least three characteristics of the sect-to-denomination phenomenon; (1) increasing in-group feeling, sustained in an atmosphere of controversy and acrimonious religious conflict; (2) the sectarian critique of worldliness, and (3) an increasing awareness of the need for organization, training, and education, to foster a more adequate and efficient growth of the movement. This early period set the major problems which Disciples of Christ were to confront. The argument on many of the points we have raised is still going on. For this reason we have to say that one cannot draw a clear line between the sect and denomination. We cannot say, just here, at this specific point, the group becomes a denomination, whereas formerly it was a sect.

Perhaps the most significant development during this early period was the increasing consciousness that Disciples were a distinct group. This consciousness grew out of the conditions which we have described; and yet, even while Disciples were engaged in furious controversies with other groups, who had absolutely no doubt that they *were* another *sect,* the new group clung to the belief that they were not a church.

> While the Reformers consistently refused to call themselves *a* church, and never claimed to constitute *the* church, they asserted for themselves a unique status. Their churches were simon-pure "churches of Christ," . . . while all others were sects. . . . They enjoyed the distinction of having no denominational name. . . . But "we as a people" became the common phrase expressive of their consciousness of kind.[36]

The members of this group knew whom they meant when they said "we." This is sufficient evidence that, sociologically, they were a sect, on the way to becoming a denomination.

CHAPTER V

The Age of Expansion:

"Views and Practices Not Commonly Received"

During the period which we have characterized as the age of expansion the three manifestations of the sect-to-denomination development which showed themselves in the earlier period continued. In these years between 1840 and 1865 the dialectic between the unity emphasis and the restoration emphasis became even more pronounced, and there was certainly no abatement of the Disciples' sense of distinctness. Indeed, one basic premise of the life of this group during this period was, You go your way, and we'll go ours. "Talk on, gentlemen," Mr. Campbell addressed the opponents of the Disciples.

> There is a day when it will be known what our motives are, and what our principles and character; and it will not be in your power to blind or prejudice the Judge of all!
>
> You are determined to wage a new war against us. . . . Adhere then to your Baptist principles, and tamper not with ours. . . . We have always shown our love of union with all who renounce human creeds.[1]

Disciples were extremely sensitive to the question of who had caused the separation from the Baptists; one suspects that Shakespeare's "milady doth protest too much" is applicable here. There is no doubt that the frequent reference to this point is further evidence of an increasing sense of separateness. Referring to the separation, Campbell said in 1843,

I think it was not at all indispensable. . . . Nothing in their system or ours compelled separation. They needed reform—radical reform . . . [but in the areas where reform was needed it could have been accomplished] without the necessity of a new denomination.

Still it may be better as it is, that a new organization, founded upon the New Institution alone, and neither upon unity of opinion, nor upon similarity of experience, should have been erected and made to witness.[2]

The separation was, as Mr. Campbell realized, a *fait accompli,* and he was not sure but what it was a good idea. The statement that "nothing in our system or theirs compelled separation" would seem, if it is true, to be a clear indication that the separation must be attributed to *social* causes, rather than to doctrinal differences.

Alexander Campbell's own account of the separation, written in 1854 would seem to lend support to this view.

It was but a short time . . . until *the abandonment of usages long cherished* by the Baptists, and the *introduction of views and practices not commonly received* by them, gave rise to so much umbrage and opposition . . . that this body were induced . . . to denounce as heretical, and exclude from their fellowship, all those churches which favored the views of the reformers. . . .

The Disciples, thus suddenly cut off from their connections with the Baptists, formed themselves every where into distinct churches.[3]

It is significant that the two phrases, "the abandonment of usages long cherished" and "the introduction of views and practices not commonly received," are introduced. This is not to deny that certain of the doctrinal differences were real and important, but it is to urge that they need not have caused a separation, as even Alexander Campbell admitted.

If Campbell's own view of the situation be accepted—the view that nothing in the religious systems of either group led to any necessity of separation—then we are forced to look for psychological and/or social causes for the separation which, in fact, did occur. Nothing is to be gained by attributing the separation to the obstinacy or cantankerousness of any of the individuals concerned. The separation of Disciples and Baptists can no more be explained in this way than the Reformation can be explained as a personal plot of Martin Luther, hatched because Luther liked the ladies and wanted to do away with clerical celibacy.

The sore point in the argument was always who threw whom out. Naturally Disciples continued to blame the schism on the Baptists, and the Baptists, just as naturally, returned the compliment. "I have no desire," said J. Creath in a letter to the *Millennial Harbinger,* "to renew unpleasant feelings between us and our Baptist brethren . . . but I was asked a few days ago, by a Baptist preacher, and am frequently asked, what did you leave the Baptists for? I answer, for the same reason that Jonah left the ship, when the sailors *pitched* him head foremost into the sea, and said he could not stay in the ship."[4]

Mr. Creath's letter, written in 1860, was only a more popular statement of an idea that had been commonly expressed by Disciples when they were asked about their status. To the question "are the Disciples a new sect?" the reply was "We answer, too, by asking a question. *Who made it?* Was it not those who excommunicated us? . . . Was it for *faith?* We fearlessly answer no. . . .

". . . If we are a sect, then, we ask, *In the day of judgment at whose door will this sin lie?* The first Christians were a sect among the Jews. But on which party does the guilt lie!!"[5] The import of this statement would seem to be that the Disciples were no longer interested in denying that they were a new sect. They seemed more interested in assigning the blame for the fact. The assertion that the Christians were a sect among the Jews is, incidentally, a correct statement of a very important principle; that a sect's existence is not a question of the truth or error of a set of principles, but rather of the social effects resulting from the fact that a group *believes* these principles and *acts upon* them.

Yet the use of the term "sect" by any group is usually not meant to apply to that group itself. It appears to be tied in with the problem of "truth" and "error," which means from the sociological standpoint the "in" and the "out" group. Without entering into the question of which view is correct, it is sociologically siginficant that in any given case "my group" is always on the side of the angels, while the others are supporting "human opinion." There are, according to this view, allowable reasons for religious separation (though schism is the great evil!). "What excuse can we have for dividing the Lord's people by questions that tend only to strife, and which are worthless, no matter how settled?" wrote W. K. Pendleton in the *Millennial Harbinger*. "But on the other hand, if this difference be founded on divine appointment, if it is the difference between fidelity to a divine ordinance and the disloyal substitution in its place of a human tradition, then let us make no compromise—declare no truce—but push the distinction to the sharpest verge of controversy, till the error is corrected."[6] The inference, obviously, is that what we stand for is divine ordinance, and what our opponents stand for is human opinions. This same in-group, out-group situation has been repeated many times in the history of religious movements.

That Disciples were sincere in this, no one can doubt. But no one can doubt, either, that this quite natural sectarian emphasis was to be the basis for an unfortunate legalism which has kept a large minority of the group from co-operation with other churches, long after the real bases for the original strife between the churches has been forgotten. One may have cause to regret that the Disciples in their period of expansion and growing strength did not realize that what they were saying about schismatics could also, with equal justice, be applied to themselves.

> Love, Christian affection, and sympathy with all the tender charities towards one another . . . these were the outward signs of union. . . . Any thing which disturbed this feeling of harmony, or broke this intimate bond of love, was schismatical. It was not necessary, that the root of bitterness should mature into an actual division . . . or the withdrawal of communion. . . . The agitation . . . of any peculiarity of human opinion, . . . was schismatical. . . .[7]

That the other groups would freely admit that what they taught and practiced was merely "human opinion" is entirely too much to expect.

A sociologically more valid critical principle, and one by which Disciples could have, with much profit, measured their own life and thought, was asserted by R. Richardson. To become a schismatic, he wrote, it is not necessary for a man to introduce an element foreign to Christianity, or to dogmatize upon the imperfect records of the past. "It is sufficient that he select some of the acknowledged evangelical truths, and exalt these to an undue and exclusive importance. . . .

". . . Sectarianism, indeed, is but another name for *narrow-mindedness*. . . ."[8] In all honesty, it must be said that exalting some acknowledged truths to an undue and exclusive importance is exactly what other groups thought Disciples were doing.

Two attitudes were struggling in Alexander Campbell's mind, and in the mind of Disciples of Christ. This becomes increasingly apparent as the story moves along. One of these, based upon the *restoration* idea, led in the direction of legalism, a religious hardening of the arteries; the other, the *unity* idea, led in the direction of a reassertion of the freedom principles incipient in the original Reformation, and was expressive of the spirit of Locke's famous *Letters on Toleration*. Each of these attitudes was to receive its due emphasis, at varying times, depending upon the needs of the moment. On one occasion Campbell, forgetting for a time the religious strife in which Disciples were involved, might write on a theme like "the Christian must be free"; but later, with other needs in mind, he would devote time to asserting that there is "nothing new in Christianity."

"Whatever may be the dangers from storms and shoals and reefs," wrote Campbell in 1847, "the home of the mariner is on the 'glad waters of the deep blue sea,' and that of the Christian is in the 'deep things of God.' Let no one presume to limit him, or erect a barrier in his way. Let no one interpose a shallow human creed, between the soul and its Author. Let the lover of truth sit at the feet of Jesus, and hear his words. . . ."[9] Yet at the same time, one cannot hear these words freely and discover new meanings and significance for them for the life of his own time. Our religion is once and for all handed down. It cannot be changed or have anything added.

> *Our whole religion, objectively and doctrinally considered, is found in a book.* Nothing discovered by any man, that has lived since John wrote the Apocalypse, is of any virtue in religion; nay, indeed, is not part or parcel of Christianity. All that can now be pretended or aimed at, by any sane mind, is *the proper interpretation of what is written in Hebrew and Greek* and translated into all the modern languages in the civilized world. Whatever in Christianity is new is not true.[10]

Significantly in the later development of Disciples, the "liberals" have followed the "we-must-be-free" idea. The extreme conservatives have tended to support the "there-is-nothing-new" contention.

The evidence shows that during the period we have called the age of expansion, the struggle between these contradictory tendencies of the Disciples movement was much on the minds of its members. Those who wanted to tone down the emphasis which had made Disciples exclusive and distinct took Alexander Campbell seriously when he told them in 1847, "I will not, because I cannot, admit that some Protestants should claim the right to unchristianize other Protestants because they presume to differ from their interpretations of certain celebrated proof-texts. . . . Every man must think for himself and act for himself, else he is but a machine—an automaton. . . ."[11] This is a time-honored position among Protestants, but one suspects that Campbell was not so "Protestant" as to allow his idea here to be applied to a favorite "proof-text" of Disciples, the one which they insist should be translated "immerse." Perhaps it could not have occurred to our Disciples forebears that if they followed this idea about proof-texts consistently they had no grounds upon which to insist that the only proper means of baptism was immersion.

Nevertheless, there were among the group not a few who were bothered by the way in which the controversy with the "sects" was being carried on. The correspondent who wrote to the *Millennial Harbinger* about "our treatment of the sects," in 1853, undoubtedly spoke for others beside himself. "I have lately been thinking of our treatment of the different sectarian denominations in the land, who profess the Christian religion, but differ from us in their views of it," wrote this troubled restoration warrior. "I have come to the conclusion . . . that in our preachings and writings, we too often speak of, and refer to, them in a harsh and severe manner—in terms uncalled for, and not authorized by the Bible. . . . We have no right to indulge in wholesale denunciation of them."[12] The spirit of exclusiveness and sectarian zeal was, in some quarters at least, cooling down to a degree. Earlier, Disciples had certainly felt that they had a right to denounce the sects wholesale; indeed, it had been not only a right, but a duty.

At least one section of the movement, then, was not so sure that the zeal for orthodoxy should be carried too far. After all, it was argued, we ought not to forget that in our earlier days we were persecuted and cast out because we were said to be disturbing the harmony of the brotherhood. "But now—*we* have become a 'Religious body.' We have our shibboleths, our 'fixed principles,' and there is danger lest we, too, shall become infatuated with the Romish conceit of infallibility, against which we said so much in those early pioneer-days."[13] From the sociological perspective used here to interpret the "natural history" of Disciples as a religious movement, we may say that no more exacting statement of the sociological reality could be formulated. We have become a religious body—with shibboleths and fixed principles which lay us open to the danger of the conceit of infallibility. Disciples, no more than any other religious movement in world history, could escape the operation of the sociological process of sect-to-denomination. The Romish conceit of infallibility was unquestionably a danger; it was to become more of a problem a few years after the period we are now examining, but even while Disciples were expanding, their very increase in numbers and influence was correlated with a tendency toward doctrinal and organizational calcification.

One way to discern this is to note a controversy in the movement which was gaining momentum and intensity with each passing year; it was the struggle over whether they ought to have fellowship with "sectarian," that is to say, *unimmersed* Christians. In this period such a controversy was a good measure and test of the conflicting tendencies in the group. Not all of Alexander Campbell's utterances, as we have amply demonstrated, supported the freedom and unity side of the Disciples dialectic; he was in many instances the strict legalist he is supposed to have been. But in one notable and important instance he gave unequivocal support to those who wanted freedom and unity. Campbell had made some casual references to "Christians" in churches which did not immerse, and for this he was reproached by a dear lady from Lunenburg, Virginia. His reply, now known as the "Lunenburg Letter," follows in part.

> Who is a Christian? I answer, Every one that believes in his heart that Jesus of Nazareth is the Messiah, the Son of God; repents of his sins, and obeys him in all things according to his measure of knowledge of his will. . . . I cannot, therefore, make any one duty the standard of Christian state or character, not even immersion. . . . I cannot be a perfect Christian without a right understanding and a cordial reception of immersion in its true and scriptural meaning. But he that thence infers that none are Christians but the immersed, as greatly errs as he who affirms that none are alive but those of clear and full vision.[14]

Had Disciples of a few years later followed the spirit, or even the letter, of this statement, the controversy over receiving the unimmersed could never have arisen. But Campbell had said other things, and Disciples as a group had thought other things, not conceivably susceptible of a liberal interpretation. Those who believed more in restoration than in unity were not slow to realize this and were able to make good use of the contradictory material.

The controversy over having fellowship with those who did things differently is not, therefore, strange in a group that was beginning to develop its own common habits and customs. It is well known that people prefer their own ways of doing things, even though there may be other ways of getting the same results. Why else would they be doing things in a certain way, except that it is obviously the *best* way—or at least that it was once believed to be the best way and is now accepted as customary? Herein are the seeds of an incipient legalism.

"That there are many Christians among the sects, I have never doubted," wrote George W. Elley, in the *Millennial Harbinger*. "We urge fellowship, or communion, with all such as are entitled to membership in the house of God. . . . Communion is regulated by the law of Christ, and by the feelings and tastes of no one. Are we pleading for a restoration of the old landmarks? . . . there must be no shrinking from the whole law of God."[15] But from the viewpoint of those who were beginning to love union and freedom more than restoration such a view would only do harm. Do not "damage this great plea for Christian union by a spirit of exclusiveness which will only allow of '*supposed* piety and Christianity' in neighboring denominations, which refuses to recognize as Christians all the unimmersed, and claims for ourselves to be Christians *par excellence,* because of a bit of accuracy on the question of baptism." This was Isaac Errett's reply to the view that only the immersed should be received. His grounds were that "A denominationalism more intense and more intolerant it would be difficult to conceive than that in which we must land, if this kind of argument is to prevail."[16] Here, too, is evidence that for some in the movement the sectarian zeal had cooled down, and they were no longer interested in exclusiveness. What had formerly been a consuming passion among the restorers of the ancient gospel was now "a bit of accuracy on the question of baptism!"

But there is more to the argument. Mr. Elley and, one presumes, many other Disciples were not satisfied. Let us be logical about this, he said. If you admit unimmersed persons to the communion table how can you refuse them church membership? Furthermore, you assert that we who oppose communion with the sects are hidebound zealots bent on saving a cold and lifeless formality. But if we are hidebound zealots, what are you? All to come, you say! "This is as liberal and as loose as the greatest latitudinarian in the land could desire. This door admits birds of every color and tribe."[17]

What was being argued here was not logic, but two very different attitudes and approaches to the meaning and purposes of religion. This is evident from Mr. Errett's reply, "We do not," he wrote, "intend to fall out with any brother because he honestly and logically, as he thinks, comes to a different conclusion on this subject from that which we have, in the same spirit, reached. . . . Christianity is not built on an ordinance. Neither Peter nor baptism is *the rock*."[18] There can be no doubt that this is an entirely different atmosphere from that in which the movement had begun. It is also the prelude to a period of intense controversy, as we shall see.

While the Disciples movement was pursuing its own inner development, and pushing its geographical and numerical frontiers out even farther, there was a steady stream of references to the atmosphere of controversy in which the group began its life. This only served to increase the ethnocentric feelings of uneasiness about their relations to the rest of Christendom in America. In 1844 the language of battle fields and conquests was still very much in the vogue. In that year, Campbell urged Disciples on in a "mighty battle still to be fought."

The old shibboleths will be erased from the sectarian banners and new symbols substituted in their stead. Many will return to Popery, and many will forsake the Babelism of partyism. . . . The two great rivals will . . . be the Pope and Human Tradition on the one side—Jesus Christ and the Apostolic Writings on the other. . . . Let us then prepare for the battle.[19]

But even fifteen years later the same consciousness of fierce opposition was still in evidence. Disciples were referred to in the pulpits and press of the "sects" as the "hydra-headed monster that disturbs the peace and distracts the slumbers of orthodoxy." "It is amusing to see how these *ordinary men* are putting on the airs of the Horsleys and the Pascals of former days!" wrote Campbell. "They seem to think, like the fly upon the wheel, that they kick up a mighty dust as they proceed! . . . They mock at us and revile us; but we shall . . . imitate Nehemiah and the ancient builders . . . who continued at the work, 'and built the wall.' "[20]

Religion, in the America of the "middle period," was apparently still something really to get excited about. At least for those who were interested at all, it made a great difference how one looked at such groups as Disciples. So much sizzling rhetoric and nasty sarcasm as is evident in the religious press of the period from 1810 to 1865 would not have been wasted on a subject which was of little importance to those who wrote about it. We may look with regret and pity upon the amount of energy that was apparently wasted in what seems to a more sophisticated age fruitless and unnecesssary argument; but this may be partly because the great questions out of which these petty arguments grew are no longer believed important. Be that as it may, there can be no doubt that when these religious parties contended so fiercely they honestly believed that great matters of heaven and hell were at stake. From the standpoint of its sociological import, this aura of the battlefield which surrounded the religion of the period has been ably summed up by one of Campbell's earnest correspondents, who signed his initials, J. H. "Praying men," he said, " 'contend earnestly for the truth once delivered to the saints'; but this is always in reference to whose *without*—not with their brethren!"[21] This man, albeit unconsciously, was a sociologist!

There is much more evidence of the continuing presence of ethnocentrism among Disciples during this age of expansion. A considerable number of items dealing with the Disciples' group consciousness could be cited, in addition to the evidence already given. Enough has been said to show that Disciples were a marching army with a strong morale and a vivid sense that the future of true religion lay in their hands. This is not a new phenomenon, but it takes on a much more lifelike aspect when it can be traced in the body of source material growing directly out of the movement itself.

CHAPTER VI

The Age of Expansion: the Continuing Battle with the World

Not only was the sense of distinctness of Disciples of Christ maintained and increased during the expansion period, but the other manifestations of the sect-to-denomination process were also inevitably revealed. The critique of worldliness and paganism was continued, though certain changes in attitude that went with the Disciples' rise in social and economic level are to be noted. A conspicuous element in this critique is the number of references which indicate that the Disciples group was extremely sensitive to the class lines that were becoming even more apparent as the years passed. Evidently, at least a part of this sensitiveness is directed at the established churches which had almost all the church members from the higher socio-economic classes.

Money is still, in 1840, as it was a decade or so earlier, the root of all evil. To it may be attributed most of the "coldness and bad times," and "many of the controversies and cases of discipline which occur in the churches." This "foredoomed and soul-withering passion for wealth" has "filled the Christian church with hypocrites, pretenders, and worldlings." This condition, moreover, cannot be remedied so long as Christians "pay undue court to men of wealth, without regard to moral worth; and despise the poor, without regard to their vices and follies."[1] Too great a thirst for riches—this was certainly to be added to the list of evils which impede the progress of the gospel. Disciples, in this period, did not doubt that "it consumes all piety, dries up all religious interest, burns out the conscience, withers the hand of Christian liberality, makes men selfish, narrow-minded, unfeeling, inhuman, and reckless of their own peace of mind."[2]

This feeling of suspicion about the evil that money can do was undoubtedly related to two factors; first, that Disciples were not yet a people who had risen sufficiently in the economic and social scale to see, without some feelings of guilt and suspicion, all the good things you could do with money[3]; and second, that Disciples were almost overwhelmingly a rural people, and this colored their attitudes toward the "big city" churches. "The American cities," wrote Alexander Campbell in 1843,

> like all other cities, are not favorable to the prevalence of pure religious influences. Like frontier settlements, they are good theatres for Methodists, and such forms of religion as require more soul than spirit, more animal feeling than Christian knowledge. Men unfortunately suppose, that because the inhabitants of cities understand trade, politics, and fashionable dress, better than farmers, and other country people, that they ought, forsooth, to be regarded as possessing superior Christian science and piety. . . . A grand and pernicious mistake! . . . The eastern and western population, living in favorable rural positions, are more learned in Biblical science, and better acquainted with the Christian Institution . . . than those with whom it has been my lot to mingle in the great cities.[4]

You people in cities, he was saying, may have all the money, and the fine clothes, but we have the religion and spiritual understanding, and this is infinitely more valuable.

This constantly recurring emphasis upon worldliness in the church was not without its relation to the attempt of Disciples to gain and hold a following, and to the fact that they were actively engaged in a struggle with other groups, most of which had a head start. Much was made of the fact that the sects and parties who opposed Disciples were filled with "gross corruption." "Practices, most palpably anti-Christian, are openly tolerated and sanctioned by both priest and laity!" it was said. "Church *feasts,* and church *tea-parties,* and church *fairs,* where all the *luxuries* of the day that can please the eye, or administer to the *gratification* of the *appetite,* have taken the place of the old fashioned church fasts."[5] Those who wanted pure and undefiled religion then, would know that the place to find it was with the group of Disciples of Christ.

But that was not entirely true either; some of the leaders in the movement were already alarmed at the signs that many Disciples were becoming acculturated to the ways of "the world" and the wiles of the "sects." "The time has been when our brethren were celebrated for knowing and loving the word of God better than any other people," wrote Alexander Campbell. "Indeed our striplings and maidens were a terror to many sectarian preachers, . . . But the case is now altered. The youths have laid by their armor as though the battle was ended, and consequently they are growing careless of their duty, and lukewarm in the cause of Christ."[6]

And that was not all! Intense in-group feelings of distinctness were involved. There was the suggestion that the ancient gospel was being laid aside for the enticements of more worldly and impure doctrines.

Those who are attentively watching the signs of the times among us, are deploring the rapidity with which some of us are assimilating ourselves, more in practice than in doctrine, to the errors of the sectarian world around us. As the Jews of old became corrupted by the Gentile nations with whom they were connected, so we are unconsciously departing, in some things, from primitive correctness.[7]

It is significant that the particular place of the young people in the problem of "apostasy" is mentioned. The sect-to-denomination process appears to involve a focusing of the effects of social change upon the second and third generations. Those in the first generation of a group's existence, having been intimately associated with the original experiences and attitudes with which the group began its existence, are more than likely to remain faithful. But the next generation, which must be "taught" the whys and wherefores of the group culture, are more susceptible to the pressures of outside forces.

Some evidence that Disciples were rising in the economic scale can be found in the references to new church buildings, and in the discussions of what kind of a building is suitable for Christian worship. Alexander Campbell, writing to his daughter in 1848, said that a Christian meetinghouse "ought to be plain and unadorned, save with simplicity and neatness. It ought to be amply spacious, well ventilated, illuminated, and heated, every way agreeable so far as convenience, health, and comfort are concerned."[8] Anything beyond this is a slander on the religion of Jesus Christ; anything like gowns or vestments would be a relic of the dark ages, of salt, oil, and holy water.

Nevertheless, a year earlier Campbell had printed an article in the *Millennial Harbinger,* the emphasis of which was that the church ought to be a fit place in which to worship.

The painful glare transmitted by uncurtained windows, revealing the naked walls, the rude benches, the rough table, and the clumsy rostrum usually met with in our houses of worship, seem illy to comport with the circumstances of the place and solemnities of religion. . . . Surely a decent respect for the service of the house of God should induce a careful attention to every means calculated to favor devotional feeling, and sanctify those rites whose mysterious import claims the undivided attention of the soul![9]

To be sure, Disciples were encouraged not to concern themselves with long-drawn aisles and fretted vaults, with clustered pillars and gorgeous tapestries—all the things which gratify a love of splendor for its own sake. Yet, "a careful attention to every means calculated to favor devotional feeling" could very easily lead to some of the things for which Disciples were criticizing other churches. Even a church "in every way agreeable so far as convenience, health, and comfort are concerned" would cost a lot more money than most of the early Disciples churches had. That such matters were being considered at all is evidence of a change in attitude in the group. One may doubt whether such things would even have been considered unless it can be assumed that there were at this time persons among our Disciples churches who were beginning to feel the need for such things as the "convenience, health, and comfort" of the worshipers. Certainly all the evidence points to the conclusion that these needs had not been considered important before.

In the light of what Alexander Campbell reported in 1853, after a visit to a certain Middle Western city, there can be no doubt that such a changed attitude had taken place. "The brethren," he said, obviously referring to Disciples,

> have just completed a spacious and comfortable meeting-house, the first erected in the city, and are intent on letting their light shine before men. Their example has stirred up other denominations, so that both Baptists and Methodists are now in progress of erecting their denominational temples. What immense sums of money are annually expended in honor of the *isms* of corrupted Christianity! . . . Not a few seem to imagine that they are glorifying the Lord that bought them, in rearing altars in honor of schisms and heresies.[10]

Is the inference, then, take pride in new and impressive buildings, if they happen to be our own? Without casting aspersions on the desire of Disciples to build churches, one may surmise that the other denominations in the city alluded to here undoubtedly felt exactly the same way about the Disciples church. It was, in *their* minds, also a monument to an *ism*. Were not a church monument to some ism it would never be built at all!

Disciples were beginning to take pride in the kind of showing they made in the eyes of the world. They may have continued to insist, as indeed they did in 1858, that "splendid church edifices are no test of splendid piety," and that "The original gospel and primeval manners and customs of the Saints in Jerusalem . . . or Phillipi would be *outre* and unendurable, in the polite circles of our modern orthodoxies,"[11] but they also wanted to be looked upon favorably by other groups in terms of material embodiments of their beliefs. One sees this in the plea to the brethren that "we need a church in Washington!"

Is it not quite a misfortune, and, indeed, a repoach upon our whole brotherhod . . . that we have not a local habitation or a name—without a house to meet in, or a desk from which to preach . . . *the primitive gospel of the kingdom and reign of the Lord Messiah!* We earnestly and ardently hope," the *Millennial Harbinger* continued, "that our brethren will make a liberal and united effort and contribution, for an object and purpose so worthy. . . . The nobility of the kingdom of heaven is superior to any other nobility. Let us have positive proof of a large class of nobility amongst us, and our boasting will not be in vain.[12]

Had not Disciples developed a sense of oneness that went beyond merely the local congregation such an appeal would never have been made. The interesting thing is that the project was conceived with a conscious recognition that the "prestige" of the group was involved. A people so important as Disciples, the appeal was saying, ought to be well represented in the nation's capital!

The sectarian critique against worldliness and paganism, in the churches and out, continued in the age of expansion. One notices particularly the number of references to the increasing prevalence of class distinctions in American society. These references cover every subject from the plea that all believers should cultivate Christian humility to the assertion that there are no social distinctions in the kingdom of God. "In the search after distinction there is often much of pride, and little of humility," states the *Millennial Harbinger* in 1852. "Our piety, if we are truly humble, will be entirely free from boasting and ostentation, for there is no greater contradiction in human speech, than to speak of a proud Christian."[13]

The assertion that there are no social distinctions in the kingdom of God can only be understood in terms of the fact that there *were* observed social distinctions in the visible church, and they were undoubtedly increasing. Had not such distinctions been observed, and had they not been regarded as jeopardizing "true religion," no such stress on the point would have been so obvious in the major religious journal of Disciples. "Pride, and extravagance of dress, and all else that tends to create *caste* among the equal members of the spiritual family, should be sternly banished from the assemblies of the saints," wrote Isaac Errett.

> While wealth is desirable for the erection of suitable houses of worship, and for the more efficient prosecution of the work of the church, let us be careful how we make gold our confidence. . . .
>
> We do not speak thus, as indulging in a sweeping condemnation of the rich. We are happy to know many men of wealth who have not been spoiled by their riches. . . . But . . . there is a peril to the church in the increased wealth of her membership.[14]

The foregoing statement still emphasizes the dangers of wealth, but with an obvious and extremely important difference. Previously we have noted how Disciples condemned worldliness and ostentation in the "sects," that is, in the other denominations. But here we find explicit evidence that the social and economic level of some members in the Disciples group was rising, at least to the extent of causing the leaders to regard it as a danger. The whole tone of the statement is significantly different from earlier ones on the subject. Years before there had been no hesitation to condemn in no uncertain terms the rich men who were corrupting the churches, but now it is added that "we mean no sweeping condemnation of the rich." We are talking about the ones who have not been made proud by their good fortune, especially (one suspects) if some of the money might build Disciples churches and support Disciples missions.

The import of much of the criticism of worldliness in this period is focused on the observed fact that money is available for all sorts of purposes, except the cause of converting the world. The significance of this would appear to lie in the implication that, while the social and economic level was rising, the devotion of the people was not increasing as well; as a matter of fact, it was decreasing. Mr. Z. Carpenter from Kentucky put it to the *Millennial Harbinger* readers this way . . .

Permit me here to ask the many who, in this exentful day, are busy in building fine and costly edifices, and adorning them with costly furniture . . . and yet, strange to tell, cannot find money nor time to aid in sending the Bible and missionaries. . . . How hard it is, even in many communities where wealth and fashion prevails; where the great majority can find funds to comply with all the polite fashions of the day—fine horses, fine and costly carriages . . . yet . . . let some faithful servant of the Lord rise up and plead the cause of the Bible . . . and see how scarce the money is then.[15]

Money was, it may legitimately be inferred, available, but instead of its being used for the spreading of the gospel, it was serving the cause of enhancing the pride and self-righteousness of the people, and of fostering what Veblen called "conspicuous waste." Such ostentatious display could only invite invidious distinctions into the church, it was argued.

The question of the use of money was likewise tied in with the continuing emphasis upon certain of the Puritanical ideas about abstinence and the denial of worldly pleasure. Tobacco, for example, was regarded as so evil that "The bare thought that he who cultivates an artificial appetite is thereby subjecting the spirit to the flesh . . . should be sufficient to induce all wise men . . . to abandon at once and forever every debasing practice of this sort."[16] But there is more to it than this emphasis upon abstinence; it was pointed out that the money we spend on "debasing habits" could have been used to further the cause of the gospel.

If one-half of what we now consume in the use of tobacco, intoxicating drinks, and other things equally useless or pernicious, were appropriated to this benevolent purpose [of spreading the gospel], how soon would . . . the strong-holds and bulwarks of Satan disappear in our own land; how soon would the wilderness and the solitary place be made glad, and the moral desert of the world rejoice and blossom as the rose![18]

Those who observed the religious conditions of this period noted with much concern the influx of worldly standards into the sanctuaries of the faithful. They may, however, have confused causes and effects when they attempted to understand the situation.

It is only when churches are in a lukewarm, or declining state, and the service of God is neglected, that young members are inclined to turn aside to vain amusements, and gay companions, to seek, on forbidden ground, something to satisfy "an aching void the world can never fill." . . .

The disposition and feelings of a renewed heart do not accord with the hilarity and mirth connected with the society of unconverted, pleasure-seeking young persons.[18]

Some confusion is evident here; for, obviously, if the young persons were not "turning aside to vain amusements" the church would not be in a declining state. It is conceivable that the churches were emphasizing their teachings, not with "lukewarm" devotion, but with sectarian zeal, which was precisely the sort of attitude not likely to influence the young people of families who were upward mobile in the social and economic scale, and who, therefore, had a wider range of interests in "vain amusements and gay companions." The temper of sectarian zeal is more akin to that of the "stern daughter of the voice of God," than to the "freedom of the Christian man." The "renewed heart" which the church leaders wanted to create was apparently a glum, duty-ridden, guilt-stricken kind of thing, not at all suitable, as they themselves realized, to "unconverted, pleasure-seeking young persons."

The worry of Disciples about the influence of worldliness upon the young people is natural enough. Already, in this period of expansion of the movement, America was becoming a class society where comparisons were increasingly being made on a pecuniary basis. It is no wonder then that D. R. Hundley could write in the *Millennial Harbinger* that no question is more frequently asked than

"What is he worth?" Is he rich in lands and houses, in silver and gold, in lowing herds fattening upon a thousand hills, or snowy sails of Commerce whitening every sea? If *aye,* then he is a man of mark—a solid man—and immediately is entitled to our respectful consideration. No question is ever made as to his *real worthiness*—whether he be virtuous and charitable; whether he honors God and loves his fellow-men; whether he has laid up treasure in Heaven. . . . Perhaps this is all very well among unbelievers, whom the God of this world has made blind. . . . But, alas! the evil is not confined to the publicans and sinners alone. . . . The Church has entered the lists to tilt a lance with the sons of Belial . . . Even ministers are not exempt from this all-pervading wickedness. . . .[19]

This is perhaps not surprising. When people come into the church they bring their economic and social position along with them. Symbols of status are not, unfortunately, parked at the door, like galoshes.

Disciples were not quite sure, during this period, how they felt about rich men and their wealth. It was, as we have seen, admitted that not all wealthy men are to be condemned, and they would be glad to have money given to advance the cause. One does not bite the hand that feeds one, but the rising economic and social level of the group did not sit easily upon the consciences of some. How the situation was to be viewed in any particular instance would seem to have depended upon the people involved and how the money was to be used. As late as 1863 the *Millennial Harbinger* was concerned about the question of "aristocracy," insisting that it ought to be kept out of the churches, and lamenting the fact that in many cases it had already gotten in. "Aristocracy," it was argued,

is based upon the "lusts of the eye and the pride of life," and is purely of this world. . . . It is hateful in the sight of Heaven, and most corrupting in the world and in the church. . . .

. . . There are thousands of honorable exceptions. . . . They are a blessing to community and to the church. . . .

A real aristocrat is the most hopeless of sinners. . . .

. . . Some churches need them, however, just as they are, on account of their *influence!* So we have aristocratic churches, with aristocratic preachers, dealing out pretty, aristocratic sermons, in aristocratic style; which means in a manner not to disturb the conscience of ungodly hearers.[20]

Already recognized was the fact that some churches were associated with the upper classes and had churches, preachers, and sermons designed and cut to fit this condition. The same "exceptions to the rule" are again noted here, as they were in an earlier reference. This is perhaps indicative that, on the one hand, Disciples were suspicious of the worldly influences with which wealth was unquestionably associated; but, on the other hand, some of them had risen enough in social position and economic status to desire the obvious advantages and power which wealth would have given their church, if they could have it without the "spiritual dangers."

The dangers were, however, very real, and there was evidence that one cannot strike matches and not expect to get fire. The church was, in many ways, accommodating itself to the social patterns of "the world" to an extent which caused many of the pious to reflect that it was difficult to tell who was in the churches and who was not. It should not be entirely a surprise then, that a correspondent wrote to the *Millennial Harbinger* in 1864, that

Worldly principles have so leavened education, and Christian intercourse as it ought to exist between families professing godliness is, in many cases, also so marred by the prevalence of worldly feelings, conformities and opinions, that young persons . . . soon learn to ask, "Where exists the difference between worldly and professing Christian society, or does such exist at all?"[21]

The realities of the world in which Disciples were expanding were concentrated upon the open-class structure, the free mobility, and the rising economic and social level of many church members. The churches were, despite the many sincere and devoted people they had as members, very human institutions indeed. The perspective of the divine was still there, but an increasing number of the church members were not only *in* the world, but *of* it, too.

Other worldly items besides tobacco, liquor, and the general dangers of wealth and ostentation did not escape the attention of the Disciple literature of the period. Books, pictures, and that old evil, dancing, were brought to the attention of the faithful as sources of the devil's power. "Bad books," said the *Millennial Harbinger,* quoting from a paper called *The Family Visitor,* "are like ardent spirits; they furnish neither 'aliment' nor 'medicine'; they are 'poison.' . . .

"Books of mere fiction and fancy are bad in their character and influence. Their authors are commonly bad men, and wicked men do not often write good books. A stream does not rise higher than its fountain."[22]

Dancing was evidently regarded by many of the "saints" among Disciples as a serious evil. A Mr. John Rogers, of Carlisle, Kentucky, spoke for more sentiment than his own when he wrote to the *Millennial Harbinger* as follows:

> But my brother, (would you believe it?) a popular preacher has come out in two numbers, in the "E. Reformer," in favor of . . . social dancing in our families! . . . I call upon you, my dear Bro. Campbell, in the name of God . . . to speak out in a voice of thunder. . . . The ways of Zion mourn; she weepeth sore in the night, and her tears are on her cheeks. All her gates are desolate. . . .
>
> . . . Is the church to tolerate . . . all this?[23]

Undoubtedly the correct answer to the question is that the church *did,* and it *does;* one suspects also that the reason was that there was nothing the church could do about it.

Apparently it was believed that pictures hung on the wall in a home might lead people into the paths of unrighteousness. "I am frequently astonished," wrote one commentator on this subject,

> at seeing the kind of pictures I meet within the houses of our brethren and "professors" of religion. They certainly don't con-

> sider the *moral influence* they are calculated to exert, or they would not suffer them to hang upon the walls of their houses. . . . Most improper amatory scenes are sometimes presented. . . . Suffer not to be about you pictures that are calculated to have a bad or immoral tendency in any way.[24]

This need not, of course, be attributed to a sectarian hangover entirely. The puritanical attitudes about sex which operated with reference to this condemnation of pictures in the home are related to the larger circle of American culture, and not simply to the religious sects as such.

The church, in its effort to oppose the worldliness we have been discussing, could exhibit an almost pathetic kind of pious moralizing. Thus the *Millennial Harbinger* addressed the youth of Disciples churches in terms of the idea that the pleasures of religion are to be preferred to those of the world. "You may regret sometimes," began an article by Timothy,

> when your mind is not sufficiently guarded, that your profession forbids you to mingle with the votaries of folly fashion, and pleasure, when the delights of the ballroom, the party, and the theatre, are descanted upon in your hearing. To feel thus is not sinful, for you are human; but to yield, makes the sin. . . .
>
> . . . Would you purchase the fierce joy of the reveller at the price of self-condemnation and deep remorse?[25]

Apparently not a few had already purchased this "fierce joy," and thought the pleasures of the church were pale beside those of the world; else why address the young people thus?

During the period of expansion one of the controversies which was later to cause a split in the Disciples ranks (or if not a split, at least a good-sized rupture) began to show itself. It was the battle over whether or not it was lawful, that is to say, scriptural, to have instrumental music in the churches. This whole question is obviously related to the critique of worldliness for it was not until Disciples began to have more economic and cultural advantages that they began to want organs in their churches. But the problem was on their minds even before the controversy became really heated. As early as 1851 we find Alexander Campbell saying his piece about the implications of organs in churches.

Roman Catholic, English Protestant, and Scotch Presbyterian churches, and even the Methodist communities . . . having all the world in them. . . . I wonder not, then, that an organ, a fiddle, or a Jews-harp, should be requisite to stir up their carnal hearts, and work into ecstasy their animal souls. . . . To those . . . whose animal nature flags under the oppression of church services, I think . . . that instrumental music would not only be a desideratum, but an essential. . . . But I presume, to all spiritually-minded Christians, such aids would be as a cow bell in a concert.[26]

By the year 1861, only a decade later, the problem had become much more serious, and could not be attacked from the viewpoint that only the "carnal" minded in *other* churches wanted musical instruments. Thus Isaac Errett felt he must warn the brethren that choirs and instruments could not be kept out by "captious objections." They must, he urged, hire music teachers to instruct the congregations in the art of singing, so that musical instruments would be unnecessary.[27] Three years later, W. K. Pendleton added the thought that he would rather never hear the good music of the organ again (he professed to be very fond of good music) than to have it interfering with the free, and heartfelt singing of the congregation. "Better," he said, "the occasional discord of an untrained voice, and more acceptable to God . . . than the sublimest swell of harmony ever uttered by the deep-throated organ."[28]

In the same year, 1864, the question was brought really into the open by the insistence of J. W. McGarvey, who carried on a furious polemic on the issue of organs in churches. Writing in what was apparently the opening blast in the fight, McGarvey gave testimony to at least one explicit item of social change and shift of attitude among Disciples. "In the earlier years," Mr. McGarvey wrote,

of the present Reformation, there was entire unanimity in the rejection of instrumental music from our public worship. It was declared unscriptural, inharmonious with the Christian institution, and a source of corruption. In the course of time, individuals here and there called in question the correctness of this decision, and an attempt was occasionally made to introduce instruments in some churches. . . .

By what standards shall we judge the question? . . . If the Scriptures do not leave us at liberty, then we have no right to appeal to expediency.[29]

It is evident that the desire to have musical instruments in the churches was increasing, and as more organs appeared the arguments waxed hotter and tempers grew shorter. Again, as in other instances, the changing attitudes were related to the rising economic and social level of the group. W. E. Garrison has undoubtedly put his finger on the real point of the situation. "When, after a generation of singing-schools taught by masters with tuning-forks, they began to put melodeons in their parlors, it was inevitable that the younger element should want musical instruments in the church."[30]

Interestingly enough, contemporary sociologists have worked out devices for measuring the socioeconomic status of families which would fit quite neatly into the context provided by this statement of Garrison. F. S. Chapin, for example, developed a socioeconomic status scale, which inventories the material and cultural possessions which families have in the living room. Behind this lies the assumption that the living room is the place where visitors are received and where the family will make its bid for social recognition. The same sort of scale has been developed for rural families by W. H. Sewell, and was first used on a sample of Oklahoma farm families.[31] A case might be made here that what applies to family living rooms also applies to church sanctuaries.

This trend did not begin until around the 1860's, so before this time there was little occasion to discuss the question of organs in the church. It has been suggested that the fight began in earnest in 1859, when a melodeon was placed in the church in the village of Midway, Kentucky. One Alexander Hibler is supposed to have stolen this "instrument of Satan" in the dark of night, and, aided by his Negro servant, Reuben, to have carried it away on a sleigh. The instrument involved in this incident is now a treasured historic relic in the Kentucky Female Orphan School at Midway.[32] This would seem to indicate that the struggle over organs was not merely an oddity of the legalistic mind, but also an issue in which social energy was expended, and "vested interests" were involved.

CHAPTER VII

The Age of Expansion:

Organizational Growing Pains

While Disciples were experiencing cultural growing pains they were also expanding both geographically and numerically. The members of the group felt this, and observed the expansion with a sense of exhilaration. "Our horizon enlarges with our years," wrote Alexander Campbell.

The field of our labor is amplified beyond all our original anticipation. Every wave of emigration from these United States, as it rolls along, carries in its bosom the elements of reformation [i.e., Disciples of Christ]. . . . We little expected, some thirty years ago, that the principles of Christian union and a restoration of primitive Christianity in letter and spirit, in theory and practice, could have been plead with such success. . . . We must say that it is "the Lord's doing, and marvellous in our eyes."[1]

The Lord, then, was causing the work of Disciples to prosper, and this was reason for rejoicing! But it is at this point that we can see traces of an important change in attitude. The change can be seen by comparing the previous statement, written in 1846, with one Campbell made in his earlier journal, *The Christian Baptist.*

In 1826 Mr. Campbell, apparently having in mind that other groups were making statements indicating pride in the progress they were making, blasted such an attitude with these words, "I have no idea of magnifying molehills into mountains, nor of consecrating the language of Ashdod into that of Canaan; . . . nor of proving that the Lord approves the present order of things, because the Methodists and Baptists annually count twenty thousand converts a-piece."[2] Just getting a lot of new members does not prove, or even suggest, that the Lord is on your side. Yet twenty years later Alexander Campbell could write that the *Lord* was giving the increase in the Disciples movement! This does not indicate that Mr. Campbell was insincere, or even inconsistent; but it does show that when conditions change, our attitudes may also alter significantly, as Campbell's certainly did when his own group began to sweep over the new frontiers.

The growth of the Disciples movement during the age of expansion was rapid. Figures are notoriously dull, and we do not propose to clutter up the text with more than a few of them. But it is necessary to clothe generalities about growth with some statistical garments. The only difficulty is that the figures available are notably inaccurate and unreliable. New movements in their early states do not take the trouble to keep accurate records or figures; they are too busy experiencing their new life to keep accurate records about it. An indication of the confusion about statistics is the fact that the figure of 200,000 members has been used by various writers to apply to the years of 1832, 1837, 1844, 1849, and 1850.[3] But using what figures are available to us the picture looks something like this. Disciples, when they split from the Baptists, counted somewhere in the neighborhood of 12,000 members; another 10,000 were added when they united with the Stone movement. It is estimated that by 1840 the total had reached 80,000 and 90,000; this figure was then increased to between 118,000 and 121,000 by 1850 (though it is urged that this figure is probably too low). In any event the number, as nearly as it can be estimated with available evidence, was about 192,300 by the year 1860. If one assumes that the base line, taken from the time of the union with the Stone group, is 22,000 members, this means that between 1832 and 1860 the membership had been multiplied approximately nine times, while the population of the country had increased only about three times its total for the same years. Furthermore, the increase owed nothing to immigration, which was certainly a factor which entered into the increase in some groups.

More important than the argument about the exact number of members in the group, since this will probably never be settled with any final and complete accuracy, is the matter of where these members were located and how they distributed themselves with respect to the urban-rural index. Disciples are not a predominantly urban movement, though they have significant churches in strategic urban and metropolitan areas, and their existence today is subject to the whole gamut of social, cultural, and economic forces which affect the religious institutions of America. The pattern of concentration in the Mississippi Valley area, and in the small towns, was set during the age of expansion. The most recent information concerning the distribution of Disciples of Christ members in the United States indicates that this pattern has continued into the present decade. As late as 1953, 78.5% of the churches of Disciples of Christ (not including Negro congregations) were located in communities with 10,000 or fewer persons, while according to the 1950 Census of population, only 49.9% of the United States population resided in communities of 10,000 or less. Moreover, churches of Disciples of Christ are firmly concentrated in states within the central geographical division of the United States. In 1953 Disciples had churches located in 46 of the then 48 states. Only in 18 of these states did they have more than 25,000 members. The six states in which they have more than 100,000 members are all located in the central part of the United States.[4]

Disciples of Christ had indeed come a long way since that obscure meeting at which the Christian Association of Washington, Pennsylvania, was formed. With their rapid growth and surprising success at spreading the "ancient gospel" had come an increased recognition of the need for organization and the formalizing of relationships which had previously been informal. This, as we have already suggested, is one of the main characteristics of the sect-to-denomination development, and Disciples were following the regular steps in the natural history of an institution. But Disciples were not unmindful of all that had been written and said by them earlier (and not much earlier at that!) about the evils of ecclesiastical authority and the zealous guarding of the rights of the local congregation.

Hence, when they set about solving the organizational problems attendant upon their expansion, they proceeded cautiously, as though walking on eggs. By 1840 the discussion of methods and procedures of co-operation which would not undermine the principles of the restoration had become general. Such matters as co-operating in evangelization efforts, organizing the Sunday church school work, and protecting the churches from itinerant and "irresponsible" preachers had to be dealt with in some way. With an increased consciousness of the need for efficiency, Alexander Campbell preferred to forget what he had said earlier and move on to the urgent problems that needed to be solved. The recognition of the needs involved in increased growth marks a new phase of the movement. It was finally realized that Disciples were here to stay, and that the problem was not so much to battle other groups for the right to exist at all as it was to organize their efforts to expand their horizons.

In 1842 Campbell addressed Disciples with the assertion that nothing was more needed in the church than co-operation and organization. "We have," he said, "the words 'co-operation,' 'organization,' and 'order' in constant employment; but who has evinced a practical understanding of them in reference to the public interests of a great community? The calls upon us for a full investigation of this subject are imperious as well as numerous."[5] Disciples were not slow to take up this question, and records are full of references to various meetings looking toward methods for cooperative effort.

Alexander Campbell himself issued what might well be called a "manifesto" on the need for organization, when he listed five strong arguments as to why organization was an imperative need. This list of points is as follows:

1. We can do comparatively nothing in distributing the Bible abroad without co-operation.
2. We can do comparatively but little in the great missionary field of the world either at home or abroad without co-operation.
3. We can do little or nothing to improve and elevate the Christian ministry without co-operation.
4. We can do little to check . . . the flood of imposture and fraud committed upon the benevolence of the brethren by irresponsible . . . persons, without co-operation.
5. We cannot concentrate the action of the tens of thousands of Israel, in any great christian effort but by co-operation.
5. We can have no thorough co-operation without a more ample, extensive, and thorough church organization.[6]

These arguments were pervasive not only because of Mr. Campbell's prestige, but also because they were arguments for something, which many in the group were already convinced was needed. The five points here are at one and the same time a statement of the problems which urgently demanded attention, and evidence of how much, from the sociological point of view, the group had grown. But the developments called for did not come about without a struggle, and without intense opposition.

The detailed rehearsal of each of the controversies that was a part of the increasing recognition of the need for co-operation would provide some extremely uninteresting paragraphs. Suffice it to say that there was increasing agreement over the *needs,* but much debate and uneasiness over the details of the *means* and *methods* for meeting these needs. The significant point is the social change involved in the process. We have already alluded to the fact that, by gradual shifts of attitude, the door had been conveniently left open for later developments. Mr. Campbell, having, as he himself said, "enlarged his horizons" (without, of course, as he thought, having changed his mind on any major principles), was ready with his answer when the opponents of co-operative efforts asked for apostolic authority for such things as missionary societies. "In all things pertaining to public interest, not of Christian faith, piety, or morality, the church of Jesus Christ in its aggregate character is left free and unshackled by any apostolic authority."[7] This is not what Campbell had said earlier, but it is certainly more in keeping with the changed conditions in which Disciples were operating.

There can be no question that Campbell had changed his mind, and that in doing so he spoke for many of the thoughtful members of the Disciples church. He showed a growing impatience with those who were squeamish about going ahead with efforts at co-operation. You can be too Protestant! he argued; this fear of the sects can be carried too far! "Our brethren, as the burned child dreads the fire, dread sectarianism," he wrote in 1847. "But this is, I doubt not, carried too far—especially when it prevents them from co-operating in teaching, or in sending their children to teach, or to be taught, in Sunday Schools. . . . Our greatest error, Protestants themselves being judges, is, that we are too Protestant in our aversions to the doctrines and commandments of men."[8] This is so striking a change in the tone of Campbell's utterances, as to be almost amazing. His early expressions of "aversions to the doctrines and commandments of men" were apparently getting in the way of progress, and it is perhaps a mark of Mr. Campbell's intelligence that he brushed them aside when they prevented what was made necessary by changed conditions.

Campbell himself gave explicit testimony to the effect of changed conditions upon his attitudes. In 1849 he wrote,

> Reformation and annihilation are not with me now, as formerly, convertible or identical terms. We want occasional, if not stated, deliberative meetings on questions of expediency in adaptation to the ever changing fortune and character of society. . . .

> . . . The public press, evangelical missions . . . and moral agencies of every sort necessary or favorable to the prosperity of the churches of Christ and to the conversion of the world . . . are probably the objects which might advantageously claim a sort of general superintendency.[9]

That, as we have already suggested, these efforts to find allowable ways to organize and co-operate were not without serious opposition, is also shown by the records. Campbell himself proceeded cautiously, despite his insistence that the needs must be met, reminding the brethren that "organization is not faith, nor humility, nor liberality."[10] But the real evidence is contained in the urgent plea that Disciples should stop wasting time on irrelevant and picayune objections. Let's get on with it! was the cry.

> Nice notions about the peculiar mechanism of church government—trembling fears of ecclesiastical tyranny—indignation at the political mischiefs that are spreading—holy terror of association with those whose social culture differs materially from our own . . . in the all-captivating and all-absorbing love of Jesus, there is such . . . a neutralizing of antagonisms . . . as to bring the lion and the ox . . . into harmless association. . . .
>
> . . . If we fritter away our strength and waste our precious time in theorizings, cavillings, oppositions, to all expedients for harmonious and effective concentration of means—*what will we do in the end thereof?*[11]

The question with which Isaac Errett ended the above statement is obviously rhetorical, for he was assuming the answer. If we fritter away our strength, the end will be the loss of the chance to evangelize the world. Behind this was apparently the American notion that a movement which does not continue to expand is already beginning to die. There was, as this statment of Mr. Errett's shows, much opposition to the efforts at organization. Those who did the opposing did not at all agree that they were wasting time. Instead, they obviously believed they were protecting the principles of the ancient gospel from being contaminated. Apparently, the chief source of the opposition to organizational efforts was with those Disciples who emphasized the restoration rather than the unity side of the dialectic in the movement. Disciples were indeed positive and explicit in what they believed the gospel to be, and it was the sledge-hammer logic of their plea which undoubtedly gave force to their evangelistic efforts. But this definiteness lends itself all too easily to the hard legalism which was implicit in the restoration effort.

J. S. Lamar later referred to Disciples of this period as follows: "They were faithful in heart to God and his Word, and yet somehow that Word had seemed to lose its loveliness to them. As it came from many pulpits, the gospel itself appeared to be clothed in the habiliments of a stern and harsh and inflexible Mosaism."[12] This stern and inflexible Mosaism was, it seems evident, the chief root of the struggle against organization and co-operation. But behind it lay the fact that a certain way of viewing the Christian gospel had become a vested interest, with which personalities and prestige were involved. Rigid legalism is the fountain from which have flowed most of the controversies which have plagued Disciples.

Disciples were also feeling the need for some kind of definition and plan of discipline, as well as for organization and co-operation. This, too, is a symptom that the movement was getting large enough to require something more than vague feelings on the informal associational level as the basis for its existence.

> Every organization implies an established authority and subordination to it. Machines have their balance wheels, compensation-pendulums, and regulators; the human system, complicated as it is . . . is in subordination to the *will;* and every association of men . . . must be subjected to some controlling authority, or it cannot live and operate as one body. . . . In whatever form, it must exist and be accompanied with power to enforce it, or confusion will ensue.[13]

When the group sought freedom to organize and to establish itself there was little, if any, talk about discipline and authority;

indeed, authority was just the thing they most wanted to be free of (though of course, as they stated the situation, it was freedom from human opinions they wanted). But now that the movement has gone a long way on the road from sect to denomination, it is realized by some of the members that what has been built in freedom cannot be held together entirely on this basis.

There is yet more to the growth of the Disciples movement than the increasing cognizance of the problems of co-operation and discipline. We have seen how, even in the first decade of their separate existence, Disciples showed an interest in the question of education for the young people of their families. They even began to argue the question of whether ministers ought to be *trained* for their work, besides having a *call* from God. Alexander Campbell gave us clear evidence that the interest in education was growing, when in 1840 he asserted that education was an essential in the furtherance of the restoration movement.

> Our volumes, one and all, prosecute the demolition of all sectarianism—the union of all God's people, upon God's own foundation. . . .
>
> The cause of education becomes a more and more interesting object in the pursuance of this plan. . . . We must have family, school, college, and church education, adapted to the entire . . . constitution of man. . . .
>
> To this subject, as essentially connected with the speed and progress of the current reformation, a more full and marked attention shall be paid. *An uneducated person is not competent to the full display of Christian excellence.*[14]

Here again, it is clear that the changing conditions had caused a shift in attitude. One cannot doubt that Campbell was expressing the view of those who realized that the younger generation, which had not participated in the original experiences of the movement, must be educated in order to understand and perpetuate the restoration traditions. The first generation of Disciples had said that education was not necessary, that all you had to do was read the plain and simple words of the Bible, but now looking to the next generation they said, "an uneducated person is not competent."

Disciples felt that they needed a college, and to meet this need Campbell published a plea to the "rich and opulent" to donate of their abundance what they could without injuring themselves or their posterity.[15] That there were those in the group who might be able to contribute to such an enterprise without seriously depriving themselves or their posterity, and to whom Campbell might address an appeal, is in itself evidence that the economic level of some Disciples was rising to some extent. The need for a college was urgent, it was argued; and it is significant that the ground on which this urgency was argued was that "good *precepts* and *examples* are no longer enough." Many persons, it was asserted, have good precepts and examples to learn from, but without training they are nevertheless "neither an ornament nor a blessing to society."[16] This was one of the chief motivating ideas behind Alexander Campbell's appeal for funds for Bethany College.

Education, it was further realized, is needed not only for future citizens and church members, but also for preachers. Disciples, at least some of them, were becoming sensitive about the uncouthness and arrogant ignorance of some of their evangelists. One suspects that they sensed the possibility that the outside world would judge them by their preachers and the kind of teaching and preaching that was done from their pulpits. Lack of training and education was no longer, as such, an indication that a person was a good candidate for the ministry, which is what might understandably be inferred from some earlier statements found in the Disciples literature.

To hear an uneducated preacher or teacher of religion . . . whose every sentence is a sin against the laws of language; who, with inquisitorial tortures, murders the King's English at every turn; and who is occasionally saying what, it is evident to all but himself, he does not mean to say—to hear such a one reproach a man of celebrity with theological errors . . . is an ebullition of human weakness and folly more disgusting than any other which I can imagine

wrote Alexander Campbell. The real point of the statement was contained in the sentence that followed. "Certain ignorant and unlearned men are wont to think that they have a Divine right to human attention . . . because of their want of human learning."[17] Mr. Richardson, one of the editors of the *Millennial Harbinger,* put much the same point in a slightly different manner, in the same year. "I have heard," he wrote, "teachers of religion inveigh, in very bad English, against learning . . . Doubtless the principle illustrated by the Fox and the Grapes had something to do with the matter . . . A tirade against learning, accompanied with the usual boast of the plainness of scripture, came with a very ill grace from one who could not speak correctly his mother tongue."[18]

Yet, while Alexander Campbell wanted Disciples to have education, he was careful to warn them that too many colleges of poor quality would be unfortunate for the future of the group. This is perhaps an indication that the need for education was now felt so strongly where it had been practically nonexistent previously that there was a tendency to dissipate money, time, and energy in efforts which could be only abortive.

One good institution well organized, well furnished with an able cohort of teachers, well patronized by the brethren and the public, is better than ten such as we are likely to have got up and spirited into life by such arguments and efforts, that tend much more to schism, rivalry, and false ambition, than to union, harmony, and successful action. I hope the brethren will . . . hear all the . . . arguments before . . . they create half-a-dozen of ill-begotten, mishappen, club-footed, imbecile schools. . . .[19]

He spoke with wisdom here. This is indicated by the fact that Disciples started an unknown number of colleges which disappeared almost as soon as they had been begun. There is much evidence that the number of colleges started far exceeded the available means to support them, which obviously accounts for the high mortality rate.

The need for education expressed itself almost compulsively. There was a strong sense that the demand for education was somehow tied in with the responsibility of Disciples in helping to meet the problems of the world. "We want men to meet the crisis and the age," the *Millennial Harbinger* sounded the call.

> Infidelity, superstition and error, ancient and modern, are everywhere around us and in our midst. . . . We as much need the knowledge of their machinery, and the use of the armory of heaven, as did the apostles at one time need the gift of tongues. . . .
>
> Schools for prophets, as well as schools for languages and sciences, are yet required, and all men feel the want of them. . . . Shall we not, then, listen to the calls of the church, . . . and, as good stewards of the manifold blessings of God vouchsafed to us, consecrate our persons, . . . our substance, to the glory of God.[20]

Disciples during this period were desirous of taking their place as the haven and training ground for future citizens and leaders, a much different interpretation of their role from the one which dominated their early sectarian existence. No longer fighting for *Lebensraum,* and well on the way toward being sociologically a denomination, they wanted a place of respectability and responsibility in religious and secular life.

It was recognized that if Disciples were to be a respected and enduring part of American life, men of more ability must be recruited for the ministry. As early as 1856 it was pointed out that much of the best talent went into other callings. "Our pulpits do not," it was said, "furnish evidence of much intellectual or spiritual growth, *nor of adaptedness to the times.* . . . The spirits that hunger and thirst for righteousness, will seek elsewhere for sympathy and encouragement—broad views of humanity—elevated views of the spiritual are rare."[21] But to provide men of broad views of humanity and elevated views of the spiritual we shall need—of all things!—a theological school. "There should be," wrote Isaac Errett, " 'a school of the prophets'—a theological school, where men of learning, and wisdom, and large experience, could impart the sum of their knowledge, from books, from life, and from their own souls, to the young, and prepare them for wise and faithful laborers."[22] No more clear evidence of the effect of social change and of how far Disciples were adapting themselves to their new conditions of existence could be provided than this. Whereas formerly it had been urged that the seminaries, or Bible colleges, as Disciples preferred to call them, were hotbeds of heresy and all forms of arrogant human learning, which led the ministry away from the essential and plain truths of the Bible, they are now recognized as a desperately needed weapon, without which no preacher was properly equipped to uphold the faith. It was now urged that schools for the education of the ministry are nothing new, that there is nothing more natural in the history of Christianity than the demand for, and the establishment of, such schools.[23]

Some members of the Disciples group, of course, opposed these trends and regarded them as a falling away from the ancient principles. They were not slow to point out to Campbell that what he was now urging certainly disagreed with what he had said earlier. In 1845 the charge was made to him in the question, " 'Have you not declaimed against Colleges and College-bred preachers in years long since gone by?' " Campbell's reply was frank and pointed. "Suppose we had changed our views [which he was not admitting] of the expediency of such institutions; what then! Must we assume the ground, Once in error, always in error! But we have not. . . . I never declaimed against learning, learned men, or Colleges."[24] Ten years later, Campbell's reply to the same charge was much more insistent that he had *not* changed his mind. "I am not conscious of any change in any Christian doctrine since I wrote the first volume of the Christian Baptist. . . .

". . . That I ever did oppose classical and scientific schools, Colleges, and Universities, . . . I have no recollection whatever."[25] It is perhaps fruitless to argue the question of whether Alexander Campbell had changed his mind. The preponderance of the evidence is that he did change his mind, but the point is that Disciples now felt different needs than they had recognized before.

The question of whether or not ministers ought to be paid still was something to argue about during the expansion period. It was increasingly realized that one of the chief reasons why some "devout, talented, and energetic" men were going to farms and workshops instead of into the ministry was that the brethren were in some sections not "sufficiently impressed with the importance of sustaining their Elders and Preachers."[26] When a group was in its infancy and had not spread over so much territory, the practice of having men who farmed during the week preach on Sundays was more suitable to the situation; but when the movement passed the bounds of a few intimate associational groups and became a clearly defined "denomination," it was necessary to have a full-time ministry if the church was to carry out its work efficiently. Even preachers have to eat—notwithstanding a favorite text that "man does not live by bread alone"—and some are even found to have families. So the question of supporting ministers was no longer a matter exclusively handled by quoting Scripture passages; it became a question of whether the churches wanted ministers at all. Perhaps this background of the argument over whether ministers should receive pay at all should be taken into account in assessing the reasons why, today, the salaries are extremely low for all but the very few ministers in the largest churches.

Though Alexander Campbell had argued in 1850 that hiring preachers may be bad, but "brethren" who do not pay their way are worse,[27] it is instructive to note that as late as 1860, a Disciples layman, J. Epps, an M.D., had examined the whole subject of payment of the clergy, and had concluded that, scripturally speaking, they need not be paid. This is evidence of the persistence of an attitude long after its relevance to the facts and conditions had disappeared. Dr. Epps's argument was published in the *Millennial Harbinger*, which is a testimony both to the attempt of that paper to give a hearing to all sides, and to the fact that a question obviously related to and affected by social conditions was still unsettled in the minds of members of the group. "Viewing the subject," said Epps, "first in regard to the names applied to the persons holding the pastor's office . . . ; second, in regard to the characteristics of these pastors . . . ; third, their duties . . . ; and finally, in regard to the nature of the truths of revelation . . . , I am compelled to come to the conclusion . . . *that pastors need not be paid to perform their duties.*"[28]

Among Disciples, many social questions were regarded as matters of opinion, since they are not treated of in the Scriptures in terms that would provide specifics for the conditions under which the group was living, and thus they should not be discussed as religious problems relevant to the ancient gospel. This is perhaps one of the chief reasons why Disciples did not split over the Civil War. A more important reason might have been that there was no central authority which could expel an individual or a church no matter what view was taken. After all, how could the local congregation split off from what it had never joined in the first place? There were many Disciples on both sides of this conflict, but no one possessed any machinery for making even a resolution of censure effective, let alone for excommunicating those who were not on the "right" side of the issue. In his careful study of *The Political Ethics of Alexander Campbell,* Harold Lunger has shown that Campbell did express his views on many questions of social, economic, and political import. He delivered himself from time to time of some forthright opinions concerning such things as capital punishment, war, and education in a democracy. In *The Millennial Harbinger* Campbell often addressed himself to the problem of slavery. Yet in all this there was a certain ambivalence. As Lunger has observed, Campbell felt tension between his role as a citizen and his role as a Christian. He did not regard the discussion of social and political issues as growing out of his concerns as a Christian.

Yet there were those in the group who wanted to deal with social and economic questions. This is evidenced by the fact that the *Harbinger* felt called upon, in 1856, to speak some harsh words about "the abuse of the pulpit."

> The liberty mentioned Gal. v. 1, is . . . a deliverance from the yoke of Satan, from the bondage which is by nature upon all the sons of Adam. . . .
>
> This is the liberty, the only liberty the clergyman is to proclaim. He is a man solemnly called and set apart to preach and teach the truths contained in the Bible, and no others. When he departs from this, he forfeits his commission. . . . The Bible says not a word about political liberty, or social equality. . . . The clergy should see to it, that it is not marred by association with any secular conception.[29]

This did not mean that the Christian was not to be concerned about the social or political condition of the country. His religion teaches him to seek the peace and tranquility of the community and to be subject at all times to its laws. But, "It is one thing . . . to exhibit the gentleness of Christ and the faithful quiet performance of duty, and quite another, to spend time, and words, and means in the promotion of objects which are merely earthly, personal and selfish."[30] There is some evidence that this attitude is closely related to, or conditioned by, the desire of Disciples that there movement not be split by the slavery controversy.

Disciples may not have split over the slavery issue, but, as we have already pointed out, there was a difference in attitude in the group which might lead to a division; the emphasis upon *unity* and the stress of *restoration* were products of two essentially different tempers and attitudes. It is about at the Civil War period that these tempers began to clash in earnest. The seeds of division, planted almost at the beginning of the movement, were beginning to sprout and show plants above the ground. The legalistic mood fostered by the strict application of the restoration notion did not set well with those who wanted to pass on to other, as they believed, more important questions than whether a given idea or practice was allowed by scriptural authority. Hence, the entrance of Disciples into the next phase of their history, the denominational phase, was almost inevitable.

Toward the end of his life Alexander Campbell wrote what might be considered a fitting summary of his own work and of the condition of Disciples. It is, to be sure, cast in literary language, but it expresses the mood of the times.

For forty years we have been not an unfaithful nor an unwatchful sentinel upon the walls of Zion, and we had, with perhaps unwarranted fondness, cherished the hope of closing our service beneath peaceful and hopeful skies. But what warrant have we to expect that our wily foe will ever sleep in his work of evil and mischief! . . .

Many seem to have passed, we trust but for a time, under the "power of the world," . . . The times are full of corruption, and the church is contaminated with the times.[31]

From Campbell's point of view "contaminated" was exactly the right word. More objectively one might say that what happened was that Disciples were reacting to, and being influenced by, the changing conditions of the world in which they lived.

CHAPTER VIII

The Sect Becomes a Denomination

Division over the Civil War had been avoided, but the threatened dissension over other issues, which had long been imminent, now broke out in earnest. Significantly, the key word in the situation is *innovation.* We have seen how, as the movement grew, and its needs changed, there were important shifts in attitude which allowed the new demands to be met. But logical consistency demanded that the restoration of the ancient gospel be just exactly that. What was wanted was an *exact* reproduction of the patterns of the New Testament church. The Disciples group, however, like every other restoration movement, adapted itself to the needs of the moment. It is no wonder then that the cry of complaint made by the legalists should center on the word, *innovation.*

Moses E. Lard, in what is now regarded as the classic presentation of the objections against change, laid down the following propositions about the "devilish" spirit of innovation. "The spirit of innovation," he wrote, "is a peculiar spirit. While coming in it is the meekest and gentlest of spirits; only it is marvelously firm and persistent. But when going out, no term but fiendish will describe it. It comes in humming the sweetest notes of Zion; it goes out amid the ruin it works, howling like an exorcised demon."[1] Discounting the value-loaded terminology this is not a bad description of the way in which innovations do occur. Mr. Lard was a realist; he recognized that you could not *argue* with innovations. They steal in, like a thief in the night, and they have done their work before you have a chance to find out what happened.

Yet the process of innovation is not without a cogent and forceful logic. Some Disciples were beginning to have serious doubts about how far you can carry the rule of following the New Testament on every point. In a period of a rapidly expanding economy, and an atmosphere of social mobility, it is almost impossible to find a specific prescription for each practice or attitude that appears to be required by the situation. While it can be viewed as the rationalization for changes that were already taking place, the argument for relaxing the demand of exact restoration is convincing and clever. Disciples had been supposed to take the silence of the Scriptures on any subject as a positive rule of prohibition against all freedom of action or obligation of duty. But, said the *Millennial Harbinger* in 1866,

> No rule could be more productive of mischief than this. That large freedom of thought and action, and that resistless spontaneity of benevolence which make a Christian a living power . . . would be cramped and stifled by so narrow a principle, till Christianity itself would become a timid and cringing thing of forms, and afraid to expand itself.[2]

Of course, it is impossible to understand either the innovations that were objected to, or the ground on which the objections were based, without referring to the social and cultural context in which Disciples were working out their history. The frontier *village,* once merely a trade and gossip center, the haven of the cracker barrel, the pot-bellied stove, and the hot political argument, became, with the advent of the railroad, the *town.* The invention of the reaper made Mr. McCormick richer and changed the traditional farming methods. Many people made a bit more money in the wake of an expanding industrial economy. With the increased prosperity came clothes a little better than last year's, and houses just a shade more modern. The extreme isolation and loneliness of the frontier were to some extent replaced by a consciousness of wider horizons and larger community to which people belonged. With an open class system and a high degree of social mobility, many of the families which had been exponents of a rugged frontier life now felt an increasing need for a more sophisticated environment, in which more and better education would be available and where more material advantages, whether as actual conveniences or as symbols of class status, would be possible. Though Disciples did not keep pace with other groups in the large cities, they shared in the general expansion of America. They, like everyone else, wanted better churches after they began to have better houses. Uncouth preachers, with no social graces and no training, were increasingly out of place. The rising demands for things which would symbolize the rising social status of the people made innovations inevitable. The general modification of the social and economic environment produced a tendency to adopt many of the customs of other churches, against which in an earlier period Disciples had inveighed.

The opponents of these changes were adept at digging up their old copies of Alexander Campbell's *Christian Baptist* and at quoting chapter and verse therein to prove that the advocates of the new practices were transgressing against the sacred principles of the founders. There is no doubt that this was occurring. This may be seen in the fact that the *Millennial Harbinger* felt called upon to refer to these people as "bibliolaters." "There is a class among us," said the *Harbinger,* "who have a sort of bibliolatry toward the Christian Baptist, and as is usual in such cases, they imagine that it has uttered many oracles, which upon a more careful study it will be found, are not to be discovered in its pages. . . . It must be remembered that . . . [Alexander Campbell] was engaged almost incessantly in the fiercest and closest conflicts with the various forms of sectarianism. . . ."[3] If, then, Campbell said anything which would be used against the advocates of innovations, it was, so the *Harbinger* implied, only because in the heat of battle he said some things which in a calm, cool hour he would undoubtedly have modified. A more objective interpretation would seem to be that when Campbell had said what he did earlier, he meant just exactly that. But as we have demonstrated, he changed his attitudes as it became necessary with changing conditions. A more realistic approach would, therefore, have been to admit frankly that Campbell did change his attitude and then argue that change is allowed.

Those who favored the changes would not admit that what they stood for really denied the principles on which the Disciples movement had begun its existence. They asserted,

> Our work is the same as that of the venerable Thomas Campbell, the cherished Alexander Campbell . . .;—the recovery of primitive christianity from the rubbish of ages and its re-implantation in society in this 19th century.
>
> But even since those masters began their work, an entire age and more of human years has gone slowly down the abyss of time. . . . We must live in this present active world and not in the world which died with our fathers. . . .
>
> The man or the people who refuse to be moulded in manners and measures by the age which they seek to mould through the inflexible Gospel, are guilty of folly as egregious as the Asiatic simpleton, who, wishing to cross Euphrates, sat down on its banks, waiting till all its waters should run out.[4]

Two irreconcilable propositions are contained in the above, which perhaps demonstrates that not logic but feelings, conditioned by the social milieu, were what were at stake in this argument. "The re-implantation of primitive Christianity in the society of the 19th century" is difficult, if not obviously impossible, to reconcile with the assertion that "we must live in this present world and not the world which died with our fathers." That there are valid principles and values contained in the life and ideas of the New Testament church can be, without much question, established. The New Testament itself grew out of the life of the early church. There is scarcely anyone who would not concede that there are some valid elements in the moral and religious universe of the New Testament. Yet it is obvious that the New Testament world also "died with our fathers." Primitive Christianity, as a complete and exact pattern, could not be restored by those who are willing to be molded, as indeed they must inevitably be, by the age which they seek to mold.

Behind this controversy over innovations was not only the question of biblical authority, but more important in terms of underlying causes was resentment over the loss of earlier simplicity. "What the older members had been used to," in which they had vested interests of personality and habit, was obviously the psychological background for the attack on innovations. This attack was focused upon such items as "open communion," the use of the title "reverend," a synopsis of the "Disciples position" written by Isaac Errett, the "oneman system," the use of organs, and missionary societies. Significantly, all of these issues grew out of the more simple and primitive frontier conditions in which the movement had its inception, and most of them, as we have seen, were related to the more obviously "sectarian" period when Disciples were struggling for a foothold in the religious world.

The question which J. W. McGarvey put to Disciples in 1868, while it may sound somewhat quixotic in view of later developments, was nevertheless pointed and certainly pertinent.

> How can men who wish to return to primitive practice engage in fairs and tableaus and other abominations so commonly employed for the support of Sunday Schools? . . . Shall societies with human systems outstrip us? . . . Our work is to check them and turn them back from their course; not to outstrip them in running after organs and compromises. The loudest call that comes from heaven . . . is for warfare, stern, relentless . . . against everything not expressly or by necessary implication authorized in the New Testament.[5]

There were others who agreed with Mr. McGarvey and they were not reticent about arguing their position. They were not, to be sure, able to muster enough strength at this time to cause a new sect to be formed apart from the Disciples group.

We have noted already that a few years previously there was a noticeable shift in Disciples attitudes toward communion with the unimmersed (and therefore, to them, unbaptized) persons. This question was to have further airing, and the continued interest in the matter serves to show more clearly how a fundamental dialectic is basic to the understanding of Disciples. The issue, as such, did not cause a division, but it brought into unmistakably clear light the opposite poles of thought and attitude which governed the Disciples' understanding of their own movement.

Significantly, Disciples did not take quite the same attitude toward the observance of the Lord's Supper as they seemed to take toward the immersion question. Certainly there was some evidence of sentiment favoring the barring of unimmersed persons from the communion table, but this never went to the limit of setting up formal procedures for exclusion. The device adopted was this. All were invited to come to the table, but they were usually cautioned to come only after having examined themselves to be sure they were in a right relationship to their Lord. This put any moral dangers involved in opening the table to everybody upon the consciences of individuals who might "examine themselves" and then come anyway. The "let a man examine himself" principle was not, however, considered applicable to the rite of baptism.

Alexander Campbell, it will be remembered, had some rather disparaging things to say, in his early editorial career, about the preachers; he characterized them variously as "hireling priests" or "reverend dandies." But with the passing of the frontier, and the rising social and economic standard of Disciples, there gradually emerged a group of ministers who, by reason of increased professional competence, more education, and noticeable social graces, could be distinguished from the laity. Not a few among Disciples still preferred, however, to stay away from the title "reverend"; or at best they wanted it used as a designation of *function* and not of *status*. When friends in Detroit presented Isaac Errett with a silver doorplate bearing the inscription "Rev. Isaac Errett," those who followed Mr. McGarvey's policy of war against everything not expressly commanded in the New Testament raised the cry of "priest-ridden" sectarianism. To be sure, the incident was soon forgotten, but the issue was still alive in the minds of some.

Evidence of how this question of the title "reverend" was tied in with social and economic change is contained in an obviously satirical item sent to the *Harbinger* from Louisville, Kentucky, in February, 1868. A newspaper had said

> The Reverend Doctor ——— will preach in the Christian church. Observing the disapprobation of the brethren present, he explained "that he was a Doctor," for he had many years ago attended a course of medical lectures; that he did not care to have any distinguishing title for himself personally, but he thought a fashionable community expected a preacher to have them. . . . The announcements were therefore made . . . that a "Reverend Doctor" would preach the primitive gospel in that city. This was the strangest paradox on record.[6]

Viewed from the sociological perspective it was not a paradox at all, but only the record of the effect of social change upon the church.

Not only had Isaac Errett been called "reverend" (though he himself had not coveted the title) but he apparently committed another, even more deadly, sin. His church in Detroit apparently had divided, and he had become the pastor of the more liberal part of the group. This church became somewhat prominent in the community, and people began to inquire as to who and what Disciples were. Mr. Errett met these questions with a pamphlet on the Disciples' position, now known as the "Synopsis." This, said the conservative restorationists, is a "creed," than which nothing can be more abhorrent. "We are told that this Declaration is not to be taken as a creed," wrote Moses E. Lard.

> When Aaron's calf came out, had he called it a bird, still all Israel, seeing it stand on four legs, with horns and parted hoofs,

would have shouted, A calf, a calf, a calf. The brethren "meeting at the corner of Jefferson Avenue and Beaubien Street, Detroit," may call their work in classic phrase a Synopsis; . . . but we still cry, A creed, a creed.[7]

It is apparent that Mr. Errett did not mean his statement to be a creed, but only an expression of how one member of the group saw its significance and its position. But whether it was a creed or not is not the important issue; the significant matter is that the extreme abhorrence of creeds which had been a part of earlier Disciples history was still persisting. To this very day, it would be extremely inadvisable for any member of the Disciples church to publish a statement of what the group is supposed to "believe" or "stand for" without affixing a prominent preface stating that he is speaking only for himself. Disciples have zealously protected the freedom which was the heritage of pioneer days.

Another center of attention in the fight against the innovations which time was forcing on Disciples was the phrase "one-man system." Not only were some members of the group sensitive about the title "reverend," but they were also jealous of their frontier patterns of church organization. In earlier days in the wilderness, preachers were scarce, and extremely few churches could get a full-time person to act in this capacity. Naturally enough, then, the use of lay elders was the way in which the church responsibility was to be cared for. Without a minister, the churches called upon the elders for both management and teaching functions. The plurality of elders was, after all, in their view obviously the scripturally sanctioned pattern, and it met the frontier conditions most satisfactorily.

The expanding life of America caught up with Disciples. More churches began to appear in towns, where a larger group of persons lived near the church building, and where a larger supply of ministers was available. Some of these preachers even had a bit of training, and the practice of having *one* man devote all his time to *one* church, instead of depending upon itinerant evangelists was on the increase. To some at least, this change was dangerous; it represented an encroachment upon the functions and prerogative of the church officers. More than that, there was fear of "clerical power." That the whole question was closely related to the changes in the social and economic milieu is demonstrated by the fact that the churches which felt the need of pastors, under whatever name, had them. Churches which either felt that they did not want a minister or could not afford to have one continued to call the one-man system an innovation.

We have already seen how the controversy over the use of organs in the churches began. There was a noticeable increase in the number of churches that introduced organs into the worship, and this naturally led to increased controversy. Again, the church did not, at this time, split over the issue, but it served to show that the number of people in the group who were no longer interested in following the New Testament for every detail of worship or organization was on the increase. Many churches were set in turmoil over the question, and in certain instances the situation was even ironical, if not actually amusing. It is reported, for example, that one St. Louis church bought a building which already had a pipe organ. When they took over, the organ was locked and never used. But the more liberal element became dissatisfied with the reactionary (or so it seemed to them) attitude of the antiorgan people, and withdrew to organize their own church, meeting in a nearby "organless" hall. So it was that the antiorgan group had an organ they didn't want, and the pro-organ group, which could use the instrument, had none. This, like many other questions, was only symptomatic of the more important fact that Disciples were adapting themselves, where necessary, to new needs created by a rising standard of living and increased economic and cultural advantages.

Viewed in this light, the contention that instrumental music should be kept out of the churches, because it may degenerate into mere musical entertainment[8]; or because its sensuousness may become a substitute for the simple worship of the apostolic church,[9] is seen to be an unconscious recognition of the changing cultural standards of individuals and families in the Disciples group. There is, to be sure, a real point in the idea that the substitution of estheticism for a genuinely ethical and spiritual religion has its dangers, but from the cultural perspective the changing standards which called for more refined content in the services of worship, including music, were to be expected. The famous magazine *Punch* came to the aid of the antimusic party here, in a rather amusing caricature of music in the churches. The story was that a clergyman was asked to take over services in a church where he had never been before.

"The Rev. Mr. Bland . . . says to the Clerk; 'I suppose a hymn is sung in the same simple manner.'

"*Clerk*—'Oh dear, no, sir; we have a very efficient choir of singers, besides three violins, three flutes, a clarionet, accordeon, horn, and my base fiddle. . . . we know Mozart's 'Twelfth Service,' and to-day we perform Purcell's 'Te Deum' and 'Jubilate,' besides our usual anthem, and, sir, you need not trouble yourself to read the Belief, for we sing that, too.'

"The Rev. Mr. Bland turns pale and asks for a glass of water!"[10]

The arguments were really symptomatic of a deep fear in the face of changes that were taking place, and not a description of what was really happening to Disciples. This is evidenced by this appeal to what is obviously an extreme exaggeration. Nothing like this, or even near it, was happening in Disciples churches.

The most important of the controversial issues was the question of what to do about increasing demands for cooperation. Here, as with other issues, the immediate point of contention was the *meaning* and *validity* of the restoration idea. As Disciples increased in numbers and became more conscious of themselves as a group which had a recognized place in the community, it was increasingly felt that the church could not discharge its responsibilities, or fulfil its missionary purposes, without organized missionary activities, in which the centralization of money-raising and some degree of centralization of responsibility would be involved. The controversy was long and involved. In many ways it was simply an intensification of arguments and interests we saw developing in the previous period. The controversy was bitter, and involved much demonstration of feelings.

Involved was a growing impatience with some of the minutiae of argument that were brought in to silence attempts to get on with the business of co-operation. "There are brethren who claim to be *pro-missionary,* but *anti-missionary society!* This is hairsplitting; a word-trick of the sophistical intellect to silence a valid demur of the conscience." The question was beginning to narrow to the proposition that if you believed in evangelistic and missionary activities you must also believe in the only means of getting them carried through efficiently, namely, co-operation, and some centralization.[11]

The controversy, however, continued for at least a generation until finally there was discernible a distinct and unmistakable line between those who believed organized co-operation to be absolutely necessary and those who continued to insist that it was contrary to New Testament practice and therefore could not be done. When this point was reached, a new sect was born, but it was not officially recognized until 1906, when the religious census of that year reported the *Church of Christ* as separate from Disciples. Actually the cleavage represented here was begun, as we have shown, as far back as the 1830-1840 period. An important footnote to the statistical recognition of what was perhaps many years before a *fait accompli* is the observation that the separation removed from the Disciples group most of those who protested against missionary societies; but it left in a large constituency of those who still believed that there was a pattern laid down in the New Testament for the church, and that Disciples, historically, *had* followed, and *should continue to* follow, it. This provides the basis for the tensions which today divide the conservatives from the liberals in Disciples.

The group was not without those who tried to hold the disintegrating segments together. These middle-of-the-roaders were unsuccessful, in the same manner in which Lincoln was unsuccessful in holding the Union together, and, like him, they felt that the continuing preservation of the cause in which they believed was more important than the issues which threatened to divide. C. L. Loos, for example, saw in the struggle over "innovations" a twofold danger.

> This tendency in the one direction is, to narrow unconsciously a great reformatory movement into a sect-formation. This may be done; and is constantly done, in the midst of the loudest protestations against sectarianism. . . . The other direction of this tendency, is to come gradually to look, first with forbearance, then with acceptance, on the sect-life before us; to become by degrees weary of the battle for unity. . . . We say for ourselves, that we have no sympathy whatever with this tendency in either direction.[12]

What Mr. Loos did not realize was that Disciples had not so much accepted the sect-life as such. What they really had done was to pass a few more steps along the road from sect to denomination. In doing this they adopted many of the customs which had already been in operation in other groups which had already passed along the same road some years before.

The sect-to-denomination phenomenon is really a *process* and not a development in which absolutely distinct lines may be drawn. This may be seen in the fact that even after many Disciples had realized the need for a less strict adherence to the restoration notion, allusions to paganism and worldliness were common. This would seem to indicate that Disciples were as yet not too comfortable in their increasing adaptation to the social and economic milieu. That the controversy over innovations should rage so fiercely is one symptom of this. One needs also to take into account that there were questions of worldliness that went beyond such items as organs, choirs, ministers, and these still bothered Disciples. To go along with this there were also more indications of adaptations and of the effects of social change. The picture, then, is somewhat confused, in that not everyone was going in the same direction. At the same time the trend was in the way of adapting the group to the needs of maintaining its now recognized place in American society.

There is a mixture of the candid and the ironical in a letter sent from Covington, Kentucky, in March, 1868.

> In this seeming struggle for pre-eminence, that party always succeeds in any special locality, who is the last to build; for some additional feature going beyond the preceding, is sure to be added. . . . We are gratified, however, in knowing that in very many instances such works have had their foundation in the true spirit of Christian liberality. . . . The expectations of good cherished, have been largely realized, in having an increased attendance from the world, on the public ministry of the word.[13]

This, we may infer, means to say that the church with the most elegant building and the latest facilities will attract more of the respectable and sought-after citizens of any community. That Disciples were not above an interest in such matters is revealed in the report of the *Millennial Harbinger* of a visit to a new church in Allegheny City, Pennsylvania. "We had the pleasure of attending at the opening of the new meeting-house," the item read. "The building is one of the finest church edifices . . . , of large dimensions, as it should be, elegant but not extravagant, and is worthy of the brethren who have built it for the service of the Lord." The local newspaper put it this way, "The building is in the Gothic style of architecture, and is entered by three large arched doorways. The roof is Vermont slate, three colors, in diamond pattern."[14]

But if Disciples were in some places building churches that might attract more "respectable" or upper-class individuals, they were as yet uneasy about having them around. Even *Harper's Bazaar* came to their aid in this matter. "The best-bred people of every Christian country but our own," read an item in the *Harbinger,* quoted from the *Bazaar,* "avoid all personal display when engaged in worship and prayer. Our churches, on the contrary, are made places for the exhibition of fine apparel and other costly and flaunting compliances with fashion, by those who boast of superior wealth and manners. . . . The fact is, that our churches are so fluttering with birds of fine feathers that no sorry fowl will venture in."[15] Not that Disciples had much of this sort of thing to disturb them, but it is at least worth noting, on the principle that where there is smoke there is fire, the problems of social stratification were beginning to be felt, even in a group that did not have great strength in large cities.

Indeed, as one Disciple complained, "Caste, in its numerous phases, social standing, and the money basis, are the all-potent criteria in the church as in the world.—Money is the God, and Fashion the Goddess, before whom so many of the followers of the 'meek and lowly one,' divide their homage and devotions. . . .

"To be poor . . . is a sorry disadvantage in the church as in the world."[16] Not all of the "evils" and disadvantages of caste were to be found, one may infer, in *other* churches; Disciples were beginning to have a share, though it was undoubtedly a small one.

The logic of those who wanted to adapt the church to the world was without doubt what one Disciples leader said it was, that what works successfully and efficiently in "carnal" things may also work in church affairs.[17] But in a church which, to all intents and purposes, grew up with America and moved west in the vanguard of the covered wagon, the logic was natural and, indeed, to be expected. Unfortunately, there is more than a grain of truth in the assertion that a good cause, to be successful, must have a substantial money basis. "That this is a *material world,* is sufficient explanation of the truth that every enterprise *must* depend for support on *material* aid," was the way Mr. Glasier put it at a Missionary Convention in Ohio in 1865. The most significant point about this was that the idea was carried one step further. It is not enough to say, Mr. Glasier continued, that the cause one believes in is true, or holy, or right, that it has the Lord's blessing and will *therefore* win the battle.[18] The cause must be implemented by the necessary wherewithal. What a tremendous change in attitude this is! Such an idea would not even have occurred to Disciples forty years before, except in terms of condemnation. But with their expansion the group could not do its work without a firm material basis.

There were other signs that the economic and cultural level of Disciples was rising. W. K. Pendleton noted in 1866 "a larger and more general liberality" in the support of college, missionary, and journalistic activities, and he urged the brethren to move on "from liberality to liberality."[19] But with this increased liberality went the same sense of uneasiness; some people were apparently getting the notion that what was wanted was money from any source, no matter how it was earned (or obtained). Those who called for increased liberality to further the growing enterprises of the church hastened to add that "unsanctified" money is not wanted. Money as such, they said, perhaps thinking of the time when Disciples had had very little to be liberal with, has no power or blessing in it.[20]

The items on which Disciples had focused their attention in the previous period, and on which a great deal of energy was expended, still continued to occupy their interest, with the stress being laid wherever the person concerned had his particular needs or desires. Those who were especially interested in education had now reached the point of asserting that Alexander Campbell had, from the very beginning, intended to establish a biblical or theological college. The board of Bethany College decided this in 1869, when it proposed to endow a chair in biblical literature at the college with a fund of $40,000. That Campbell had wanted a theological school was, it was stated, established by the documentary evidence at hand[21]; though it is difficult to see what the evidence could have been, in view of Campbell's earlier attitudes about learned clergymen.

Others, who were concerned about the ability of Disciples to meet the demands of their expanding work, still talked about the failures in the movement caused by a lack of organization.

Our former failures have sprung less from the illiberality of our brethren than from the childish expectation that one man, a corresponding secretary, could manipulate 3,000 churches by writing letters to them, by seeing what few of them he could on the railroads. . . . This was about as sensible an undertaking as it would be for you to try to collect the taxes of West Virginia by writing letters to all taxpayers.[22]

That the question was now being argued on the basis of what would best get the job done, rather than whether the New Testament sanctioned the arrangement, is sign of a significant shift in attitude.

The separation from the Baptists, having been for so long a time an accomplished fact, and now so far removed from the focus of attention, was seen in a much more mellow light, at least by those who favored the more liberal policies. "We have never thought that there was a justifying reason for the separation . . . ," wrote W. K. Pendleton. "It has ever seemed to us, that a larger spirit of charity and Christian toleration might have prevented it. . . . Our opinions are often held superstitiously, that is, religiously rather than rationally; and hence, when they are oppugned, we dogmatize about them, and denounce our opponents. . . . The gospel is giving us a freedom that is revolting against this hoary error."[23]

This statement is a good introduction to the next phase of the Disciple movement, in which an outstanding characteristic was a noticeable cooling down of zealous sectarian animosities. The controversies which had dominated the movement were now being seen in a more calm light, suggesting that they were receding from the consciousness of Disciples, as those who had been the leaders in the warfare were beginning to pass; one supposes that they may have found peace and reconciliation in heaven, where, it is reported, the theological and religious differences are relatively insignificant. The other aspect of this more tolerant attitude is that those who still wished to be contentious *within* the group were increasingly drawing themselves off into their own group.

To the very end of the period the view that Alexander Campbell had never intended to start a new sect was staunchly maintained. He only meant, it was asserted, to reform the existing groups with respect to their errors. "But prejudice, envy and clerical bigotry are hard things to persuade, and still harder to contend against, and so the strife commenced, and for more than forty years, went on, with a zeal . . . that in calmer years, both sides must regret."[24] That the Campbells did not intend to begin a new sect is undoubtedly true; but the developments we have traced show that not all the prejudice, envy, and bigotry were on the side of those who opposed Disciples. A fair respect for facts should compel even the most passionate believer in the Disciples way in religion to acknowledge this.

Moreover, it should be pointed out that while the controversy was raging, Disciples showed no signs of regretting it. Only when the struggles began to appear to deal with issues no longer having any point did the "calmer years" arrive, when both sides would do their regretting. The right of Disciples to a place in the religious life of the country was no longer questioned, as it certainly had been earlier. Others still opposed their views, to be sure, but wherever they could convince people, their right to do so was not seriously challenged. When the rest of the world acknowledges the right to exist, belligerency and zeal are no longer accurate definitions of the situation, and they tend to recede when no longer regarded as necessary or useful.

Even so, there was still an urgency in the attempt to maintain the sense of the Disciples' distinctive place in the religious world. When W. K. Pendleton laid down his pen and closed the books on the *Millennial Harbinger,* he said,

> Outward corruption is pressing us into closer communion, and the almost infinite requirements of theological speculation are com-

pelling us to recur to the simple foundations of the Apostolic Church. The powerlessness of sectarianism is constraining us to search anew for the power of Primitive Christianity. . . .

. . . As we grow stronger in numbers and powers let us also become free of Sectarian unity and exclusiveness.[25]

What began as a furious period of controversy ended with all the signs that the sectlike traits of the group would increasingly disappear, while evidences of the denominational status of the group would multiply. This is, in fact, what has happened, although the picture is more complex than the mere statement of it would imply. From the 1870's on, the descendants of the Campbell-Stone movement were to talk and act more like members of a denomination and less like sect-group adherents. With respect to the surrounding society and culture, they were to become less isolated and antagonistic as they found themselves more able to affirm the values they saw expressed in secular contexts. In their relations with other religious bodies, they were to become more tolerant and appreciative. The sociological consequences of this situation are the subject of the two chapters which follow, and the ethical and organizational challenges which result from it will be our concern in the concluding chapter.

CHAPTER IX

The Growing Awareness of Denominational Status: Consolidating the Gains

"The Disciples have wanted to avoid being a denomination and still try to escape applying the word to themselves. But in spite of this they have to be named and designated and denominated. The census bureau, annual reports, year books, church councils, and similar occasions make it necessary to recognize the denominational status."[1] Yet there has been resistance to this, with the result that the "group-image" and the sociological reality are often seriously in disagreement. This has been clear for some time. In fact, as early as 1937, *The Christian-Evangelist* referred to the matter as "The Dilemma of the Disciples."

"The Disciples of Christ," said the editor,

> came into being largely as a protest movement against the divided state of Christendom. It was never the intention of the fathers of this movement to organize a new denomination. . . .
>
> And yet today the rest of the Christian world views the Disciples of Christ as a denomination among denominations. . . .
>
> And must we not candidly admit that we have most, if not all, of the earmarks of a denomination? We are a separate people,

requiring our members to come out of the other religious bodies if they would join us. We have our own separate corporate existence. . . .

This then constitutes the dilemma of the Disciples. In the eyes of the religious world and to all common-sense minds we are a denomination. . . . yet justifying our existence on the grounds of our plea for Christian unity![2]

The Christian-Evangelist, speaking the mind of many Disciples, has continued to regard being a denomination while supporting a plea for Christian unity as a dilemma. However, an occasional tendency toward slipping back into the view that the group is not a denomination should be noted. For example, an editorial in 1943 makes a claim which is difficult to reconcile with the growing recognition that the movement is a denomination. "We have no denominational tradition to perpetuate, no theological dogma to defend, no ecclesiastical office to cherish, no special interpretations to uphold."[3] And as late as 1947 the editor regarded the charge that Disciples of Christ were becoming a denomination with some surprise. "It is amazing," he said, "to hear the accusation that Disciples of Christ are tending toward denominationalism. That is the last frenzy of the religious introvert. There is no more likelihood the Disciples of Christ will accept a denominational status than that the United States will become a monarchy."[4] If the sociological account of the sect-to-denomination process is accurate, it is not a question of whether Disciples "accept" the status. The only question is whether the process has actually taken place.

Sociologically, the sect has to choose between two courses. It may deliberately elect to create a "city set upon a hill," to remain aloof, to keep itself unstained by contact with the world. In order to maintain the purity and unchanging state of its way of life, the religious group must deliberately isolate itself from the larger society and culture. The Older Order Amish of Pennsylvania have succeeded to a degree in pursuing this course. But the ultimate success of such an attempt entails conditions which most descendants of the Campbell-Stone movement are probably not willing to fulfill. Even in the Amish situation, the maintenance of the culture has been dependent upon the retention of agriculture as the only suitable occupation for Amish people. Rural life preserves the maximum possibility for cultural isolation.

Amish culture is a particularly relevant illustration. The major principle of this culture is conformity to the patterns of the Bible, not simply in matters of church polity but in all things. The Bible, taken literally, is regarded as the source of all values. A subsidiary principle is that nonconformity is required in all situations where worldly standards conflict with those of the Bible. Social contacts with out-group persons are to be held to the minimum. The Christian is to have as little as possible to do with unbelievers, since they are potential sources of contamination.[5]

This procedure was theoretically possible for Disciples of Christ. But it was not followed. There is a second course of action available. This was the one taken. The religious group may attempt to take its place among other groups, and to win converts to its way of thinking. Once this choice is made, the group becomes subject to all the influences which play upon human groups. When Thomas Campbell's "voluntary advocates of church reformation" found themselves unwelcome among the Presbyterians, they made an alliance with the Baptists, but this too proved unsatisfactory. The new group withdrew and began to go its own way. No serious effort was made to establish an isolated subculture which could preserve the new reformation unsullied from the world. Instead, the group rolled up its collective sleeves and began to contest the Baptists and Methodists for the place of prominence in the evangelization of the frontier. Once this decision was taken, the involvement of this new group in the sect-to-denomination process was virtually inevitable.

Awareness of the denominational status of Disciples of Christ has come slowly and reluctantly. "The length to which they go to avoid accepting 'denominational' status is interesting. According to the dictionary, any religious group which has separate identity can be termed a denomination. But to avoid the use of this word there have been substituted such terms as 'our communion,' 'our people,' 'our movement,' or 'our brotherhood.' "[6] The use of such terms to designate the group is an attempt—perhaps unconscious but nonetheless real—to dodge the sociological facts of life.

In two separate instances during 1957, editorials in *The Christian-Evangelist* acknowledged that the use of such terms as "brotherhood" or "movement," when employed to avoid using the word "denomination," is an avoidance mechanism. Concerning the term "brotherhood," "we have a suspicion that it is a sly way which the communion has of providing a substitute for the word 'denomination'—a term which is rather anathema in Disciple circles when applied to themselves."[7] The use of "movement" to indicate the Disciples in-group has also been viewed as a semantic escape. "The term 'movement' as used among Disciples, seems to have been invented largely to escape the necessity of calling themselves a 'denomination.' "[8] Two decades before, the attitude toward the use of such terms as "the brotherhood" had been quite different. For in 1938 it was suggested that "Our aversion to naming ourselves as a denomination or a sect has driven us to this more meaningful term."[9] The attempts to avoid sociological realities, while understandable, have not contributed toward the growing sense of maturity which is so essential in a religious movement that wants to be relevant to the needs of the twentieth century.

Frederick D. Kershner was undoubtedly correct in asserting that "if Thomas Campbell, when he produced the 'Declaration and Address' in 1809, had possessed the remotest inkling that he was starting a new Protestant sect, which within a hundred and thirty years would 'reach a notable place among the half-dozen largest denominations of America,' he would have stopped right there."[10] But Thomas Campbell did *not* have that inkling, and the group he helped to originate *has* achieved a notable place among American Protestant denominations! Disciples have shared the fate of other groups in Christendom. No doubt Martin Luther, had he really understood that his action would lead to the splitting asunder of the Church Universal, would never have nailed his Ninety-Five Theses to that church door. Equally so, John Wesley, if he had known that he was originating the Methodist Church, might have gone a bit slower with his class meetings and open-air preaching. Of course Thomas and Alexander Campbell and Barton W. Stone did not *intend* to create a sect that would later become a denomination! But this is what has happened.

Since the 1870's, when the denominational status of Disciples was already quite clear, an examination of the major literature of the movement and consideration of important trends in its life reveal evidences that two crucial sociological processes have occurred. One of these, to be discussed in this chapter, is the mounting evidence for, and growing acceptance of, the status of being a *denomination*. The other is the emergence of an *institutionalized sect* within the group, crystallizing around an explicit rejection of denominational status, and an attempt to "restore" the Restoration Movement to its "original" purposes. This emerging institutionalized sect will be the subject of the following chapter.

In tracing these processes, the device of looking first at the internal dimension and then at the external dimension will be employed. By the internal dimension we mean the developments with respect to attitudes toward polity, structure, and organization. The external dimension refers to how the denomination and the institutionalized sect regard the surrounding society and culture and seek to establish relationship with it, and their attitudes toward the problem of unity with other religious groups. Clearly, the internal and external dimensions of these processes are intimately tied together. Yet it is useful for purposes of analysis to separate them.

I

The Internal Dimension: Organization

Commenting on the characteristics of organization, the sociologist R. K. Merton writes, "A formal, rationally organized social structure involves clearly defined patterns of activity in which, ideally, every series of actions is functionally related to the purposes of the organization. In such an organization there is integrated a series of offices, of hierarchized statuses."[11] Even in earlier decades, Disciples had begun to recognize the need for development of organized procedures, though they did not articulate this recognition in formal sociological terms. As one approaches the past three decades, the necessities of rational organization and the penalties which the lack of it brings have been increasingly emphasized. This is one aspect of the growing awareness of denominational status.

"Jesus left a task, but he said nothing about the method" is how one commentator on Disciples affairs put it. "He did not tell them [his followers] just how the church should be organized, or what the nature of the worship should be. . . . There was not uniformity of method in the apostolic age."[12] In 1906 the issue was stated as one of deciding between organization and anarchy. An early missionary leader, speaking of the Constitution of the Christian Woman's Board of Missions, said,

> If one person, or set of persons, has the privilege of interpreting the spirit of the Constitution, then every member should have the same privilege, and the result would be anarchy or the absence of government. . . . The principle involved is the same as that over which our terrible civil war was fought: the question as to how far each State had a right to be governed by its own interpretation of our National Constitution.[13]

Not only is the rationale for organization based upon the premise that Jesus did not specify a method, and upon the understanding that it is necessary in order to avoid anarchy. Even the leaders of fifty years ago went further than the pioneers did in suggesting that insistence upon the autonomy of the local congregation was not functional in a multigroup society. Charles T. Paul asked in *Missionary Tidings:*

> What do we gain, by asserting and so strenuously maintaining the autonomy, the absolute and imperious independence of the

local congregation, if thereby we sacrifice our cohesion as a body and weaken our cooperation ability. Perhaps some leader can show us the folly of magnifying forms that belonged to the peculiar conditions of the first century, and thereby missing our share in the great tasks of the twentieth century, through organization and leadership comportable with the vastly different conditions which obtain today.[14]

Evidently, for many Disciples the need to justify what seemed to be required organizationally in terms of the way things were done in New Testament times gave way to an increasingly frank appeal to pragmatic grounds. *World Call,* in its very first volume, sounded this note. "Nothing is done in the old individualistic way," began an article entitled "The Call of the New Day." "For the winning of the war we organized not merely the army but the nation. . . .

"Can it be otherwise in the vaster, more delicate, more complex task of the Church of Christ? . . .

"We must organize, organize, organize. . . .

"Then the whole strength of the entire brotherhood must be mobilized and hurled against the opposing line of ignorance and sin."[15]

There was, to be sure, a certain naïvete in all this. For in the same year *World Call* made the interesting assertion that "all who completely give themselves with consuming passion to Him and to the discovery and accomplishment of His program for the world will find questions of Church polity, ordinances, and methods already settled or easy of solution."[16] This is true if one makes the assumption that the phrase "give themselves with consuming passion to Him" implies a standard for dealing with questions of polity, and that "the accomplishment of His program for the world" refers to a clear and unambiguous blueprint, containing organizational and procedural norms. Unfortunately, the acceptance of such assumptions has not proved to be possible for a great many Disciples.

The frequent discussion of the rationale for, and the periodic attempts to answer criticisms of, organizational procedures suggests that, together with increasing awareness of the need for organization went a continuing sense of uneasiness about it. The Executive Committee of the United Christian Missionary Society, in its report to the Board of Managers for 1921, points out that this society "is probably the most thoroughly representative religious organization in Christendom"; with its structure "wrought out by our people, in convention assembled, after prolonged study and deliberation," and its constitution containing "every safeguard for democracy which the wisdom of the Brotherhood could devise," and eliminating "every possibility of 'official control' or of 'Secretarial dominance.' "[17] Was someone, then, suggesting that the organized missionary work was being carried on undemocratically, subject to an undesirable official control and secretarial dominance?

There apparently was a need for the emerging leadership elite to point out that organization is *not* opposed to liberty, and therefore that bolting brotherhood conventions and withholding support from the regular agencies is actually destructive of the common ends.[18] They answered criticisms of the expenditures of official agencies by analyzing the concept of "overhead" and indicating that the overhead of the United Christian Missionary Society is actually below that considered essential and proper for operations of its size.[19] They were disposed to remind the faithful that, while the aim of the work is the simple one of converting men to Jesus Christ, the task itself is extremely complicated and difficult, requiring wise and well-trained administrators who will conduct the enterprise in a businesslike way.[20]

In advancing the aims of Disciples of Christ, there is need, as one writer expressed it, to take certain chances and embrace some dangers.

> One might say, "There is too much centralization here. Too much power is vested in a few people. Putting large powers in the hands of a few human beings is a dangerous thing to do."
>
> And that is very true. There *is* danger here; but it is the inevitable danger unavoidably attached to every great enterprise that involves a large number of people. . . .

. . . But the possibility that power given to a few may go to their heads and make autocrats of them is not a fraction so weighty as the certainty that we shall get little or nothing done if we give authority to no one.[21]

When the issue is put in these terms, it is very far from being a consideration of whether what we propose was done in New Testament churches. Yet a Disciples state secretary put the issue squarely on the line when he asserted, "There is no more dangerous . . . heresy among us than that the local church is the only divine agency revealed in the New Testament.

". . . The missionary, educational and benevolent agencies of our brotherhood are honest efforts to properly express in organized life the universal ideals of the gospel."[22] The real issue is one of the merits, functions, and procedures of organization, considered on their own terms. Many Disciples want the additional assurance of having New Testament sanction.

The appeal to New Testament sanction is a strongly felt need even among some who are most aware of the pragmatic nature of the situation. In some instances, the need for organization for its own sake and its grounding in the New Testament are combined, so that one supports the other. This argument was stated as late as 1958. "To be a New Testament church means to organize for service. . . . It means to be a functioning organization. Elders and deacons are fine. . . But, just as they were added when they were needed in the first church, so we also add any kind of office which is needed to help spread the gospel of Jesus Christ. This is to follow the teaching of the New Testament regarding church organization."[23] Thus, the warrant for doing what we have decided is necessary on other grounds is really in the New Testament after all. Finding this warrant is a quite functional procedure in a group purporting to "call Bible things by Bible names,"and, in this instance, to do Bible things in Bible ways.

Rather than state the case in these terms, one might appeal to a crucial *fait accompli* in Disciples history. "When the . . . Disciples of Christ rejected the binding character of the silences of the New Testament, they opened the door to all kinds of organizational change."[24] If the whole area of matters which are not discussed in the New Testament is open for free choice of latter-day Christians, all the leeway required to justify consideration of organizational procedures on pragmatic grounds is provided. In a sense, this rejection of the principle that nothing should be done by a Christian—or a Christian church—which is not expressly commanded in the New Testament means that a search for the germ of a modern idea or approach in some subtle interpretation of a New Testament passage is not necessary. So organizationally, those Disciples most aware of the denominational status of their movement have arrived at the point of maintaining that the aim—spreading the gospel throughout the world—may be carried out by means and measures which seem to be dictated by the needs of the times, and the social and political realities of the society.[25]

This still leaves them with a whole set of crucial problems. The achievement of freedom from a legalistic regard for the New Testament does not, in itself, solve the difficult problem of building and perpetuating a democratic polity in a complex industrial society. The perplexing dilemmas of freedom and order, and hierarchy versus democracy, remain. A tightly structured bureaucracy of the Roman Catholic type is not a live alternative. Yet neither is the extreme, even antisocial, individualism which is a product of frontier American heritage. Will the fear of hierarchy so influence Disciples thinking that they will be reduced to a state of impotence because of an unwillingness to adapt to conditions in an organizational society? This is the crucial question. In 1930 A. A. Honeywell could suggest: "There has been little serious discussion on how to have strong, effective, organizations and at the same time to have them democratic."[26] The attempt to settle such questions on scriptural grounds had perhaps continued for so long that the effort to consider twentieth-century problems in twentieth-century terms was somewhat hampered.

Yet there is little doubt that a new mood toward questions of organization among Disciples was making itself felt. Only five years later, in 1935, the editor of *The Christian-Evangelist* articulated this mood when he pointed out that "A settled, mature society demands intelligent, efficient co-operation, and it is into such a society that we are now moving in America." The editor also went on to state what, in his opinion, follows from this.

The time has come, therefore, when the Disciples of Christ should abandon the myth that the only protection a local congregation can have against ecclesiastical domination is inefficiency in overhead organization . . . [and] face anew the whole question of how free groups of Christians can best be organized for furthering the work of the Kingdom in a mature and stable society.[27]

Such "facing anew" has gradually involved a willingness to assert that finding divine sanction or New Testament authorization for methods and procedures is no longer necessary. Instead, organizations are to be judged by "their Christ-like purposes and works."[28] Organizations in missions, education, benevolence, church erection, and pensions for ministers need not be patterned after some New Testament plan, but they do need to accomplish their work efficiently. One may appreciate the length of time it took Disciples to arrive at this point in their thinking. The movement originated in a frontier context where the aversion to ecclesiastical hierarchy was pervasive. Later, it was to become evident that sheer individualism and local autonomy are not, in themselves, sufficient protection against abuses, nor do they solve the problem of freedom and order.

Apparently, the New Testament does not speak about many questions of method and procedure, so, in a group ideologically committed to the New Testament as a basis, such questions may logically be placed in the realm of opinion. Even so, one notes the presence of a bifurcation of attitude. This has tended to polarize the group around awareness of being a denomination at one extreme, and the attempt to perpetuate an earlier stage in the history of the movement, at the other. For if methods and procedures are matters of opinion, then the Christian is free to accept or reject them without compromising the aims and purposes of the group. Some have argued from this premise that anything which implies connectional relationships of local congregations, or necessitates a hierarchy, should be viewed with suspicion. At the denominational pole, Disciples have tended toward the notion that this premise lays upon them the responsibility of creating, as rapidly as possible, whatever means or procedures are needed.

The difference between these two approaches lies not in the fact that one part of the group absolutely rejects organization and the other part advocates it, but rather in the respective attitudes taken toward the problems of organization. Some, because of their basic suspicion of anything beyond the local congregation, tend to see any moves in the direction of institutionalizing or structuring as a kind of creeping encroachment. Others, less concerned about autonomy, eagerly search for new ways to get the job done. The search for the middle ground between these extremes in Disciples thought and practice continues. Among those who consciously recognize that Disciples of Christ are now a denomination, the signs point toward an increasing tendency to consider such questions in explicit and candid sociological and political terms. Those who retain a considerable residue of suspicion of organizations will, paradoxically, continue to crystallize around a tightly structured core of the faithful who would like to see things the way they were in an earlier day. That is to say, they will increasingly organize to fight organization.

II

The External Dimension: the World

The growing awareness of denominational status is seen also in the changing attitudes of Disciples toward the society and toward other religious bodies. With the gradual shift from the cultural periphery to the cultural core of life in American communities, Disciples are coming to share in the general acceptance of "this world" as the arena in which God works, to a much greater extent than they have previously. "Can any one doubt . . . that we are on the verge of a wondrous advance? Let us be no longer slow in responding to God's call. He has parted the waters for us to pass over to victorious conquest. Let us linger no longer among the flesh-pots of Egypt. He is with us, and we shall know no defeat."[29] So spoke a missionary leader of some fifty years ago. One may surmise that she had in mind both the advance of the Christian cause in general, and the success of Disciples in particular, when she indicated that it was no less than God himself who carries the banner.

The feeling that Disciples were to play a major part in the Christianization of the world was to become stronger as the years went by. The emergence of a "social gospel" can be traced in detail in the literature of the movement. As might be expected, there was concern from the first as to whether such an emphasis is justified by the New Testament. "The social gospel," wrote one socially minded Disciple, "is the message of Christ to the individual, not as an atom in a vacuum, but as a social center; it is the message of Christ addressed to the environment of the man as well as to the man. . . . But is it Scriptural? Yes, it is the fulfillment of the scriptures, for it brings into the central foreground the ideal of the Kingdom of God, the central teaching of Jesus."[30] This was written in 1913, in the period when Walter Rauschenbusch was developing a "theology for the social gospel," as an aid to "christianizing the social order."

This strain of thought among Disciples very early took the form of stating in various ways that "the ethic of Jesus" is the solution to the world's problems. The first issue of *World Call* sounded a note which was to recur many times. "The decision stands out so sharp that all the nations can see that only the principles of Jesus are practical."[31] And only a few issues later Alva W. Taylor, the outstanding early contributor to Disciples' social consciousness, asserted that "the Church's business is to promote the Jesus idea in the world."[32]

Disciples were not retreating from the world. Neither were they embracing it, for the concern was the redemption of the social order by persuading people to accept the principles of Jesus and to "apply" them in all areas of society. "Unredeemed America," awaiting the healing balm of Jesus' teachings, was the theme of the Presidential Address before the American Christian Missionary Society, which F. W. Burnham gave in 1919.[33] Denominationally minded Disciples have expressed the need for their group to work at this kind of task ever since, although they have not been so quick to set about developing realistic strategies and tactics to implement the values to which they appear to be committed.

Such matters were, of course, dimly perceived in principle. Alva Taylor, for instance, noted that it was not enough to operate on the principle of keeping our children away from "the evil influences of their environment." Why not, he asked, "abolish some of the evils" and "practice moral and social sanitation as well as physical prevention?"[34] This was, in effect, to say that the Christian who is concerned to redeem the world from evil cannot confine himself to symptomatic treatments. He has to look for the roots of the evil, and devise ways of digging these roots out and killing them. This was an important principle, but its implementation has never been very clearly defined in the expression of Disciples' social concern.

The reiteration that "Jesus is the answer," like a theme with variations, continues unabated down to the present. The impression is often given that, somehow, if only we can get enough people to "believe in Jesus," the problems of the world will take care of themselves. Among the versions of this idea are a number which suggest a general interest in the social application of the gospel. "Christianity is the only solvent for the great problems which confront us. . . . Can any one read the utterances of the prophets of God and doubt that the helping to solve such problems [industrial, race, and international relations] is in the province of Christian leaders?" said the 1921 report of the Board of Temperance and Social Welfare.[35] The President of the International Convention in 1922 delivered the judgment that "The church of our Lord holds the golden keys of righteousness and justice and peace by which life may be steadied and come to have once again the normal mind, with restored Christian perspective."[36] The editor of *World Call* put Disciples squarely on the side of the social gospel when he asserted, "Jesus came to launch a constructive spiritual revolution. This involved a radical transformation of human nature and society, in the building of a new social order which he called the Kingdom of God."[37]

Some were aware that the attempt to make the gospel relevant to social issues faced serious opposition. The fact that "there is no guarantee that those converted to a gospel of personal salvation will welcome a gospel of social salvation,"[38] was duly noted. The tendency to disavow the responsibility of the Christian for devising strategies for implementing his social concerns is characteristic of many Disciples. The charter for this disavowal was well stated by an executive of the Board of Temperance and Social Welfare. "I have no blueprint of such a social order," he said. "As a Christian I am responsible for setting forth its moral imperatives, pointing out the possibility of its achievement and indicating the source of power for the task. Social engineers—sociologists, economists, industrialists, political scientists and technicians must bring it about. My job is to point out the need and to indicate the way. It is the job of those who control our resources to see that it is done."[39] This is perhaps a somewhat more sophisticated version of the notion that if we can somehow permeate the atmosphere with Christian ideals the kingdom of God will come.

Disciples seem concerned that the church should address itself to social and political matters. They often seem equally concerned that the words addressed to the world shall never say anything specific. The following is an illustration typical of many in the literature. Speaking of the church and social reconstruction, a Disciples minister said,

> It is no part of our contention that the church should attempt to formulate a program for the reorganization of our economic life. . . .

First, it must prod the conscience of the American people and arouse their hot indignation against the injustices and cruelties of our society. . . .

Second, it must affirm the sacredness of personality and demand that the nation's economic life be organized primarily to conserve human values. . . .

Third, it must demand that the child shall be the greatest asset of the nation and its most sacred trust. . . .

Fourth, it must demand that the pagan and immoral distinction between a "leisure class" and a "working class" shall be annulled. . . . This is not economics, nor is it politics; it is simply "pure religion and undefiled."[40]

In this statement the intense interest which Disciples have in their society, and their rejection of attempts to escape from the world, or to regard it as irrelevant to the Christian, is revealed. So also is their acceptance of the illusion that such matters are nonpolitical. The statement suggests certain problems. When the Christian's conscience has been prodded, and his hot indignation aroused, what shall he do? Nothing relevant to removing the injustices and cruelties is indicated. When the Christian has affirmed his faith in the sacredness of personality, to whom does he address his *demand* that the economic order be organized in ways which will recognize this sacredness? If the distinction between the leisure class and the working class is immoral, what is to be done to erase it? When such questions are considered, the belief that we are dealing exclusively with "religion, pure and undefiled," and not with economic and political realities, is nothing less than incredible.

In terms of their development of a social conscience, Disciples exhibit denominational behavior. They do not turn away from the world as a place of defilement, but seek ways to relate to it positively. Disciples, generally speaking, would affirm the judgment of the editor of *The Christian-Evangelist* about this. "The Christian church has a message concerning human relations as well as about man's relation to God. . . .

". . . They must be keenly sensitive on all matters, political, economic, and social, which afflict and trouble men."[41] In 1958 the editor rejected attempts to limit the Christian gospel to personal salvation. Answering the question "Dare We Limit the Gospel?" with a ringing negative, he said that "a frequent criticism made of the church today is that it should 'stick to the gospel' and leave the problems of society at large alone. According to this point of view . . . the Church is to be concerned chiefly with personal salvation. . . . To the state is assigned the sole responsibility of the application of ethics and morals to the realm of political and human relations. . . . The danger for the Christian in this kind of division of responsibility is that it violates the very essence of the meaning of the gospel itself."[42]

In the judgment of an executive of the Board of Social Welfare, Disciples began in the 1930's branching out from a preoccupation with internal issues to an interest in social questions. "Anyone who has attended the International Convention with any degree of regularity for a decade or more must be dull of mind indeed if he fails to perceive that significant changes have come over the Disciples during that time," wrote James Crain in 1938. "A change of direction began to be observable about the time of the Washington convention in 1930. At first it was faint—no more than a suggestion that we were beginning to think along new lines. Such issues as world peace, international good will, Christian ideals in race relations, temperance and the like began to come to the front. . . . Theological quarrels receded into the background. . . . Thus the Disciples . . . have passed from internal bickering to concern for human redemption."[43] The obituary for theological quarrels and internal bickering may have been premature, but the noting of increased interest in social questions is certainly accurate.

Yet this judgment must surely be qualified in the light of the more recent convention of 1956. Assessing the events there, the executive of the Board of Social Welfare was less than pleased with the demonstration of social concern. "Where have Disciples of Christ moved because of the convention?" he asked. His answer was not reassuring.

Not far, I am afraid, in the area of social justice and concern for human welfare. No one was offended, I imagine. Few were challenged. . . . The watchwords were moderation, poise, and balance. . . .

. . . There was no intent to avoid the issues. But somehow, by common consent it seemed, there was an understanding that no one should, too seriously, challenge anyone else.

"Above all," Disciples seemed to be saying, "let us do or say nothing that would divide the brotherhood, give us 'bad publicity' or embarrass our leaders." . . . We dealt with major issues. We dealt with them tenderly, judiciously, sedately. . . .

A rereading of . . . major speeches of the convention leaves one with the feeling that social issues are far from the major concern of Disciples of Christ.[44]

The difference between this 1956 estimate of Disciples concern for making their gospel relevant to social questions, and the earlier one of 1938, reflects the gradually emerging consciousness that increasing consideration must be given to strategies and tactics by means of which Christians can implement their values. The growth of the awareness that the Christian gospel is both individual and social, and that individuals cannot finally be redeemed unless attention is paid to the social and economic context in which they live, is clear in the literature of Disciples. Further developments await the raising up of a group of strategists who can show the group how to move from the level of sentiment and ideology to that of organized and effective expression in the actual processes of the society.

Reporting on ideas expressed at a Christian social action conference, a Disciples social action leader noted the tendency to state issues in terms of *social* agencies and *social* problems. The reason? "Because . . . our world is becoming more and more interrelated into complex social structures which may either blight or serve human life. . . . the old take-up-an-offering-and-give-a-Thanksgiving-basket reaction of the churches and all the individualistic, haphazard, slip-shod ways of working which it epitomized have now been formally repudiated by the churches as inadequate, childish responses to man-sized social problems."[45] The increased understanding of the complexities of implementing the Christian ethic in an organizational society which this statement suggests is reflected in the thinking of some Disciples, but for the most part such an understanding has not materially influenced the relations of Disciples as a group with the surrounding society.

The development of such understanding will undoubtedly be hampered by two major influences: certain characteristics of the history and organization of Disciples, and the socioethical dilemma of the denomination as a type of religious group. A crucial point is the tradition among Disciples that things not expressly commanded in the New Testament are matters of opinion. This, as we have seen, made it possible for Disciples to consider certain matters of organization on pragmatic grounds. It would appear to have a somewhat different implication for social ethics. Social concerns are, in terms of the tradition, matters of opinion. The Christian can take them or leave them, and be no less Christian for all that. This tradition has been expressed structurally in the fact that the only means through which Disciples can speak their minds in any united way—the International Convention—has no binding legal status. It is a voluntary assembly, with no more status than individuals or local churches are inclined to give it. In practice this has meant that convention resolutions and actions represent the attitudes of those who prepare them, and possibly of those persons who are in attendance at the convention and happen to vote upon the resolutions. One cannot even say for sure that the resolutions really speak for all the persons who vote for them, since the process of approval is often perfunctory and hurried.

Attempts to change the organization and meaning of the convention have been made. At least once there was an experiment with an official delegate convention. This proved to be abortive. The official delegate proposal has been reintroduced at various times. There is currently some agitation to consider it again. The device of having the resolutions committee consist of widely acknowledged leaders from different sections of the country, known to have divergent views about the issues likely to be considered, has certainly helped to give a more representative character to the resolution-making process. Some have wondered, however, whether it does not also help to account for the number of platitudinous resolutions which say little beyond putting Disciples on record before the public as being in favor of virtue.

A step in the direction of better communication was that of having materials and study guides dealing with social issues which may be given attention in convention actions distributed some weeks in advance. Thus, members of local congregations could be made aware of these issues. Yet none of these devices, with the possible exception of the official delegate convention—if it could be made a truly representative deliberative body—really alters the fact that Disciples are not equipped organizationally to exert anything but moral suasion and appeals to good will. And this in a society where the groups whose purposes are effectively realized tend to be highly organized on behalf of those purposes, and to possess an intimate knowledge of political dynamics! Disciples are a denomination in organizational terms, but their structures do not yet function adequately on behalf of social concerns which many Disciples are willing, at least on the verbal level, to affirm.

What we have referred to as the socioethical dilemma of the denomination is also likely to hamper the rapid development of strategies and tactics for the implementation of Christian social action among Disciples. The extent to which this is true is difficult to assess, but the influence of this factor seems clear enough. The denomination, because of its very success as a religious group, is always in danger of succumbing to the temptation to be a cultural mirror, reflecting the values and attitudes of those whose coming into the movement has made that success possible. The more the denomination turns its face away from the sectarian tendency to reject the world, or to remain aloof from it, the greater is the possibility that it may accommodate its ideology to the views of those of its members who have achieved the highest degree of socioeconomic success, and who therefore have the greatest stake in the maintenance of the societal *status quo*. The sect, because of its tendency to regard the world as evil, is usually without any power to influence the world, yet it often functions to preserve values and ethical motifs which are a precious part of the Christian heritage. The denomination, since it has created devices and structures with which to influence the world, has greater potential for implementing its values than the sect, but it has less impetus in this direction if such action challenges the conditions in the society which have enabled it to gain influence. To the extent that this situation is operative, it will act as a deterrent to the development of effective strategies, and as an encouragement to the passing of resolutions which articulate on the verbal level the social consciousness which is so evident among Disciples.

There is another facet of the dilemma of the denomination. Within the movement, there is great concern that nothing be done which would "divide the brotherhood." If the description given of the 1956 convention is reasonably accurate, the things done or not done, the things said or not said, take on a profound significance. Efforts are being made to hold potentially dissident elements in coalition, in the hope that eventually they can reach agreement on the issues which divide them. No denomination wants to lose a sizable portion of its membership. In this context, doing things "decently and in order," setting up moderation, poise, and balance as the goals of the proceedings, and the adoption of a policy of not seriously challenging the views of others all become understandable. The great issues with which a responsible denomination must deal in our kind of society *are* controversial. The question of appropriate strategies and tactics is controversial. So, in effect, those in the group who are inclined toward the development of procedures through which the social concerns of Disciples might be more effectively expressed, are hampered by intragroup necessities. What they are proposing might very well upset the delicate balance by which segments of the group are held together. The crucial question is whether, if this situation continues, it means that Disciples are frozen in a sitting-down position. The reference is to the matter of developing techniques of Christian social action, but the same point might be made about other issues which endanger the intragroup unity of Disciples.

III

The External Dimension: the Denominations

A major item in the ideology of Disciples of Christ is the great passion for the unity of Christendom. They may have oversimplified the causes for disunity—attributing it to what they called "human creeds," and insisting that all that was necessary for unity was to go back to the Bible—but no group has surpassed this one in efforts to bring about Christian unity. The famous formula, "The Church of Christ is essentially, intentionally, and constitutionally one," was actually a statement referring to the church "universal and invisible," since it clearly could not have described the existing situation. Yet this "impossible possibility" has been a strong motif in much of Disciples history.

As their sectarian zeal and sense of exclusiveness began to diminish, Disciples looked for new ways to express their feelings about the importance of Christian unity. They became less and less insistent upon their special interpretations of the Christian faith, and more appreciative of the contributions of others. Ida W. Harrison, an early twentieth-century missionary leader, expressed the thought that Disciples could not attain the heights of spiritual greatness until they learned to appreciate the good in other religious groups. "If we would attain to the heights of the spirit of union," she wrote, "we should not only review our own past, . . . we should also take note of what is noble and Christlike in those great bodies with whom we would now come into closer fellowship, and be willing to learn of them."[46] Many Disciples approached the task of achieving Christian unity with a mood of almost naïve optimism. Even forty years ago, a Disciples leader in unity efforts could write, "It now seems all but assured that the blessed day for which the Disciples of Christ have been praying and pleading for a hundred years is about to dawn. This is undoubtedly the supreme issue now before our people."[47] There is no doubt that wherever efforts at co-operative activity between denominations were occurring, Disciples were to be found in the vanguard.

This eagerness to co-operate with other denominations was not always greeted with enthusiasm. Some thought that such co-operation indicated a less than desirable concern for the ideological position of the movement. Looking back upon his years as editor of *The Christian-Evangelist,* J. H. Garrison commented,

> . . . the paper has always been a staunch advocate not only of the right, but the duty of the Brotherhood to engage in co-operative missionary work. . . . It has also been one of the things for which we have stood to plead for more fraternal relations among all Protestant bodies of Christendom in so far as we could do so in harmony with our plea. This feature of the paper has brought upon it a great deal of criticism.[48]

Evidently, some Disciples thought that the phrase "in so far as we could do so in harmony with our plea" covered more territory, and excluded a great deal more, than J. H. Garrison did. So strong did this feeling of uneasiness about the extent of our co-operative efforts become that it was one factor in the emergence of the institutionalized sect in the movement.

There was a certain degree of ambivalence about Disciples participation in such co-operative activities as comity agreements on the mission field and in local communities, as well as participation in the Federal Council of Churches. Many Disciples were proud that a member of their group, Edgar DeWitt Jones, was elected to the presidency of the Federal Council. Yet the picture is somewhat clouded by the apparent failure of Disciples to undergird their enthusiasm for Christian union with tangible support. In 1932 Frederick D. Kershner commented that "The relations of the Disciples of Christ to the

Federal Council have been more or less unsatisfactory from the beginning. Owing to an entirely erroneous impression of the purpose of the organization, our people gave it only grudging support and came very near imitating the dog in the manger policy of the Southern Baptists by staying out altogether."[49] And *World Call,* expressing its confidence in the abilities of Edgar DeWitt Jones, felt compelled to add that it remains to be seen whether the group which gave him to the Federal Council will give him the kind of support he needs. "No communion has talked more about the necessity for union than the Disciples. Yet their action has not always been in harmony with their profession."[50]

Still, nothing can gainsay the fact that Disciples have contributed some really outstanding leaders to the efforts toward church co-operation and union, at all levels from the local community to the World Council of Churches. Participation in the World Council was advocated even by some whose devotion to the special "plea" of Disciples was rarely questioned. Thus Frederick D. Kershner could write in 1934 that

> . . . we would like for everybody to join our own communion, and thus create unity, but as sensible beings we know that this is not going to happen short of the millennium. The best we can hope for at present is an approximation of the ideal of the type furnished in the constitution of the World Council of Churches. . . . It involves no sacrifice of principle with regard to ordinance, or any other item of faith. . . . Christians everywhere should become better acquainted with the program of the World Council, and should do their best to promote it.[51]

When the new National Council of Churches was formed, Disciples participation in it could be interpreted as the thing which they would do quite naturally. Said one Disciples leader, "*Our concern for unity is no longer peculiar.* . . . One could not help feeling that, though they might not have imagined anything quite like this, Barton W. Stone and Thomas Campbell would have been happy at Cleveland."[52]

The impression that Disciples behaved more and more like a denomination, and less and less like a sect, in their relations with other religious bodies is supported at numerous points in the literature. The mood of seeking every possible way to achieve unity and co-operation with other groups has increased, and this mood has been accompanied by a noticeable lessening of the need to insist upon Disciples uniqueness in the religious world. The presidential address at the International Convention in 1946 stated an approach to the problems of Christian unity which continues to gain momentum.

> Sometimes there are those who bemoan the fact that we are not as unique as we were in an earlier period. Why should this be a source of grief? . . . One of our first concerns should be to help work out a world strategy for Protestant Christianity. . . . There are two general directions in which any one of us may go. . . . We may adopt the superiority, "I know it all" . . . attitude and separate ourselves from those who differ. . . . We may say . . . "I am firmly convinced of the scriptural correctness and spiritual efficacy of my own religious convictions. . . . But Christianity is an enormous matter. I am sure that I see through a glass darkly."[53]

The very way the issue is stated indicates a spirit greatly different from that in earlier periods of Disciples history. The admission that "I am sure that I see through a glass darkly" bespeaks the point of view of a denomination.

Those among Disciples who cluster at the denominational pole, and those who gravitate toward the institutionalized sect, seem to be in agreement at one crucial point. George Walker Buckner, Jr., has stated the point on which there is agreement. "Christian unity and church union are not one and the same." He then proceeds to draw the following inference. "Unity must come first. Without it union can never be. Unity leads to cooperation and understanding; and these are prerequisites of any effective kind of united church. Unity and cooperation, and even church union, do not, as some suppose, require uniformity of belief or practice."[54] So we can co-operate even with those with whom we disagree in matters of belief or practice! Yet this inference is not clear to everyone, it would seem. Starting from exactly the same premise—that unity and union are not the same thing—we can just as logically arrive at an opposite conclusion. "Before real honest-to-goodness unity can appear, we must solve the problem of basic beliefs. . . . When people agree to hold different basic beliefs, and only to co-operate in humanitarian activities, and have such main objectives as seeking prestige and power to influence legislation, they have precluded any possibility of realistic unity."[55] Before we co-operate, we must be sure we agree as to belief and practice.

The sect is concerned first to be sure that its ideology and its customary ways are not compromised. The denomination is willing to hold agreement in beliefs in abeyance while practical means of co-operating are devised, in the hope that out of this process unity can emerge. In this respect, the members of the group who are most willing to answer to the designation "Disciples of Christ"—and who are not disturbed by the fact that the "D" is a capital and not a small "d"—tend to constitute a denomination among denominations.

CHAPTER X

The Rejection of Denominational Status: the Emerging Institutionalized Sect

For a sizable portion of the descendants of the Campbell-Stone group, the "dilemma of the Disciples"—that the movement is now a denomination, yet justifies its existence on the grounds of a plea for Christian unity—is no dilemma at all. As a matter of fact, "there is a considerable body of us within this fellowship for whom there is no such dilemma. . . . For us unity and restoration of the New Testament faith and order are identical and a church that approximates that New Testament standard can not be denominational except in the sense that all Christianity is denominational."[1] This judgment was shared by a number of members of the group who let the editor of *The Christian-Evangelist* know how they felt about his dilemma.

To acknowledge the existence of the dilemma is actually to disavow the purposes of the Restoration Plea. At least this is the view of those who object.

. . . I do not believe we are in any "dilemma" except that brought about by preachers who refuse to preach the *"Gospel of Christ* which is the power of God unto salvation to every one that believes."

What we need is preachers who will preach the gospel that will save individuals and not "a gospel" that will tickle the itching ears of the Sectarians. . . Yes, if we are in a "dilemma" it is the fault and weakness of the preacher and not with our plan or plea.[2]

There really is no dilemma if only the group will stick to its original aims. But there is more to it than this. Those who think there is a dilemma are confused. They seem to think that the Christian Church is advancing some *human* program. Not so! "We are not offering *our* religion, but *Christ's* religion! We are not offering *our* way, but *his* way!" Thus, you who talk of dilemmas of Disciples are "sponsoring and laying the foundation for one of the most soul-wrecking divisions since the fourth century."[3]

One reader of *The Christian-Evangelist* wondered what the editor was up to. "Did you drop this bombshell on the brethren merely to watch some of us squirm," he asked, "or did you do it for the purpose of proving that 'The National Weekly of the Disciples of Christ' no longer believes the principles on which the Restoration Movement rests?"[4] The discussion of the "dilemma of Disciples" apparently touched a tender nerve. The literature of the movement reveals that an enormous amount of attention has been paid, in the past few decades, to the question of whether the Restoration Movement, which proposed to eliminate sects and denominations, was in fact itself becoming a denomination. Not a few members of the group were disturbed by what they thought was happening.

The suspicions of those who saw Disciples becoming a denomination were indeed well founded. Disciples have, in fact, become a denomination. Yet a considerable number in the group have rejected this fact. In this process, they have tended to crystallize around a few focal points of doctrine and polity, and to develop an increasingly well-defined and identifiable group. This group is attempting to turn back the clock, to arrest the development of the movement at a stage much closer to the original situation out of which it emerged. They "reject" denominational status, and in the process take on the characteristics of the *institutionalized sect.* In denying the sociological facts of life, they inadvertently set in motion a new sociological process, the emergence of a distinct and clearly distinguishable group. The marks of this process are revealed in the language of those who participate in it.

"Do you really believe you can wean the whole 'Disciple' group away from their Campbellian-born love for the plain New Testament church?" a reader from Ohio asked *The Christian-Evangelist.* "Or is it your intent to further divide the Restoration Movement? . . . Of course, I may be mistaken, but it seems to me you must know that the increasingly sectarian tenor of your policy is more likely to result in a clear-cut distinct division between those who desire complete sectarian status, and those who are just as eager for a return to the position held by our fathers prior to the Civil War."[5] The phrase "sectarian tenor of your policy" here means "your tendency to treat Disciples as a denomination." The reference to "those who are eager to return to the position held by our fathers" is, in the sociological sense, an implicit acknowledgment of the existence of a definable group, and not merely a collection of individuals who happen to share some isolated feelings.

This polarization in the movement is understandably upsetting to members of the group. "I wonder when and where we came to the parting of the ways," said one layman from Kansas. "When did the Church of Christ begin to be the Disciples' church? Who started this divisive movement? And why does it continue when such a large element among the Disciples of Christ reject it and resent it?"[6] The process continues because, far from rejecting and resenting it, a large number of descendants of the Restoration Movement find that what has taken place meets their religious needs. No one intended that the sect-to-denomination process should occur. Neither did anyone consciously desire that some members of the group would draw together into a closely knit in-group to express their preference for the predenominational period in the history of the group. Yet this is what the evidence reveals.

Those who prefer the predenominational stage are quite sure they represent the core of the tradition. They are equally convinced that the Church of Christ and Disciples of Christ are departures from this core. Speaking to this point, the editor of *The Christian Standard* writes,

In 1906 a large number of these churches . . . crystallized around the name "Church of Christ" and the prohibition of musical instruments as aids to congregational singing. In 1920 another large group began to crystallize around the name "Disciples of Christ," a missionary society, a publishing house, and a convention. . . . The "International Convention" and by inference its reporting agencies, abandoned all pretense of being associated with an undenominational movement, and began to act as the "official" "clearing house" and "voice" of a "Disciples of Christ" denomination.[7]

A few years later, the point was reinforced in even stronger terms. Those in the movement who are trying to realize "the unity of the Spirit, in the bond of peace" are, so to speak, caught between two insistent factions. Those who will not fellowship with other Christians unless they remove the organs from their churches, and those who represent brotherhood agencies as official are equally "sectarian." They limit themselves to those who have accepted "human authority" in their religious expression.[8]

Those who admit to being Disciples, and who are most likely to be aware that the sect-to-denomination process has been operative in their movement, are often quite as sure that *they* represent the main body of the group. This makes the task of interpreting statements, such as the following, difficult. Commenting on the International Convention in 1926, W. R. Warren said,

There were differences of opinion on many matters, but a common devotion and fidelity to the one Christ and to the supreme and immediate necessity of making him known to all the world and giving him complete sway in our lives, compelled the granting of one another the largest individual liberty in Christ. . . .

. . . From time to time some may go out from us because they are not of us but the great body of Disciples of Christ is moving on with united purpose and triumphant power.[9]

To what do the expressions "some may go out from us because they are not of us" and "the great body of Disciples of Christ" refer?

Regardless of who is going out from whom, and irrespective of which portion of the group is *really* the main body, the emergence of both the self-conscious denomination and the institutionalized sect is quite clear. The use of these concepts is intended to be objective and descriptive. Yet one cannot help being aware that such concepts become embroiled in the emotionally charged atmosphere which surrounds the processes being described. Still, the concepts do have objective sociological meanings, and their use is never intentionally invidious. This should be kept in mind as our account proceeds.

A highly articulate group within the Restoration Movement has set itself clearly in opposition to what it refers to as the claims of Disciples of Christ. By defining Disciples as an *out-group,* those who reject denominational status gradually emerge as an *in-group.* The point cannot be overemphasized. When a reader wrote to "The Counsellor's Question Box," a column in *The Christian Standard,* with a question concerning "the part Alexander Campbell, founder of 'The Disciples of Christ Church' played in the field of missionary societies," he received in reply a commentary on the mistaken assumptions of his question.

You will pardon my correction of the statement, "Alexander Campbell, founder of the Disciples of Christ Church." Mr. Campbell was just one of a number of people from different denominations to advocate the unity of Christians by a return to the simple teaching and practice of the church as recorded in the New Testament. Neither he nor any of the men associated with him in the protest against denominationalism ever consented to the formation of another sect. . . . Some who have entered into the heritage of the pioneers, do accept a denominational status, and call themselves "Disciples of Christ" in a sectarian sense. They have repudiated the basis upon which the movement was launched.[10]

The verb used here—"repudiated"—is actually not strong enough.

This is one of the saddest, most tragic developments in our . . . times—the movement to restore New Testament Christianity *subverted* by those who denied its basic principles. . . .

Within the denominations . . . is a host of Christian people who love the Lord Jesus Christ. . . . These people are Christians. . . . They are also disciples of Christ. . . . There will always be a Restoration movement, because there will always be people who know and who will want to share the joy of being Christians, nothing more and nothing less.[11]

So the original purposes of the Campbell-Stone movement have been subverted, and those who have been parties to this subversion have become a denomination. Yet the faithful need not be dismayed, for there will always be a group who are loyal. How shall they achieve their aims? By drawing closer together with those who "want to share the joy of being Christians, nothing more and nothing less!" Plainly, this is the charter of an emerging institutionalized sect.

Although we are aware of the dangers involved, we shall employ, in what follows, the term *Restorationists* to refer to this institutionalized sect, and the term *Disciples* to indicate the denomination within the movement. Restorationists see Disciples as having slowly but surely departed from the faith of the founders. In fact, Disciples have much in common with "Wrongway Corrigan." "Twenty-first-century historians may write a church history which will include very little mention of the Disciples of Christ denomination. . . . The account will say that the 'Disciples' denomination . . . has stepped back into the denominationalism which it spoke against. . . . Its concluding sentence will be: 'And the great majority of Christians refused to be called the sons of "Disciples" choosing rather to share ill treatment with the people of God than to enjoy the pleasures of denominational sin and ecclesiastical power for a season, accounting the reproach of Christ greater riches than the treasures of denominationalism.' "[12] The identification of "We" and "They" could scarcely be clearer.

How did Disciples get into this condition? They accommodated to the surrounding society and culture, and "flew in the wrong direction" with "the denominations." This need not be, say the Restorationists. More individuals and churches are learning this all the time.

For many years an unfaithful leadership has tried to force denominationalism upon free churches of Christ. We have seen churches and preachers succumb rather than resist, lose their freedom in Christ, and with it their evangelistic zeal. . . . But an increasing number of congregations served by faithful ministers who refused to play the hireling, and by informed elders who were true to their trust, have thrown off the shackles of a sectarian leadership, and have stood squarely on solid New Testament ground.[13]

A few years ago, *The Christian Standard* outlined in a remarkably perceptive way how a sect emerges. The process includes the following phases: overemphasis upon a few peculiar phases of doctrine to the minimizing or elimination of others, introduction of peculiar practices in worship or polity, the insistence upon sectarian peculiarities leading to the defense of false positions, and the building of vested interests around which crystallize a sectarian organization.[14] This was designed to explain how the Church of Christ and Disciples of Christ departed—one to the right and the other to the left—from the heritage of the nineteenth-century movement to restore the New Testament church. Yet it applies with considerable accuracy to the emerging institutionalized sect of Restorationists.

There was some awareness of this possibility. As early as 1936, a member of the brotherhood from Ashland, Kansas, felt compelled to raise the question of whether the antidenomination had become a distinct group. "We have always claimed," he wrote, "that we were not a denomination. . . . But the sin of it is that we are so opposed to denominationalism that we become a denomination."[15] A correspondent in 1958 made the charge more specific.

> The group of Christians calling themselves the "undenominational churches of Christ" are a denomination! Although you insist that you have no formal or official organization, by common consent you have a publishing house, training institutes for your ministry, and a program of national and international missions. . . . There is a building of personal relationships, a certain exclusiveness and distinctiveness that the group claims for itself, and now formal associations that certainly mark the "undenominational churches of Christ" as a denomination.[16]

Technically, the incorrect sociological concept is employed here, but the description points to the process which we have been discussing. We must now look more in detail at this emerging institutionalized sect.

I

The Internal Dimension: the Suspicion of Organization

For several decades, the Campbell-Stone movement has exhibited a healthy fear of bureaucracy, a mind sensitive to the dangers of organization. "We must watch and pray to be kept pure in heart. . . . Organizations, human plans for good in every age, have met with disaster because of human weakness. . . . We know that there has been no perversion of the objects of any of the organizations planned to promote the restoration of primitive Christianity in our day. But, are even we entirely immune?"[17] This is how Annie E. Davidson put the issue in 1907. The latter-day Restorationists are not as confident as she was that there has been no perversion of original objects. Contemporary Restorationists would applaud what J. H. Jowett put forward some forty years ago. Said Jowett, "We organize more than we agonize. We are more intent upon multiplying machinery than we are upon enriching our fundamental power. . . . We are more concerned to confer with one another than we are to hold great communion with God."[18]

Not a few in the movement viewed attempts to provide structure as a plot to develop a superorganization. One who felt this way put it as follows.

> Though big Barnabas sold all and started the pension fund in the first church, it was for all as they had need. The United Christian Missionary Society has us by the neck. They send us sad-looking posters for our auditorium and a bill for about 10 per cent of what we can raise for all purposes for a whole year.
>
> Now these preachers will join this superorganization, and together they will excommunicate every church that can not or will not come across.[19]

The danger referred to here was often put in terms of the concept of ecclesiasticism. Christians may, in their desire to advance the cause, come together to co-operate. Yet they must do so as individuals. The attempt to bring local churches together as units of some organization is a road to serfdom. It is the beginnings of ecclesiasticism, yea of dictatorship, and a totalitarian church. This is not an objection to co-operation, or even to organization, but rather to "the totalitarian church."[20] However, Restorationists do reject, and with emphasis, co-operation with those whom they interpret as being disloyal to the charter of the movement, and organizational structures they believe are controlled by those who do not share their image of the group's history.[21]

Among several large Protestant groups there is a tendency to refer to organizational headquarters as "the Vatican." Among Lutheran Church (Missouri Synod) people there is a droll habit of speaking of "the Vatican" in St. Louis, and Methodists are often heard to remark about Nashville in the same manner. Restorationists, however, find nothing at all droll about this. Their feelings about Indianapolis are deep-seated, and there is no hint that little pleasantries are being engaged in. A Restorationist from Los Angeles notes with obvious pride, "The Lord has a few thousand faithful saints who will never bow the knee to the United Society. In fact, there is just as much authority for that hierarchy in Rome as there is for that one in Indianapolis."[22]

The structure is regarded as illegal, immoral, and as an absurd pretension. It is a human institution, to which no faithful Christian need have any *necessary* loyalty. One will find it difficult to retain either "liberty in Christ" or to be true to New Testament polity, if he acknowledges that any official agency or organization beyond the local congregation has any claim upon him.[23] In fact, most of the people who support such organizations can be conveniently divided into two major classes—those who have departed from the true faith and give support for personal or professional reasons, and those who are simply not informed as to the issues. In the first group are the "liberals" and the professional religionists. The second group includes preachers who fear retaliation if they object, some misguided women, and a number of persons who are indifferent or have been sold a bill of goods.[24] The possibility that many who support the organizations do so because they believe structure and hierarchy to be essential in contemporary society is apparently not considered, or is regarded as inconsequential.

The feelings of Restorationists are based upon a clear, well-defined ideology. If one accepts the initial premise in the argument, it is difficult to find logical flaws in it. "Organization is, basically, planning and performing common projects in an orderly manner," said one Restorationist. But then he jumps from the question, "What is organization?" to the question, "What does the New Testament say about organizations?" The first question involves a sociological and political discussion, and the second is an exercise in exegesis. "There is no record in the New Testament of any organizations for Christian work or fellowship except the congregations of Christians. . . . No teaching in God's Word would appear to condemn additional organizations. . . . When God speaks neither in favor nor to oppose any particular action it is then left up to the individual to decide its merit. . . . No organization in the Lord's work can, without changing the New Testament pattern, be given authority over any Christian person or congregation."[25]

Restorationists, it appears, want as little as possible to do with organizations. They are inclined to attribute most of the difficulties in advancing the Christian cause to the setting up of organizations beyond and above the one explicitly authorized in the New Testament—the local congregation. Nothing more than this is really needed, they urge, and anything more than this only means trouble.[26] The idea that any additional organization or structure might be needed is a human opinion, not supported by God's Word.[27]

This ideology is used to buttress a great fear of organization, and to interpret what organizations and their functionaries do as an attempt to place churches and ministers in bondage. Even the sending out of materials dealing with what Disciples leaders called "The Crusade for a Christian World" could be interpreted as an effort "to bring every local church into denominational bondage in every department of its activity," and as a "highly financed and closely organized assault upon the freedom of the local church."[28] Some agencies within the movement were started by "Bible-believing and Christ-honoring" Christians who thought they might help to further the work. These agencies have, however, been taken over by a "clique" which wants them recognized as "official" and which is disloyal to the purposes for which the agencies were created.[29]

One official, the state secretary, appears to be most vulnerable to attack as an agent of "the hierarchy." Sociologically, he occupies a status for which there is an ambiguous and shifting definition. His role-behavior, then, is likely to depend upon whether he possesses attractive personal qualities. He may achieve considerable prestige, and he may make a fine contribution to the work of the churches. But he must be eternally alert to the possibility that he may be pressing his claims farther than local churches will allow. He may also incur the wrath of ministers who feel that they have not been treated fairly. Two ministers expressed in 1932 what many have felt since. One, who styled himself "a warm friend of the secretary," said that "some of us preachers . . . can't help feeling that we have been discriminated against, when, after we have established satisfactory relations with some church, the State secretary . . . comes on the scene, and boosts some other fellow into 'his job.' And this for no apparent reason other than the fact that he will hoorah for 'our brotherhood literature.' " We must, however, sympathize with the secretary. "How can the poor secretary help it, since he is one of the wheels of the great machine?"[30] The other minister was not so sympathetic. His picture of the state secretary is that of a man who is an agent of the superorganization. "When a plain preacher of the gospel of Jesus Christ is in their respective States and does not 'scratch the back of the United Christian Missionary Society by the State mission route,' he is dubbed a trouble-maker if not actually black-listed. He is a trouble-maker indeed . . . because he spends his time preaching the gospel instead of catering to said Society."[31]

In the eyes of many Restorationists, the state secretary is the representative of those who have sought to "denominationalize the brotherhood." His main work is to propagandize local congregations on behalf of "official agencies" of the denomination, which means, of course, Disciples of Christ. His primary concern is not to help the work of local churches, but to build up contributions to agencies which have not been able, on their own merits, to elicit adequate support.[32] More than this, he is in collaboration with those who want to introduce departures from the ideas of the founders. He may not be a "modernist" or a "liberal" himself, but he plays along with them just the same.[33] And so it goes. The state secretary occupies exposed territory, and he is evidently a ready target for the expression of suspicion about organizational developments in the group.

Above all, the facet of organization which elicits the most comment and arouses the most fears is the International Convention. On Restorationist principles, the convention can hardly be more than a gathering of individuals for inspiration and mutual stimulation. If a member of the group speaks of the convention as "our convention" he is advocating denominationalism. The convention cannot be "ours," since it cannot possibly *represent* a movement which is made up of individuals and congregations.[34] Actually, the convention does not represent, it *mis*represents. It creates the impression that this group is simply another denomination, eager to work out plans of merger and union with *other* denominations. The convention, by lending support to the notion that its officials speak for "the denomination," gives the world an erroneous idea of the principles which the group came into being to espouse.[35]

The passing of resolutions concerning social and political questions disturbs Restorationists greatly. From Dallas, Texas, comes a forthright statement of the objections:

> A number of these resolutions have no bearing whatsoever upon the work of the Church and the Convention should have nothing in its meeting other than the things that further the cause of Christ. . . . The resolution which deals with the race relations is entirely out of order. . . . The Convention was silent on the liquor problem which is, as every person knows, the scourge of the human race today. . . . The thing for our ministers and the church papers to do is to confine themselves to the advancement of the cause of Christ and let issues which divide the brotherhood alone.[36]

One notes with interest the assumptions of this approach—that resolutions on social questions have no bearing on the church's task and do not further the cause of Christ, that discussion of race relations is out of order but liquor ought to have attention, that issues which divide the group should not be considered. These assumptions appear significant in the light of the fact that they are stated over and over again in the literature. We do not, say many Restorationists, go to the convention to discuss the problems of the world. We go to "hear Christ exalted."[37]

The proposal for a convention made up of official delegates is regarded as opening the door to ecclesiasticism. "Once we agree to have such delegation of the power of the local congregations, we would be bound to accept the votes of such a convention as the votes of the churches. And how far is that from ecclesiasticism. . . . Who is to guarantee the autonomy of the local church after it has sent a delegate into such a gathering?"[38] The great fear is that a delegate convention would appear to commit the group. Restorationists are not impressed with the assurances that a delegate convention would not necessarily be binding on the local church. If an official convention speaks, its pronouncements will become formal declarations of "the denomination."[39] Furthermore, all this talk about convention machinery is beside the point. It is taking the group away from its allegiance to the conviction that "we have a definite, God-given task and a peculiar message to a divided church."[40] "The business of a Christian convention is simply the preaching of the gospel. All Christians are interested in that."[41]

The suspicion of organization and structure can almost succeed in rendering a group incapable of responding to its environment. Yet the fear that the organizational tail may wag the ideological dog does perform an important function. There is always the danger, in any organization, that the preservation of structure may become an end in itself. As early as 1933, a perceptive observer of organizational trends in the movement stated this point with clarity. Jacob H. Goldner, addressing himself to "The Craze for Organization," noted that "Organization is indispensable in our modern life; however we have gone to extremes and have become overinstitutionalized. . . . There is constant danger of making the institution an end instead of a means."[42] Restorationists would, it appears, argue that this point justifies an extreme suspicion of any structures beyond the local congregation.

II

The External Dimension: the Critique of "Worldliness"

The denomination, as a type of religious organization, maintains a certain degree of tension with the world. While it has experienced a considerable amount of accommodation to the surrounding society and culture, at some points it remains critical. The accommodation process has proceeded far enough that the group begins to face what we earlier called "the dilemma of the denomination." Yet there still remains a considerable feeling of "over-againstness" with respect to the world. This is what keeps reminding the members of the group that the kingdom for which they hope has *not* come, that they still face the difficult problem of being *in* the world but not *of* it. One should note, however, that as the group moves out of the sect stage, the tension with the world is experienced more in terms of crucial social and political questions, and less in terms of private and personal morals. At the institutionalized sect pole of the movement, Restorationists have clearly articulated an arresting of this process at a stage earlier than is the case with most Disciples.

The feeling of "over-againstness" has been well stated by Frederick D. Kershner.

> The world may have changed since Jesus was in it, and the "ambitious ecclesiastics and sectarians" may be wrong in thinking that there is any need of salvation, at the present time. Nevertheless, some of us are still able to note a line of cleavage between the spirit of the world and the spirit of Christ. When the latter begins to "get along nicely with the former" we suspect that there is something wrong with the situation.[43]

In the midst of the great depression, a member of the executive committee of the Board of Temperance and Social Welfare was afraid that the spirit of Christ was already getting along too nicely with the spirit of the world. He suggested that "it is quite apparent to many that, as presently constituted, the Protestant church is too entangled in the old order itself to be of much help."[44] The question was also raised as to whether Christians were not too often guilty of adopting the device, well known to students of animal life, of protective coloration. Said James G. Van Buren, "It is only natural for us to want to blend into our religious, cultural, and national surroundings. . . . We seem in some areas, just another fundamentalistic group, in others just one among a number of placid, ritualistic, and liturgical churches; in still other locales, we appear to be a kind of sweet-scented ethical cultural society."[45]

The issue of blending in with the surroundings was put with delightful irony by a writer who identifies himself only as Thistle. Thistle's work is reminiscent of the skill of Alexander Campbell in cutting through a swamp of pretense with a machete of satire. Thistle, who addresses his communications to a fellow named "Down," delivered himself of a brief discourse on chlorophyll.

> I've had my fill of chlorophyll
> I'm tired of smelling sweet
> I'll risk a chill or getting ill
> But I'll have nothing green to eat.

After all, Down, how silly can we get? . . . This chlorophyll epidemic is a sample of the manner in which people are carried away by tides of popular hysteria. . . . This should serve to remind you, friend Down, to be wary of being swept off your feet by the latest fad, whether it be in diet, dress, politics, or religion. . . . I don't know that it is always a good thing to have a cross on top of our church buildings, but I am sure it's much preferable to a weather vane. We need to be "rooted and grounded in love" so that we may, indeed, be saved from being blown about by every wind.[46]

A movement dedicated to the advancement of New Testament Christianity cannot afford to be blown about by every wind, nor can it completely make peace with the world, short of that world having become the kingdom of God. "There is a peace which Christ bequeathed to his followers," wrote the editor of *The Christian-Evangelist* in 1957, "but it is born out of sacrificial suffering and loyal devotion to the cause of the Kingdom of God. . . . Unless the Church is at war with the world about it, aggressively attacking the evils within our pagan society set to destroy us, it has little resemblance to New Testament Christianity."[47] In one sense, the Christian can never be without a feeling of estrangement from much that goes on in the world. Yet this says nothing specific about the identification of the aspects of society and culture from which the Christian is to dissociate himself, and against which he is to carry on a war unceasing. On this point, the descendants of the nineteenth-century reformation exhibit considerable disagreement. The institutionalized sect within the movement carries on a critique of worldliness which is almost a carbon copy of the one described for earlier periods.

What are usually called "worldly amusements" come in for a considerable share of attention. When, nearly thirty years ago, the Linwood Boulevard Christian Church in Kansas City became a "community church" and started showing movies and having parties, an editorial warning was issued. "The Church of Christ is not intended to provide amusement, pleasure, nor even fashionable culture for its members and the community. The Church's sole work is to preach the Gospel and teach men the commandments of Jesus."[48] These worldly things are unthinkable in the church. They are only a little, if any, better outside the church. "We are anxious," said a correspondent from Tennessee, "to have our brethren express their convictions on the propriety of Christians engaging in the worldly amusements . . . such as dancing, card-playing, cigaret smoking and attending the demoralizing movies. . . . Many . . . contend that the above-mentioned things are not sinful; that customs are constantly changing, therefore we are at liberty to change our practices. But God is unchangeable, and if it was sinful to engage in worldly amusements threescore years ago it is sinful to-day."[49] Sin, like beauty, may be in the eyes of the beholder, but if the beholder is God, that puts a different construction on the matter.

So many evil things are going on that it is difficult to decide which one ought to have attention first. One minister expressed the view that while dancing is bad, and is hurting the church, card-playing is even worse. This evil, he said, is sweeping through our congregations, and even elders and deacons have been caught holding the tell-tale cardboards in their hands. The recommendation seems severe, but one can be sure the intentions were serious—clean house, and rid the churches of those who will not stop such harmful practices.[50] Movies, too, are near the top of the list of forbidden things. A correspondent from Washington, Pennsylvania, wrote that he did not see any reason to make a distinction between good movies and bad ones. Only sinners are employed in the movies, and even if they produce decent pictures, a not very likely possibility, we should not be parties to such pollution. "Christ called us from 'among the world' and when he comes for his bride he won't take it from the theater-going crowd."[51] James Crain, of the Board of Temperance and Social Welfare, was of the opinion, in 1933, that the movie industry was dominated by pagan ideals and barnyard morality. He accounted for the financial plight of the industry by suggesting that "this flood of sex and liquor propaganda has gone to the point where the decent section of the community has rebelled and prefers to stay at home rather than go to the movies and be entertained by gutter filth."[52] One could add that he is not likely to change his opinion on the basis of what the industry has produced in the twenty-five years following his statement.

Even in the days before the paper-back, the flood of literature regarded as evil was disturbing. Books are all right, said the editor of *The Christian-Evangelist*. In fact, a clean, healthful book has all the sweetness of roses bathed in dew. Yet nothing is more revolting and poisonous than a depraved book. The criteria of the depraved book are not made too clear, but whatever else a depraved book is it is "Christ's Deadliest Enemy."[53] Still, the high standards of purity which *The Christian-Evangelist* set for what should be allowed to appear in print were considered low by some readers. A. Preston Gray, of Kingsport, Tennessee, noted that this journal included, as a contribution to "humor," the following item. "A colored girl had just been baptized in the river. As she came to the surface she cried 'Bless de Lawd, I'se saved! Las' night I was in de ahms of Satan, but tonight Ah'm in de ahms of de Lawd!' 'Sistuh,' came a baritone voice from the shore, 'how is yo fixed up for tomorrow ebening?' " Said Mr. Gray,

"Then we wonder why people do not take matters of religion and the ordinances seriously. But I have heard ministers of the gospel make sacred things the brunt of their blasphemous levity. One then should not expect more of a modernistic semireligious journal."[54]

Gambling and the use of tobacco were also in the catalogue of worldliness.[55] But without doubt the issue which has most exercised the faithful is dancing. The views of many were stated by the editor of *The Christian Standard.* "Can there be any doubt," he asked,

> in any honest person's mind as to the purpose of the modern dance? Is it not perfectly manifest that the modern dance is a device for inflaming the sexual passions and for gratifying to some extent the base desire for promiscuous sexual relations? . . . Colleges . . . once marked by the high religious tone with which they supported their training for Christian service, are now enmeshed in this worldliness, and explain it by the claim that even the Christian homes demand it for their children.[56]

This interpretation was advanced in 1934, but as late as 1956 jazz and the current craze of rock'n'roll were described as demon-worshiping carnality, and it was averred that the introduction of festering yaws, sleeping sickness, and elephantiasis into our culture would hardly be more dangerous.[57] In the intervening years, a steady stream of comment refers to the dance as evil.[58]

The cruciality of dancing as an index of worldliness is seen in the flood of response to the appearance of the following news item in *The Christian-Evangelist.* "Before a blue silk backdrop, solemn-faced and nervous, 15 bare-footed girls . . . presented dancing interpretations of familiar hymns . . . at the regular Christian student congregation meeting in the educational hall. . . . Garbed in draped gray silk and plain black silk tunics and trousers, the church dancers . . . went through ensemble formations symbolizing supplication, humility and prayer."[59] When the avalanche of criticism descended, the editor of *The Christian-Evangelist* pointed out that the whole thing had been distorted by a newspaper reporter who did not bother to get the facts straight, and suggested that before the brethren "let fly" they should hear the other side of the story.[60] The minister remarked that "regardless of what it is called—pantomime, tableau, or dance—the program was fine. The young women were properly clad, serious in their attitude, and did their part with dignity and sincerity."[61] Some of the saints were not about to subscribe to this effort to give Christian sanction to such sinful activities. From Corvallis, Montana, came the following lament. "May Brother ---------- repent and may God forgive him for his mistake. I have been made to blush over the criticism about the so-called Christian Church. . . . I suppose they partook of the Lord's Supper after the dance. Brother ------------ knows his Bible better than that. If he doesn't he had better get out of the pulpit."[62]

Since the question of the minister's knowledge of the Bible was mentioned, it should be noted that a member of "the brotherhood" from Ohio experienced difficulty in locating the scripture passages to which the objector from Montana referred. A Mr. Gatchell wrote that "if our dear enthusiastic brother 'subscriber' of Corvallis, Montana . . . will kindly inform us of the chapter and verse where the Master either forbids or condemns dancing" he would appreciate it.[63] But whether Jesus explicitly approves or condemns dancing is not really the point. When girls attempt to express religious emotions in the dance, this is not divine expression, but human expression. Is the Word of God, or the thoughts and feelings of men, the standard for worship?[64] When the church sanctions behavior which gives the appearance of evil, then the church, not the world, is to blame for the resulting sensationalism.[65] At any rate, so much were the feelings of the brethren aroused that even two years later the question was asked "Can any sane thinking person, Christian or otherwise, conceive of Christ having girls, pretty or not, clothed or not, dancing in the synagogue to interpret the song of Moses or the Psalms of David?"[66]

With respect to amusements, the critique of worldliness can be stated in terms which do not condemn, out of hand, specific activities, but state some principles by which the Christian might judge whether, in the given instance, his participation is allowable. When the issue is put into this context, the shift from the sectarian to the denominational view of worldliness is evident. Most recently, the matter was stated in this way by the minister of an urban congregation. He pointed out that today's amusements are subject to criticism by the Christian because they are largely spectator rather than participator activities, they are largely commercialized, they are dominated by sensuality and sex, they display too much of a tendency toward violence and sadism, and they are shallow and superficial.[67] One or more of the "worldly amusements" may be ruled out by the use of these criteria as guides, but the issue is not prejudged. None of the criteria, for instance, except possibly the first one, would have forbidden "that dance in the church."

The question of education has continued to come in for its share of attention. For Restorationists, there is a real doubt about whether education is simply another indication of growing worldliness. Are the church colleges engaged in a process of "garnishing the tombs of the prophets who made them," and "rejecting the essential spirit and teaching for which they gave their all"? As for the ministers trained in these schools, "better no ministry at all . . . than a ministry . . . steeped in worldliness and disposed to compromise with it."[68] The church college may even be an enterprise "projected to distract the attention of the brethren from the great work of leading the lost sheep of Israel back to the Great Shepherd."[69] We must, say the Restorationists, get back to fundamentals, taking the Bible at face value, and remembering that Jesus left the teachings in the care of uneducated people. The educated ones are only trying to make the interpretation difficult.[70]

Our friend Thistle flays those educated ministers who are putting on airs. "We are," he said, "about to be 'doctored' to death." What he thought about this is made clear. "I don't care if they're earned, unearned, given, stolen, purchased or assumed—all 'doctoring' among Christians seems questionable to me. . . . Let our preachers learn all they can . . . but leave the 'doctoring' to the physicians."[71] Many of the brethren were made nervous by a tendency for ministers to use their education to set themselves apart in a special category. "Such an 'aristocracy' might be excusable," said one letter to the editor, "if founded upon superior spirituality, greater learning, more 'talents,' or hard work. But seldom is this the case."[72] You may have a whole briefcase full of diplomas, and a closet full of academic hoods. We still cannot be sure that you are God's man.

The sectarian critique of the ministry reaches its heights with the *coup de grace* administered by Thistle. One is here reminded of Alexander Campbell's "Third Epistle of Peter." Thistle related the fictional applications of a certain preacher for vacant pulpits:

> Understanding that your pulpit is vacant I'd like to apply for the position. I have many qualifications I think you'd appreciate. I can preach with power and have had some success as a writer. There are those who insist that I'm a good organizer too, and I've been a leader in most places I've gone. . . . I don't have any accredited degree from any college in this country, though I did do considerable studying in foreign schools. I am unmarried and over fifty years of age. I have never preached in one place for more than three years at a time and in some places I've left town after my work caused riots and disturbances. I'll have to admit I have been in jail three or four times. . . . However, if you feel you can use me I'll do the best I can for you.[73]

Needless to say, no pulpit supply committee extended a call. One did want to know who this ex-jailbird was. The answer was "the Apostle Paul."

The critique of worldliness was also brought to bear upon the signs that socioeconomic distinctions were creeping inside the doors of the sanctuary. In 1919 an article in *World Call* asked the question: "Which Course Is Most Pleasing to Christ?" It compared a church "where the Lord's business is transacted," and where the building is convenient but very plain, so that missions rather than furnishings have first claim on the budget, with churches which center their attention upon outclassing rivals and having the most ostentatious place of worship in the neighborhood.[74] And a year later this same journal was to suggest another question—"Are the Disciples Christians?" Impressed by the increasing numbers, wealth, and influence of our people, *World Call* wanted to know if the same increase could be observed in their Christian character.[75] Yet in the same year it was pointed out that we need not fear putting too much money into our church buildings. For the world judges the church by the symbols it provides.[76] This was followed, in 1922, by a call for a Bureau of Church Architecture.[77]

Awareness of worldly standards of success, and of the status symbols which express them, was made clear by statements of those who were sensitive to such matters. Chauncey R. Piety set forth the theme pointedly in 1931:

> I knew a cultured and aristocratic congregation, and some of its members boasted of its class, saying, "Hand-picked fruit is the best." I am anxious for the church to save the rich and the cultured, but I hold that the present situation is unholy and unhealthy for the church life. The cultured and refined would be better to draw the poor and the neglected to their bosoms. One of them said, "I don't see why we should be running after the miners; they're not going to do anything for us."[78]

Others among the brethren were to return to this theme from time to time.[79]

In 1938 a sociologically perceptive observer of what was happening in Protestant churches in America expressed his views about the "social sources of denominationalism" in a communication to *The Christian-Evangelist*. He was concerned about the social and cultural factors which, even more than religious and theological differences, were contributing to the divided state of Christendom. The more-established Protestant churches are, he said, moving toward unity under the leadership of middle and upper class members. Meanwhile, lower socioeconomic groups are not finding their religious needs met in the programs of the "respectable" churches.[80] The editor himself turned to this theme in 1958 when he discussed class segregation.

The insidious danger in this class segregation is that it has become unconscious and is being generally accepted as the norm in denominational life. The principle is expressed in the trend of the churches to move from the inner city and follow the trek of the middle classes to the suburbs. The result is to leave other religious bodies—also class segregated—to care for the needs of those of more limited means.[81]

Here again, the critique of worldliness can take on a denominational, as contrasted to a sectarian, direction. The concern about the social sources of denominationalism is definitely a facet of the critique of worldliness, but at a level far different from the concern with private vices.

In fact Restorationists, who are most often involved with the critique of worldliness at the sectarian level, seem singularly unconcerned about the influence of socioeconomic success upon the churches, if we may judge by a recent editorial. Asking the question, "What's Wrong With Success?" the editorial comments that

> It has become the fashion in certain circles to belittle success. The local church that has large crowds in its worship services . . . that builds bigger buildings to house its growing congregation, and whose offerings fill its treasury, is somehow suspect, as though such success indicates an emphasis on material things rather than on the spiritual. . . . What is wrong with organizing a congregation as efficiently as possible to do the work of a church of Christ is supposed to do?[82]

The reply to this can only be "nothing," but one may doubt whether the issue has been fully comprehended within the context of efficiency.

The literature contains numerous other items which might well be included in the discussion of the critique of worldliness. Space does not permit the inclusion of further material on this theme. This topic is certainly one of major interest to the latter-day descendants of the Campbells and Stone. The reason for this is undoubtedly that the critique of worldliness lands us right in the middle of the ethical implications of religious faith and belief. One cannot, after all, deal with the sect-to-denomination process without seeing that this is a matter of crucial significance. To the theme of ethical implications we shall return in the concluding chapter.

III

The External Dimension: the Gospel Is Not Social

For Restorationists, the "social gospel" is a creation of "modernists" or "liberals." Jesus' work was with individuals. He did not put forward any social gospel. The early church was concerned with the resurrected Savior, and with converting men to him. Christians may choose to participate in campaigns for social reforms, but the church, as such, should not be a part of this.[83] The church should stick to its proper business—evangelism and edification.[84] When the church enters into the political arena it supports man-made laws, and thus compromises the laws of God. The church cannot afford to engage in such bargains.[85] What is more, the problems which social gospelers seek to solve through social action will be solved eventually if the church is successful in its task—taking care of sin in individual lives.[86]

Social gospel enthusiasts seem to think the church is a Meddlesome Mattie or Polly Pry, which ought to exert pressure upon legislators to pass laws to erase the inequalities in the society. They seem unaware that the early church did not waste its time with efforts to reform society. It had more important things to do.[87] Social gospel preachers are actually planting the seeds of theological and social radicalism. People who contribute money to the United Christian Missionary Society should know that they are supporting an effort to undermine the free enterprise system. The same goes for the World Council of Churches.[88] These people would do better to spend less time trying to change society, and more time doing what Jesus did—changing men.[89]

At least one influential Restorationist thinks that social gospel advocates are trying to rewrite the Scriptures. "Let us see," he says, "how a 'social improvement gospel' fits into the New Testament. John 3:16 would have to be 'revised' to read: 'God so loved the world that he gave man the impulse to make the world a better place in which to live.' In the description of the gospel in 1 Cor. 15:3 we might read, 'Christ died that we might see the value of democracy, the evils of wealth, and the need to reform penal methods.' Romans 1:16 could be rearranged thus: 'I am not ashamed of the gospel of Christ, for it is the power of man to abolish race prejudice, and attain a warless world.' John 14:2 would read, 'In my Father's house there are many low-cost housing developments.' "[90]

Many social gospel advocates are as aware as are its critics that Jesus did not teach a social gospel. They would point out that the criticism misses the point. Jesus indeed was concerned with individuals. But, say the social gospel supporters, Jesus' concern for individuals cannot be implemented in our kind of society unless we attempt to change the structures and institutions which help to make individuals less than Jesus wanted them to be. Jesus was concerned not just with *individuals,* but with *persons.* To make individuals into persons, it is necessary to be concerned with the context within which this process occurs. Jesus was not concerned with this context because he expected God to take care of that matter. In the twentieth century, we cannot expect some eschatological consummation, and therefore *we* must take the initiative. Another difference between the denominational and the sectarian view of the world is suggested here.

IV

The External Dimension: the Denominations

With respect to the two crucial motifs in the history of the Campbell-Stone movement, Disciples have increasingly tended to emphasize *unity,* while Restorationists, as the name implies, have been more concerned with *restoration.* One should not infer that Restorationists have not been, or are not now, concerned about unity. They emphatically do not understand the situation in this way, and it would be a distortion to reject their self-interpretation at this point. Disciples and Restorationists agree as to the centrality of the search for unity in their movement. There is lively disagreement between them as to the importance to be attached to the basis upon which unity is possible. Restorationists, in general, hold that Christian unity is possible only on the basis that the New Testament teachings concerning ordinances and polity, as they understand them, shall be the norm. Many Disciples are at least willing to consider other proposals, and to interpret the New Testament in a broader and more liberal sense.

The "oral tradition" of the movement contains a story which expresses the strong feelings Restorationists have about "our Plea." "John Sweeney and Isaac Errett were conversing about the Restoration movement many years ago, when it was just beginning to get well under way. Bro. Errett said to his companion: 'Bro. Sweeney, there is just one thing I fear about our movement; that is that there will come a day when we shall raise up a generation that does not know what it is that we have started to do!'"[91] "What we have started to do" is to end the disunity of Christendom by ceasing to require anything in the realm of doctrine and polity except what the New Testament teaches. The "plea, the plan, and the purpose" are inseparable. The *plea* is for the unity of Christians, the *plan* is the restoration of the church of the New Testament, and the *purpose* is the evangelization of the world.[92] When the plea and the plan are dissociated nothing but trouble can result. The plea for unity comes to naught if its basis is not insisted upon.[93]

Through the years an increasing number have drifted away from the faith of the fathers, until now we have actually raised up a generation "that does not know what it is that we started to do."[94] Had we continued to hold that all questions of authority were settled when we accepted the Lordship of Christ, all would be well. Then the one faith, hope, baptism, and mission would be crystal clear.[95] If one is true to the principles of the founders, he does not doubt that the New Testament contains the pattern or norm for the church, nor does he question the premise that we must build according to that pattern.[96] To those who ask, "Have we outgrown the Plea?" the answer must be a resounding "No!" Some, to be sure, act as if they had outgrown the plea, but in this they show their preference for human opinions rather than God's ideas.[97] People like to debate about these things, but the facts are that Restorationists "stand for 'the truth,' the *whole* truth and *nothing but* the truth."[98]

The claim of Restorationists, that we now have that generation that does not know what it is that we have started to do, can be substantiated. Many Disciples feel that the nineteenth-century reformation, to meet the needs of the twentieth century, must in some respects change its character. In the present context, this means that some of them wonder whether the Plea has to depend upon the Plan. Even in 1932 Edgar DeWitt Jones suggested that Thomas and Alexander Campbell, Walter Scott, and Barton W. Stone were, after all, human and did make mistakes. He was inclined to think that "perhaps one of these was an attempt to find in the New Testament an exact model, perfect, which if we would be perfect, we should duplicate and reproduce."[99] They were, however, right in their dream of Christian unity.

Disciples have entertained the possibility that we may have been worshiping a slogan, for when we look for the New Testament *church* what we find is New Testament *churches*.[100] The tendency toward "Bible only" Christianity is susceptible to the danger of literalism and proof-textism, which is the mother of dogmatism. This, in turn, is perhaps one of the chief reasons for the dissension and disunity within the movement.[101] Some Disciples even admit that "believer's baptism" and local autonomy are "matters of opinion" just as are many other points of doctrine, ordinance, and structure.[102] Most recently, it was suggested that our Plan for realizing the Plea for Christian unity has already been undergoing a period of agonizing reappraisal, which has yielded a judgment such as the following.

What then do we mean by "Restoration"? If we mean the re-establishing of the church in form and procedure as it was in the days of the New Testament . . . our effort is both futile and trivial. But if by "Restoration" we mean the breathing anew in our time of the spirit and life of that early church—then may restoration be swift and complete![103]

In recent years, a growing number of Disciples have, as a leading Restorationist charges, come to regard the restoration of the New Testament church as "inadequate, irrelevant, and self-righteous."[104] The literature makes this abundantly clear. Such assertions are, in the minds of those who make them, attempts to preserve the contributions of the movement to the religious world. Restoration, in this light, is inadequate because it is too small a piece of territory for advocates of Christian unity to defend; it is irrelevant because, far from being unitive, it is divisive (as A. T. DeGroot pointed out); and it is self-righteous because it lifts our own understanding of things into a place of prominence unbecoming of humble seekers after unity in Christ. For Restorationists, such thoughts are obvious departures from the faith.

After all, Christian unity could be achieved in a generation if professing Christians would stick to the honest study of the Bible, and not keep company with those who are trying to find reasons for looking elsewhere for guidance.[105] Instead, "the liberals" are seeking to take what was "built up by the sacrifice of those who dedicated [it] for the proclamation of Christianity as a revelation with a Savior and imperious King, and . . . prostitute these riches to serve ends that these same pioneers died opposing."[106] If people are not going to support the one thing which is the movement's excuse for being, the Plan, then what is the point?[107] People may indeed display fine Christian characters, but the issue is the proper position to be held by those who are part of the movement.[108] Divisions are brought about by those who introduce questionable procedures and doctrines, and who refuse to suppress departures from the faith.[109]

Previous chapters have demonstrated that sectarians see themselves as engaged in a great warfare. The literature of the past three decades amply illustrates that this feeling of battle has been preserved by Restorationists. Said one stalwart warrior in 1950, "In this dark hour of the Restoration movement, let us raise the battle cry, 'Pass the ammunition and we'll all stay free.' "[110] We must have done with the business of Christians sitting "by the watercourses of Reuben piping to the flocks while their brethren jeopard their lives even unto death."[111] We shall give no quarter to those who compromise with the Gospel, and who claim support for their efforts while surreptitiously undermining the faith.[112] The infidels who are subverting the tradition must be routed, and we shall not continue to have fellowship with apostates and unbelievers.[113]

Restorationists devoutly pray for, and earnestly seek, the unity for which the pioneers in the faith worked. They see no possibility, however, of achieving this unity on any basis other than the restoration of the New Testament church. They are inclined to think that Disciples confuse *unity* with *union,* and that for the sake of union—the coming together of denominations into some kind of federated structure—Disciples are too willing to compromise their beliefs. When Christians achieve unity, say Restorationists, they will not really need union. Unity here means sharing a common understanding of the ordinances, polity, and work of the church. When all come to share the passion for Christ, and for the essentials of his gospel, the only kind of unity that matters will have been achieved. Church union is actually irrelevant and unnecessary. Thus the question, "Why do the independent churches of Christ oppose the World Council of Churches?" can be answered simply and logically. "Churches of Christ, which understand and have remained loyal to the ideal of the Restoration movement, and the World Council of Churches do not have a common goal. The one movement pleads for a restoration of the unity which obtained in the apostolic church. That was unity of fellowship in Christ, as individuals. . . . The leaders in the effort to restore New Testament unity did not advocate 'church union.' "[114]

One understands, then, why comity arrangements—the assignment of territories within a community to given denominations with the understanding that no other group is to move in—are regarded as "cartel systems among religious groups," involving the assumption that one denomination is as good as another.[115] And one knows why efforts toward achieving church union are sometimes viewed as a desire for "union at any price." This is how the statement of a Disciples college president that he would submit to Episcopal ordination, if this was all that was standing between the two groups, was interpreted.[116] Even the sending of an official delegate to the World Council meeting at Lund belongs in this context.[117] For Restorationists—the emerging institutionalized sect within the movement—anything less than the restoration of the New Testament church is a departure from what the movement was born to stand for. For many Disciples—the increasingly self-conscious denomination within the movement—the restoration idea is of no special moment. They do not understand themselves as advocating union at any price, but they think of restoration, if they think of it at all, as irrelevant. They may even entertain the suspicion that it is a form of carrying out the motto, "Let's compromise and do it *my* way."

V

The Denomination, the Institutionalized Sect, and the Unity of the Brotherhood

To those fully aware of the great passion for unity which played so large a part in the origins of the Campbell-Stone movement, the thought that a polarization process has occurred is disturbing. With one large segment of the group gravitating toward an increasingly self-conscious denomination, and another rapidly emerging as an institutionalized sect, the prospects seem dark indeed. Yet we should remember that "the

Disciples were born in a climate of schism, and have never enjoyed a period of complete unity."[118] The contemporary situation is not new. It has been with us ever since the beginning, in one form or another. One still may be uneasy about the fact that, in the present, the "climate of schism" bids fair to produce some extremely rough weather.

This possibility has been faced realistically. Thus, Stephen J. England has recently said: "It is at least possible that our past has generated a chain reaction of division which may continue until the entire group disintegrates. . . .

". . . Our people are almost at the tragic point of admitting that we will unite, within ourselves, those who think alike on secondary matters. . . .

". . . We have been forced, by the twin compulsions of social structure and of human incapacities to bear our witness as one of the separate Christian groups. . . . At the same time we are required . . . to witness for the unity of all Christ's followers. These two requirements pull us in opposite directions."[119] It should be noted, however, that when men are convinced of the truth of what they stand for, or when, from vested interest or institutional inertia, they continue to maintain a position, they are reluctant to admit that it is a question of "secondary matters." For what is *secondary* to one is *primary* to another. The polarization within the Campbell-Stone movement has not occurred with respect to merely peripheral concerns. The different understandings of polity, the functions of the church, and the approach to Christian unity, reflect greatly divergent pictures of the world, and of the way in which the Christian gospel is to be related to that world.

This point of view may appear to militate against the efforts of those who desire, above all else, the "unity of the brotherhood." This is not necessarily the case. The mediator's role is not made more difficult by recognition of the facts. Too often the mediators have seemed to be parties to an illusion—that if problems and disagreements are not mentioned they will eventually just go way. How else does one account for the constant references to the idea of not raising issues which might "divide the brotherhood." This approach is rather like treating a brain tumor with aspirin tablets, or curing a deep-seated neurosis by positive thinking. Some seem concerned that in our efforts toward unity with other denominations we may be guided by the question of what we may have to give up. They have argued that this would result in a union based on the lowest common denominator. What has been insufficiently noted is that the don't-raise-divisive-issues approach to intragroup unity will tend to produce exactly the same result. The unity of the brotherhood is greatly to be desired, but not too much progress toward this goal will be made until, once and for all, the issues which divide us are brought unequivocally and deliberately into the open and looked at for what they are—profound differences about God, man, the church, and the society, and the relations among these.

A brief word must be said concerning our use of the sociological concepts of *denomination* and *institutionalized sect* as interpretive devices. The concepts refer to stages in a social and cultural process—the changing of the sectlike religious group in the direction of the *church* or *ecclesia* type. Our use of these concepts may have created the impression that there are two—and only two—subgroups within the movement, that a given individual or congregation is either Disciple or Restorationist. This is not our intention, and it would be a distortion of reality to present this as a model of the situation. The denomination and the institutionalized sect described here are the static extremes within which a dynamic social process is occurring. Neither individuals nor congregations can be neatly divided between the types suggested. The picture is one in which, on a significant number of issues, members of the group will tend to gravitate toward one type or the other. But there is no *necessary* and *logical* consistency about the process. Between the two clear-cut sociological groupings at the extremes are a considerable number of members who may be pulled first one way and then the other, depending upon the issue under consideration, and the definition of situation which is operative at the time.

Our hypothesis would be that the tendency of given individuals or congregations to gravitate toward the denomination or the institutionalized sect will vary with such factors as rural-urban location of community, socioeconomic class level of congregation, educational level of members, the degree to which members are sufficiently informed about the issues to become concerned about them, the direction in which the minister and elders lean, and the peculiar history of the local church body. Each of these variables needs further testing, but the factors indicated appear to be the relevant ones. We have used these sociological concepts because we believe them to be useful as interpretive tools, and not because there is any intrinsic merit attached to them. There is no intention to treat the concepts as neat pigeonholes into which the facts must be forced.

CHAPTER XI

Disciples of Christ and the Future: in Search of a Strategy for Implementing Social Concerns

When Isaac Errett, in the 1860's, looked back upon the reformation of the nineteenth century, he expressed his feelings of pride in that fine phrase, "At one and another trumpet call of reformation, multitudes came forth from Babylon."[1] And indeed they did, for the movement continued to grow and prosper until today, nearly one hundred years later, it is one of the largest religious bodies in American Protestantism. We pay this great pioneer of the faith no disrespect if we suggest that, at the beginning of the sixth decade of the twentieth century, our problem is not so much to find ways of looking back with pride as it is to find ways of moving ahead with effectiveness.

With this in mind, the most relevant starting point appears to be the hypothesis that the growing awareness of denominational status within the movement will continue to increase. If this hypothesis is correct, the problem of the group is that of becoming mature and responsible *as a denomination*. The implication of the sect-to-denomination process has often been that a group, once it has reached denominational status, inevitably settles down into comfortable respectability, developing a kind of provincialism-with-divine-sanction, and consolidating its institutional success. Yet there is the possibility of another issue from this process. Becoming a denomination *might* mean instead the development of responsible Christian citizenship, both individually and institutionally. Viewed in this light, becoming a denomination would represent a challenge and an opportunity, and not a mere accommodation to the world. In this final chapter, then, we look to the future of an increasingly self-conscious denomination.

The heart of the sect-to-denomination process is the way the religious group relates itself to "the world," how it views the encounter of its goals and values with the surrounding society and culture. In a sense, the key context within which a religious group develops is social and ethical. The sect-to-denomination process occurs as one result of the fact that, in the process of relating itself to society, the religious group finds its values influenced and changed. If it attempts to grow and prosper, it seeks also to convert others to its values, and in this attempt the nature of the group itself changes. For a group which defines itself as Christian, the crucial problem is how does one implement Christian values in a world that is not Christian?

A useful frame of reference for approaching the way Disciples of Christ have gone about answering this question is that provided by Albert T. Rasmussen. He has suggested that there are three major ways in which the Christian may relate himself to the world: through hidden influence, through love and concern in personal relations, and through co-operative social action. Those who relate themselves to the world by means of the hidden influence tend to regard their faith as a private dialogue between the individual and his God. There is no real necessity that what goes on in this divine-human encounter be articulated in any action in the world. This is to relate to the world by withdrawing from it. At most it is to identify the Christian ethical life with inner attitudes, kindly intentions, and good feelings.

In the second way of relating to the world—through the practice of love and concern in personal relations—the emphasis is upon the belief that, if Christians as individuals witness to their faith by acting through love, this will eventually usher in the kingdom of God. The third way of relating to the world—through co-operative social action—is clearly based upon the realization that acting through love in personal relations will be inadequate for expressing a Christian influence. Of this Rasmussen well says, "If Christianity is going to exert genuine influence and guidance in a world of dynamic social movements and of mass communications, it must enter the struggle for men's hearts and minds. . . . (W)e must also develop channels of influence into our communities and out into the broad context of social life in which our moral climate and our behavioral patterns are formed."[2]

The editor of *The Christian-Evangelist* set forth a quite similar view of the ways of exerting Christian influence in the world in a recent editorial. "From the very beginning of Protestantism," he said, "there have been two characteristic attitudes which Chistians have taken toward society. There is the individual, 'pietistic' emphasis which urges Christians to hold themselves aloof from the world, having nothing to do with politics. . . . But far more dominant in Protestantism has been the conviction that, while individuals must be saved . . . there is an equal Christian obligation to help redeem the social order."[3] There may be reason to doubt the judgment as to which of these attitudes has been dominant in Protestantism, but the interpretive device is a useful one.

Where do Disciples of Christ fit in this pattern of ways of relating to the world? Certainly the first type—the hidden influence—is not characteristic of this religious group. For whatever else they have been, this people of God has never intentionally been escapist or egocentric. The second way of relating to the world—through love and concern in personal relations—comes very close to an expression of the stance of Disciples toward the society in which their history has been pursued. Their emphasis has been upon the inculcation of Christian values and perspectives to individuals who, because they are Christians, will so act as to bring about the desired social results.

This attitude is clearly expressed in the thought that "if we are careful to win the individual, give him the vision, correct his conscience and give him the pace in walking with God, we need not bother about society at large, idealism, or civilization. . . . The hope of national and social redemption rests upon individual redemption."[4] And it comes out even more forcefully in the statement that "while in legislatures and congressional halls men are wrangling and fuming about this, that, and the other, . . . the Christian thinks and acts with no one to drive or coerce him. He is *free* and works with a glad spirit to build up the Kingdom of God."[5] Actually, implementing our Christian values in the world is not so difficult. We can do it easily, if we just tell people how nice it would be.

> Clear, firm, faithful, warm-hearted preaching . . . kindled and accompanied by the Holy Spirit would correct the vagrant, doubtful, hesitant mood of the hour and bring people into a good understanding of Jesus Christ . . . and cure the ills of society, in a half-dozen years. If we had the courage to let methods and machinery go for awhile, and *preach,* we could soon bring the age of might and power to the churches.[6]

With this context in mind, we can see the significance of the point which Harold Lunger makes concerning *The Political Ethics of Alexander Campbell.* "For Campbell there was no basis or motivation for . . . Christian social action. . . . 'The Church cannot constitutionally undertake to reform the state. It may seek to convert the citizens; but can never assume, by any political expedients, to reform the State.' It apparently has no responsibility for giving its members guidance on matters of practical Christian citizenship or leading them . . . to a better understanding of the issues."[7] What was true for Alexander Campbell has also been true, in large part, for his religious descendants. This situation is not, as Chapter IX has indicated, a result of the fact that Disciples have not developed, over the years, a well-articulated social consciousness. Clearly, the constant reiteration of the theme that Jesus' ethic is the answer to all our social and political ills shows a genuine social concern. Disciples have a social stance consonant with their growing awareness of denominational status, but they have not made great progress in designing ways to implement their gospel in the society. They have too often believed that the relevant method is the expression of love in personal relations, or the expression of moral suasion through the passing of resolutions. There are three main facets of this situation, which indicate that Disciples might profit from seeing themselves as "in search of a strategy for implementing social concerns."

I

The Nonpolitical View of Politics: Individual Moral Virtue Solves the Problems*

Those who believe that the expression of love in personal relations is an adequate way of exerting Christian influence indulge in the luxury of believing that moral values can be implemented effectively apart from the political and social context. An important premise of this view is that the most important thing for the Christian is that he be "righteous" and "virtuous," which means that he adhere to certain private virtues or pursue a few single "moral issues" apart from the complex social matrix in which they occur.

A good illustration of this is that many Christians, when they express opinions concerning politics, talk as though the only issue is the personal morality of the candidates. In at least one important state election, I have heard quite a few

*In this and the following two sections, I am indebted to a group of social ethics students now or formerly at Yale Divinity School, including William Lee Miller, Kenneth Underwood, Robert Lynn, Edwin Becker, Ernest Lefever, and William Muehl. My discussion is certainly indebted to their work, as illustrated by the issue of *Social Action* entitled "The Christian Faith and American Politics," XVIII (November, 1951).

Christians say that they were going to vote for a certain candidate because "everyone knows that he is a 'family man' and a 'good Christian.'" When asked what this means, they say that he attends church regularly and teaches a church school class. One may doubt whether the possession of such admirable private virtues is evidence of qualification for office. A more basic consideration would be whether he understands the complex social and economic situations of our time, and has command of the necessary political skills to implement his program.

According to some Disciples, one does not need any technical skills or profound knowledge of the situations into which he wants to project Christian values. For "our God is concerned with our fundamental attitudes. If they be right and honest, he can leave the rest to us. He is concerned not about what decisions we finally make but that we be actuated in all things by the spirit of love and truth and justice."[8] Even in dealing with international relations, we need nothing but the spirit of Christ in our hearts. "We do not propose to enter into the political side of the question," said a group of missionary leaders, "but will confine our efforts to a peace propaganda based on the teaching and spirit of Jesus. We will study the New Testament and accept its teachings concerning peace."[9] When the Christian goes into the voting booth, his criterion for pulling down the levers is "the will of God," which he can easily discover by reading the Bible and learning what Christ said. Thus the Christian voter will conclude that "everyone of us can find some good man on whom there is no smell or taint of liquor for whom to cast our ballot."[10]

The price paid for this nonpolitical view of politics is that the morally pure play into the hands of those who do have a policy and who are not so concerned about their virtue. William Lee Miller has well expressed this when he says, "The nonpolitical Protestants can be so manipulated because . . . they choose candidates by narrow and predictable and nonpolicy criteria: personality, religion, abstemiousness, 'morals,' or attitude on rigidly doctrinaire . . . issues."[11] Dependence upon the cultivation of individual moral virtues actually betrays the very values it is designed to uphold, since it does not reckon with the fact that the effective decisions about which values shall be implemented in the society are made in the sphere of *politics* and not *morals*.

When one considers the history of the American frontier, which was so important in establishing the stance of Disciples toward the society, it is not surprising to find this dependence upon individual moral virtues and implicit rejection of politics. This frontier individualism was quite congenial to the agrarian society of the early nineteenth century. Yet, as Kenneth Boulding has made so clear, we live in a postorganizational revolution society, characterized by mass movements—big labor, big business, big agriculture, and big government. The moralistic, nonpolitical view of politics reflects the sectarian beginnings of Disciples of Christ. The continuance of this approach in the midtwentieth century, however, is a survival of sectarian traits in the period of denominational status.

Disciples need to modify their naïve moralism in the direction of political realism. There is some ferment with respect to such matters. This is indicated by the spirited exchange that took place in two articles in *The Christian-Evangelist* for 1958. These dealt with the resolutions on social issues which are passed at the International Convention. Ralph B. Shank, in criticizing the practice, emphasized that the social action concern departs from the main purpose of the church in relation to society—to make better men—that it reduces the church to a political-pressure group, that it may be a violation of the principles of church-state separation, and that it carries the seeds of division.[12] Virgil E. Lowder, in approving the practice, asked the question, "Is it not naïve to believe that individual Christians, without any organization or structure, without coordinated effort, without a united witness, and without channels of cooperation, can make a sufficient impact upon crucial social problems in a world like ours to alleviate or solve those problems?"[13]

World Call, in 1950, published an article in which the statement of Thomas Keehn, legislative representative of the Congregational-Christian Churches, to the effect that "Protestant churches could set forth Christian principles more effectively if they would put registered lobbyists in Washington," was quoted.[14] Reference was also made to the reputation which Protestants have for being "antivoters"—that is, they are known for being against liquor, gambling, and war, but it is difficult to tell what they are for, except possibly for virtue. There are some indications, then, that the nonpolitical view of politics is being recognized as inadequate. Yet, by and large, it is still prevalent among Disciples.

II

The Lone-Ranger Theory of History

For some months in the later 1950's, the television screen and the radio were filled with a steady diet of "Westerns" and detective stories. Commentators noted this trend and responded to it with varying degrees of enthusiasm. The most perceptive of these commentators remarked on the fact that these programs seemed significantly related to the mood of the American people. The hypothesis was that these stories answered to an important need of contemporary individuals—the need to find some way to reduce the complexities of the mass society to manageable proportions. The detective story and the western simplify good and evil by personifying it. The forces for good are, in these highly stylized and ritualized dramas, pure and unambiguous. They are pitted against the forces of evil, which symbolize whatever has gone wrong in the community. This is, then, a modern morality play.

In the real world, the ethical issues are complex and ambiguous. One often chooses, not between good and evil, but between two alternatives, each of which contains a mixture of good and evil. Nikolai Berdyaev has expressed this point in terms of "the tragic and paradoxical character of the moral life." "The tragedy," he writes, "lies not in the conflict between good and evil, the divine and the diabolical, but in the conflict between different kinds of good and value—between the love of God and the love of man, the love of one's country and of one's nearest and dearest, the love of science or art and the love and pity for men, and so on."[15]

The Christian who takes a nonpolitical, moralistic view of society and ethical problems sees social questions as a struggle between "the good" and "the bad." The good is seen in individuals who, because of their private moral virtues, act as the moral pillars and defenders of righteousness. The bad is seen in individuals who, because of their private vices, uphold unrighteousness and undermine virtue. This view of the moral life as simply the struggle between the good *individuals* and the bad *individuals* may be characterized as The Lone-Ranger Theory of History. The Lone Ranger, a fictional radio and television character, solves quite complex problems, and defeats vast quantities of evil, with the help of his Indian companion. He is, therefore, a convenient symbol for a highly individualistic theory of history. All we need to solve complicated problems is the appropriate Lone Ranger.

Our tendency to accept some version of this view of history is an illustration of commitment to the expression of love and concern in personal relations as the way of exerting Christian influence. No one can gainsay the fact that the influence of one person upon another in a face-to-face encounter is a most important one. Yet it is also a fact that this personal influence is only partial. It does not touch the heart of many of the issues where the Christian influence apparently does not reach. Not only are we constantly dealing with people who are not personally known to us, but we often make decisions which affect the lives of other persons who could not possibly be in a personal relationship with us. Our ability to express love and concern for the neighbor depends more upon our knowledge of the intricate structures of economic, social, and political life than it does upon our personal moral virtues.

III

The Three-Monkeys View of Life: Compromise Is Evil

The nonpolitical view of politics and the Lone-Ranger theory of history seem to require a kind of abstract moral purity. This emphasis leads to the belief that compromise in politics is corrupt, or even that politics as such is evil. At this point, the morally pure Christian asks not the relevant question—what can be accomplished in the real world?—but the irrelevant question—is my position pure and right? Like the three monkeys, he hears no evil, sees no evil, and speaks no evil. The Three-Monkeys View of Life, since it is convinced that the sphere of the ethical life is the virtuous conscience of the individual, finds it distasteful to admit that Christian values might ultimately be served by the compromise of opposed interests and demands. Yet it is through politics—and only through politics—that society is organized and governed.

The policies that are actually operative in any community are the result of the give-and-take, the compromise, of the contradictory interests and values of the groups which manage to get themselves heard. In the light of this, the position taken by one Disciples minister, speaking the minds of many others, appears strangely out of contact with reality. "Did Jesus ever qualify his position?" he asked. "Did he ever make any exceptions? Did he say 'my method will work except in a crisis?' He set a straight course. . . . *Living* out true Christianity has *more power* than all the armies in the world trying to safeguard the principles and teachings of Christ."[16] The question is no longer "What would Jesus do?" but "How, in view of present realities, can the values which Jesus advocated best be implemented?" "No compromise" is an impossible rule, for clearly "politics is the art of the possible."

The struggle over the values and principles which will be implemented in the life of the community goes on. The bargaining, the pressures, and the inducements which become a part of the process of compromise are uninformed by the values which the nonpolitical Christian represents, since he insists that his cause must not be sullied by contact with impurity. Yet only values which are implemented by power can be actualized. If we do not reckon with this fact, we succeed only in allowing others to fill the power vacuum created by our refusal to participate in the processes of the real world. The nonpolitical Christian, in his zeal to drive out the visible demon, does not reckon with the seven other demons which may come in its place as a result of his failure to understand the complex interconnections of events in society. Disciples tend to fit all too well into this pattern. If they are really serious about exerting a Christian influence in the society, they will need a great deal more than a campaign to build several hundred new churches in which individuals will be taught the nonpolitical view of politics, the Lone-Ranger theory of history, and the Three-Monkeys View of Life.

IV

The Communication of the Gospel: Is Anybody Listening?

A few years ago, William H. Whyte, in a book by that title, asked the question, "Is Anybody Listening?" His context was not the communication of the gospel of the Christian religion, but the gospel of American business. Whyte pointed out that even with the greatest sales apparatus ever known, business was perplexed as to why its message was not getting across. So businessmen were asking, quite understandably, "Is anybody listening?" This question might well be asked about the attempts being made by various religious groups to communicate the Christian gospel.

One of the main enterprises of Protestant groups is certainly the communication of a gospel. It could even be said that this is the main function of these groups. So what any denomination accomplishes in this area is a crucial matter. Yet we find that most Protestant groups—including Disciples—are depending upon the communications tools of the premass communications society. Kenneth W. Underwood, a student of communications from the point of view of implications for religion, has summarized the weaknesses of Protestantism in the communications field.[17]

First, the church press has become largely ingrown. Like the sermon on temperance Sunday, it reaches only the people who are already in the fold. Too often the issues discussed have relevance only to matters with which a small minority of the members of the group is concerned. The church press, when it does discuss the great issues of our time tends to deal with these issues in terms of how they affect the maintenance of the religious group and its immediate concerns. The endless series of articles in Disciples publications on immersion and the Lord's Supper, and the discussions of the social issues of the day in terms which largely reflect the intellectual confusions indicated above are illustrations of this.

Second, the churches have developed very little in the way of materials which would help people to evaluate and understand the popular media from the standpoint of Christian ethics. For the most part, efforts in this direction have been confined to moralistic criticisms of the mass media for sensationalism or the presentation of "immoral" material. Disciples need to develop some writers who can communicate not more tirades about the effect of given amounts of female nudity, but a profound understanding of the way in which the media afford insights into the society and culture they express. More important than the "sexiness" of Jane Russell is the fact that her banal statement that "God, when you get to know Him, is a livin' doll" is interpreted as a reason for being concerned about religion.

Third, Protestant groups give little indication that they understand the variety of social groups and audiences in American society. The messages sent out in the attempt to communicate the gospel seem uniformly innocent of the findings of recent studies of audiences. A recent study of the communications process concluded that "Mass communication takes place in a social matrix which is a dynamic composite of religion, national origin, culture and social class. Every given member of the radio and television andience occupies a position in this matrix and in addition is often in the process of changing his position. This position will strongly influence his attitude toward the content of a message on radio or television."[18] What is needed for effective communication is a policy which reflects a cogent and adequate theory of the audience to be reached, which in turn depends upon a meaningful theory of society, culture, and personality. Major attention must be given to identifying the groups to which any message is to be communicated.

Fourth, there is little recognition among Protestants of the basic principles of communication. In some respects our understanding of communicating the gospel seems to be based upon the injunction, "he that hath ears let him hear." William H. Whyte, in referring to the failure of business to communicate its "gospel" to America, quotes sympathetically the following passage from Dostoievsky. "If the people around you are spiteful and callous and will not hear you, fall down before them and beg their forgiveness; for in truth you are to blame for their not wanting to hear you." Our confidence that we have the kind of truth that is the salvation of man should not betray us into the false position of unwillingness to master the disciplines and techniques by which this truth can be communicated.

The encounter with the mass media is apparently something more than merely learning to write bright, smart advertising copy. It is certainly more than wearing a blue shirt and remembering to smile at the television camera lens. Yet in the study of the communication of religious messages on radio and television mentioned above, the researchers found little concern over the really profound impact of the mass media upon the situation in which the clergymen function. We are living in an age when a virtual revolution has occurred in the communication process and we seem to regard it as of no more importance than the latest change in fashion.

The central task is that of moving from a peripheral understanding of the communications process as a set of gadgets enabling us to do more efficiently the same old thing, to a crucial understanding that effective communication in this age may require an almost total revamping of strategy. What Wilbur Schramm has recently argued concerning the general situation in mass communications applies with peculiar force to a religious group endeavoring to find a stance relevant to society. Wrote Schramm, "The present is a time of important change in mass communication; . . . a time of change is a time for redefining standards and responsibilities; and . . . these new standards and responsibilities . . . are defining a new philosophy of public communication for the United States."[19] If the next few decades find Disciples unprepared to participate meaningfully in this time of redefinition, and if they do not develop adequate strategies and tactics for communicating, they will find themselves sorely out of touch with the ongoing pace of life.

V

Where Do We Go From Here?
Some Suggested Directions

In the concluding section of *The Political Ethics of Alexander Campbell,* Harold Lunger writes,

> The Christian today can well begin where Campbell began, but ought not to stop where he stopped. . . . Campbell actually *discouraged* Christians from discussing social and political questions *as Christians,* and opposed their joining with others outside the church for any form of Christian political action. . . . The result of this policy was to leave it to the individual Christian to resolve the conflict between his duty as a Christian and his duty as a citizen as best he could . . . , and to leave the public issues themselves to be settled largely on the basis of economic, social, and political interests, with no effective means of bringing religious and moral influences to bear upon them.[20]

Finding a way to bring religious and moral influences to bear upon the public issues of our time is the key to achieving maturity and responsibility as a denomination.

The following suggestions are advanced as a tentative statement of some objectives which, if attained, would help to guard Disciples against denominational stagnation. *First,* considerable thought should be given to the emphases stressed in the training of ministers. The need of our times is a ministry consisting of men thoroughly competent not only in the traditional disciplines of biblical studies, theology, and church history, but also in the understanding of what psychology and the social sciences have learned about personality, society, and culture. To have a call to the ministry, and to have a mastery of the Bible, are simply not enough to enable the minister to do the kind of job he must do. The communication of the gospel involves a genuine dialogue with "the world," and it is true as never before that the minister cannot hold up his end of this conversation without a thorough understanding of his culture.

The implication is certainly not that there is less need for training in biblical studies, theology, and church history. The point is that we can no longer pretend that these studies alone really prepare a man for the ministry. Nothing at all short of the best knowledge available in the understanding of human behavior, and of the societal and cultural contexts in which the ministers' role is to be carried out, should be considered good enough for the training of Disciples ministers in the years ahead. Some very encouraging things are being done along these lines, but much more remains to be done so that these essential understandings are not merely peripheral to the main concerns of theological education.

Second, in view of the cruciality of the communications situation, Disciples need a group of men who are thoroughly at home, not only in the techniques of mass communications, but also in the understanding of the communications process in its fullest dimensions. This could well mean not men trained in theological seminaries but men well grounded in work at the graduate level in such fields as journalism, radio and television, and creative writing. One of the difficulties at this point has been that persons who have interest in various fields of communications have not been sufficiently oriented religiously to make their training and talents available. Or, to turn the issue around, persons with competence in the field of religion have not been in possession of adequate training to transfer this competence into the communications area.

Ideally, what is needed is a group of men sufficiently endowed intellectually and motivationally to be willing to undergo the discipline of seminary training plus the doctoral degree or its equivalent of experience in various fields of communication. There is a real opportunity for the theological seminaries to pioneer in this enterprise, not only by affording students at least a minimal experience with the communications fields, but by working out programs in connection with nearby universities and colleges in which students with talents in these directions might develop both theological and communications competence. At the moment, not too much is being done here.

Third, since they live in a multigroup society, Disciples need to establish linkages in as many ways as possible with all the significant groups in the society, and not simply with those represented in the membership. One possible clue to the too-ready acceptance of the nonpolitical view of politics among Disciples is that they do not understand the pressure and interest groups in the society. Knowledge of what the labor movement represents, for instance, is often derived from what a friend of a friend said about something the plumber who came to fix the leaky faucet told him. Disciples have not developed any real and effective communication with the great foci of power in American society—labor, agriculture, business, and government.

Seeking meaningful contact with, and understanding of, the various power groups in the society does not imply an acceptance of the point of view of any of them. What is involved is the recognition that Disciples will not be in any position to exert a Christian influence in the world if they are not in close touch with the sectors of the society where the crucial decisions are being made. In this regard, most of the efforts are piecemeal, and they too often amount to the naïve effort to harass government officials with threats of what

Protestant voters will do if the administration persists in sending an ambassador to the Vatican.

The irrelevance of some Disciples efforts is pointedly emphasized by James West, in his comments about the churches in Plainville. Said West,

> Not even in the Christian Church, which stands proudly aloof from the emotionalism distinguishing the others, are discussed any of the important problems of agriculture, ethics, and human relationships that actually face the community. The real resident "reformers" (for example, the county agent and the vocational agriculture teacher) all go to church as a way of keeping "in" with the community, to lessen criticism of their work, but not one of them would dream of attempting to make of any church, or of any preacher, an instrument or ally to help further their work.[21]

What West implies about the irrelevance of the rural church to the real problems of people might also be said in varying degrees about dealings with the other significant groups in the society. Dependence upon an ethic of love and concern in personal relations has perhaps rendered Disciples insensitive to the need to enter into relationships with the groups which struggle in an arena of conflict and compromise. When they have expressed concern it has tended to be of the sentimental variety, not related significantly to the concrete issues concerning which decisions are being made. At the other extreme has been the tendency to render inadequate judgments with respect to various groups involved in the struggle so that one or the other group emerges as the villian or scapegoat. Establishing real lines of communication with the significant interest groups would help to overcome the tendency toward either sentimentalism or moralistic judgmentalism.

Fourth, Disciples need to institutionalize their dealings with the relations between the gospel and the world. This can best be done at this stage by introducing the concern for social action into the organizational structure of the local church. This would mean that each church, along with its committees for evangelism, finance, building and grounds, pulpit supply, and missions, would have as a part of its regular structure a group whose major concern is the study of ways to relate the gospel to the community. Without the implementation of the social action concern into the formal structure of the church there is every indication that a disembodied gospel is being preached.

In the organization of the church, as also in its patterns of benevolence, there are crucial clues to what is considered important by the members of the congregation. Not to include the social action dimension in the structuring of the work of a congregation in the community means ultimately that the other important tasks of the organization suffer, since they tend to be placed in the context of maintaining the institution for its own sake, rather than in the context of total outreach of the gospel on behalf of which the congregation speaks. Roger Shinn, speaking of the interrelations among evangelism, stewardship, and social action, has well said,

> To see any one of these activities apart from the others . . . is to corrupt the very purpose we aim to emphasize . . . Evangelism comes to mean adding names to the rolls. . . . Stewardship generally gets connected with the budget. In evangelism most congregations are rejecting the commission to preach the gospel to every creature in favor of preaching it to some types of creatures. In stewardship . . . the faith that God has entrusted to us His world . . . becomes the pretentious declaration that we will use to suit our prejudices even that portion of the world specifically dedicated to God. . . . It is false to say that the congregation(s) . . . are doing a good job of evangelism . . . and stewardship . . . but are falling down on social action. Everything the church does is of evangelizing significance.[22]

And to this one might add that everything the church does not do which would help it to make its life and work relevant to the actual concerns of men in all sectors of the society is of evangelizing significance, in the negative sense.

The plea for establishing social action as a part of the regular structure of the local congregation needs to be stated carefully. All too often the impression is created that social action means espousing certain pre-established views on such issues as race relations, foreign affairs, and labor-management relations. The social action emphasis does not stem from the prior acceptance of any set of doctrinaire conclusions about particular issues. Its only prior commitment is to the fullest possible understanding of the relation between Christian ethics and the concrete problems of men in the present society, and to the devising of ways in which Christian influence might be exerted in connection with these problems. Full recognition is afforded the possibility that committed Christians may disagree in the realm of strategy and tactics, and to the certainty that *the* Christian position on any issue is not to be identified absolutely with any opinion arrived at by finite men.

There are certain objections to the institutionalization of the social action concern, and these must be frankly faced. One of these is that the consideration in the church of the crucial and controversial issues in society will be disruptive of fellowship. There is this possibility, but one might ask this question—what kind of Christian fellowship is it that is bought at the price of suppressing and ignoring the real interests and prejudices that divide men? Is it not a fact that the really important issues of life—including those in which religious people are involved—are all controversial, and if we must refrain from discussing them, we are reduced to talking about inanities like the weather? The fellowship which rests upon the tacit agreement never to mention the things which divide men is actually an insipid and lifeless sham. The Christian fellowship which cannot cope with the world of contentions and pressures, transcending it but certainly not ignoring it, is a glass house at which people will understandably throw rocks. It is after all in the give-and-take of a real confrontation of basic issues that the pride and inordinate self-concern of men are checked and counterchecked, and it is only in this way that the essential understanding which is the basis of true fellowship can be produced. The minister and others who make social action their special area of concern must handle the situation with tact, to be sure, but the fear of contention and disruption of fellowship should not be a ground on which the social action emphasis is rejected.

Another objection to implementing the social action emphasis in the structure of the congregation is actually a restatement of the first two positions concerning the exerting of Christian influence in the world. This objection takes two forms. In one form, it says that social action is not the business of the church; the business of the church, and especially of the minister, is to witness to and preach the gospel. This is to depend upon the "hidden influence" for the expression of a Christian impact upon the world. In its other form, this objection says that social action is unnecessary, for if we preach the gospel to individuals they will be saved and go out into the world and "do right." To the first form of this objection the answer has to be that God works his "hidden influence" in the world through committed men who will, not only the goals and purposes of the Christian ethic, but also the relevant means and techniques. To the second form of this objection, the answer is really to restate much of what has been said. The expression of love in personal relations is admirable—it is even essential—but, given the situation in the world, explicit attention must be paid to the various contexts and structures in terms of which individuals live. So an essential part of the witness to, and preaching of, the gospel is the concern for social action. Committed Christians may certainly disagree about what specifically follows from this, but it is difficult to see how they can be Christians and reject the proposition that an effective witness to the gospel requires social action.

Herman Reissig has suggested that the social action committee of the local congregation should consist of individuals who exhibit the following characteristics:[23] they should be active members of the congregation; they should be persons convinced that Christians need to make a serious effort to relate their faith to the social issues of the time, and that the church, *as church,* has the responsibility to assist its members in this task; and they should be imaginative and resourceful persons, who are not using the committee to push the panaceas in which they are personally interested. Ideally the social action committee should represent as many interests and orientations as happen to be present in the congregation. Just as there may be individuals in any congregation who have talents, skills, and knowledge which may be useful in other areas of the church's concern, such as finance and evangelism, so there may be those who have special gifts for articulating the Christian concern for social action. Such persons should be sought out and encouraged in their efforts to give expression to this part of the life of the church.

There have been indications that Disciples are beginning to see the importance of implementing their social concern by making it a part of the structure of the church. One minister explicitly recognized this need when he pointed out that, in addition to worship, education, pastoral service, evangelism, and missionary outreach, an important function of the local church is that of constructive social criticism. "The local church must," he said, "provide enlightened leadership, popularize and direct organizations which will labor for such things as equal opportunities for the minority groups, law enforcement, liquor control, just international relations, and good citizenship."[24] The implication was that this function of constructive social criticism was to be carried out by giving it a place in the organizational arrangements of the church.

Christian social action, Ruth E. Milner pointed out in 1952, must concern itself with the task of changing the social order so that severe maladjustments and acute needs in the lives of individuals will not occur. This means that a community-conscious church will provide a place in its program for consideration of social issues. The possibility that this may introduce controversy is frankly recognized.[25] Local congregations should, an editorial in *World Call* insists, attempt to put into practice the pronouncements set forth in our conventions.[26] The Christian action committee is said to be responsible for guiding the local church in the task of relating its faith to all the problems of the community.[27] The churches must plan for definite programs of action.[28] All of these statements represent ideas presented in Disciples literature since 1946. They illustrate the growing realization of the necessity of social action, if the goals and purposes outlined in the Christian gospel are to make a difference in the world.

VI

Conclusion

How shall Disciples approach their place in the religious world at this stage in their history? They have arrived at a time when it will be even less necessary, and certainly less relevant, to place so much emphasis upon "our distinctive witness." Disciples need to worry less about the logic of their position, and more about finding practical ways to draw closer together with those who, by reason of common social and cultural needs, are congenial. Disciples have a secure place in the religious world, and their distinctive contribution has now become a part of the heritage of all Protestant Christendom. They can justify this secure position by becoming the most mature and responsible among the denominations. This will require a mood, not of self-conscious defensiveness lest their voices not be heard in the arena of claims and counterclaims, but of expansiveness and eagerness to bear a witness to Christian values in the world which shall point to the kingdom beyond all divisions.

Those who first responded to the nineteenth-century trumpet call of reformation left their religious descendants an exciting and challenging heritage. The dream of a united Christendom, and of a kingdom of love and righteousness and peace, is still before them. Their motto might well be stated in the words of one of their founders. "We are a weak band, an humble beginning; but so much the better," wrote Alexander Campbell. "Such were they of Galilee—such were they of Saxony—and such were the founders of this great nation. With the spirit of God in our hearts, with heaven in our eyes, and the Bible in our hand, our God assisting us, 'we shall leap over a wall,' and 'put to flight the armies of the aliens.' . . . If the time be come he will establish the work of our hands; if it be not we shall not lose our reward for having attempted it."[29] To your tents, O Israel! The trumpet call of reformation is sounding!

NOTES

Introduction

1. J. Wach, *Sociology of Religion,* p. 197. Copyright 1944 by the University of Chicago. Used by permission.
2. K. Davis, in introduction to W. J. Goode, *Religion Among the Primitives,* (Glencoe, Illinois: The Free Press, 1951), 11. Used by permission.
3. *A Study of Rural Society,* (New York: Houghton Mifflin Co., 1952), 375. Used by permission.
4. See, for example, the pamphlet published by the World Council of Churches and titled significantly "Social and Cultural Factors in Church Divisions" (1952).

Chapter I

1. From "Denominational Maps," by Simeon Stylites, copyright 1948 by the *Christian Century.* Used by permission.
2. H. R. Niebuhr, *The Social Sources of Denominationalism,* (New York: Henry Holt Co., 1929), p. vii. By permission of the publishers.
3. *Ibid.,* p. 27.
4. J. M. Yinger, *Religion in the Struggle for Power,* (Durham, North Carolina: Duke University Press, 1946), pp. 18-19. Used by permission.
5. *Ibid.,* p. 31.
6. H. R. Niebuhr, "Sects," in *Encyclopedia of the Social Sciences,* (New York: The Macmillan Company, XIII), 624.

7. R. Park & E. Burgess, *Introduction to the Science of Sociology,* (Chicago: University of Chicago Press), p. 872. Copyright 1921 by the University of Chicago and used by permission.
8. *Ibid.,* p. 873.
9. *Ibid.,* p. 204.
10. *Ibid.,* p. 871.
11. E. T. Clark, *The Small Sects in America,* (Nashville. Abingdon Press, 1949), pp. 16-17. Used by permission.
12. As quoted in Yinger, *op. cit.,* pp. 117-18.
13. H. Richard Niebuhr also emphasizes this as an important factor. Cf. *Social Sources of Denominationalism.*
14. It is this group of "legalistic" sects into which Disciples of Christ most nearly falls.
15. Clark, *op. cit.,* pp. 22-24.
16. *Ibid.,* pp. 20-21.
17. H. Becker and Leopold Von Weise, *Systematic Sociology,* (New York: John Wiley and Sons, Inc., 1932), pp. 624-28.
18. L. Pope, *Millhands and Preachers,* (New Haven: Yale University Press, 1942), p. 118. Used by permission.
19. *Ibid.,* p. 121.
20. *Ibid.,* p. 121-22.
21. Reprinted by permission from James West: *Plainville, U.S.A.,* Columbia University Press, 1945, p. 146.
22. Pope, *op. cit.,* pp. 122-24.
23. J. M. Yinger, *Religion, Society, and the Individual,* (New York: The Macmillan Company, 1957), pp. 150-52. Used by permission.
24. Cf. his paper "The Sociology of Secularization: Religious Groups," *American Journal of Sociology,* LXI, (1955-56), pp. 121-28.
25. J. Wach, *Types of Religious Experience,* (Chicago: University of Chicago Press, 1951), pp. 187-208.

Chapter II

1. W. E. Garrison, *Religion Follows the Frontier,* (New York: Harper & Brothers, 1931), p. xi. Used by permission.
2. F. J. Turner, *The Frontier in American History,* p. 2. Copyright 1920 by Frederick Turner; Copyright 1948 by Caroline Mae S. Turner. By permission of the publishers.
3. *Ibid.,* p. 207.
4. J. Leyburn, *Frontier Folkways,* (New Haven: Yale University Press, 1935), p. 194. Used by permission.
5. C. C. Cleveland, *The Great Revival in the West,* (Chicago: University of Chicago Press), pp. 29-30. Copyright 1912 by the University of Chicago and used by permission.
6. W. W. Sweet, *The American Churches,* (Nashville: Abingdon Press, 1948), pp. 22-23. Used by permission.
7. B. B. Tyler, *History of the Disciples,* American Church History Series, (New York: Charles Scribner's Sons, 1894), pp. 1-3.

8. Cleveland, *op. cit.,* p. 120.
9. Those who discredited or made fun of the revivals were all lumped together under the flexible and blanket term "deist." Such people are mentioned frequently in the revival accounts.
10. *Biography of Eld. Barton Warren Stone,* pp. 36-37.
11. B. B. Tyler, *op. cit.,* p. 17.
12. From the letter of Archibald Alexander in the Appendix of W. B. Sprague, *Lectures on Revivals of Religion* (New York, 1833).
13. From *Biography of Eld. Barton Warren Stone,* p. 45.
14. *The Millennial Harbinger,* 1862, p. 127.

Chapter III

1. Garrison, *op. cit.,* 101.
2. *Christian Baptist,* VII, 626.
3. E. Gates, *The Early Relation and Separation of Baptists and Disciples* (Chicago: Christian Century Company, 1904), 40.
4. *Christian Baptist,* I, 36.
5. *Ibid.,* III, 242.
6. *Ibid.,* III, 249.
7. *Ibid.,* II, 166-67.
8. *Ibid.,* I, 43.
9. *Ibid.,* IV, 295.
10. *Ibid.,* II, 133.
11. *Ibid.,* II, 136.
12. *Ibid.,* III, 223. The correspondent unconsciously showed his knowledge of some of the forces that operate to modify customs when he added, "Though I am not convinced of the necessity of weekly communion, not seeing how it could be kept so often in our back country, owing to our scattered state of living . . . yet I think that whenever it is observed, it should be done according to the primitive model."
13. *Ibid.,* III, 223.
14. *Ibid.,* IV, 313-14.
15. *Ibid.,* VI, 531.
16. *Ibid.,* I, 73.
17. *Ibid.,* VI, 508.
18. Rufus Babcock, editor, *Memoirs of John Mason Peck* (Philadelphia, 1864), 111.
19. *Christian Baptist,* VI, 536.
20. *Ibid.,* I, 17.
21. *Ibid,* VII, 571.
22. *Ibid.,* V, 451-52.
23. *Millennial Harbinger,* 1830, 542.

Chapter IV

1. Garrison, *op. cit.,* 130.
2. In 1833 one E. A. Mills was expelled from the Baptist church at Eagleville, Ohio, because "he will not consent to abandon the reading of Mr. Campbell's *Millennial Harbinger.*"

3. *Christian Baptist,* V, 452.
4. *Millennial Harbinger,* 1830, 5.
5. *Ibid.,* 1831, 358.
6. *Ibid.,* 1834, 619.
7. *Ibid.,* 1831, 3.
8. *Ibid.,* 1831, 174.
9. *Ibid.,* 1837, 149.
10. *Ibid.,* 1834, 216.
11. *Ibid.,* 1831, 45.
12. *Ibid.,* 1834, 60.
13. *Ibid.,* 1831, 113-14.
14. *Ibid.,* 1833, 140.
15. *Ibid.,* 1834, 134.
16. *Ibid.,* 1837, 91-92.
17. *Ibid.,* 1830, 474.
18. *Ibid.,* 1836, 335.
19. *Ibid.,* 1830, 313.
20. *Ibid.,* 1834, 317.
21. *Ibid.,* 1835, 428.
22. *Ibid.,* 1834, 373.
23. *Ibid.,* 1831, 23-24.
24. *Ibid.,* 1837, 365-66 (italics mine).
25. *Ibid.,* 1835, 96.
26. *Ibid.,* 1838, 157.
27. *Ibid.,* 1939, 404.
28. *Ibid.,* 1839, 261.
29. *Ibid.,* 1830, 91.
30. *Ibid.,* 1830, 200-201.
31. *Ibid.,* 1836, 120-21.
32. *Ibid.,* 1831, 131-32.
33. *Ibid.,* 1835, 199-200.
34. *Ibid.,* 1831, 75.
35. *Ibid.,* 1835, 474.
36. Garrison, *op. cit.,* 146.

Chapter V

1. *Millennial Harbinger,* 1841, 409-10.
2. *Ibid.,* 1843, 5-6 (italics mine).
3. *Ibid.,* 1854, 188.
4. *Ibid.,* 1860, 330.
5. *Ibid.,* 1855, 618-19.
6. *Ibid.,* 1865, 22.
7. *Ibid.,* 1860, 8-9.
8. *Ibid.,* 1849, 151-52.
9. *Ibid.,* 1847, 316.
10. *Ibid.,* 1848, 280.
11. *Ibid.,* 1847, 220.
12. *Ibid.,* 1853, 207.

13. *Ibid.*, 1864, 169-70.
14. *Ibid.*, 1837, 411.
15. *Ibid.*, 1862, 40.
16. *Ibid.*, 1862, 131.
17. *Ibid.*, 1862, 175-76.
18. *Ibid.*, 1862, 227.
19. *Ibid.*, 1844, 4.
20. *Ibid.*, 1859, 499.
21. *Ibid.*, 1842, 130-31.

Chapter VI

1. *Millennial Harbinger,* 1840, 275.
2. *Ibid.*, 1842, 45.
3. Though, as we saw in the previous section, the door had been left open for this realization, and it already existed to some extent, Had money been available, Disciples would undoubtedly have accepted it, despite their doubts about it.
4. *Millennial Harbinger,* 1843, 64-65.
5. *Ibid.*, 1844, 247-48.
6. *Ibid.*, 1846, 249.
7. *Ibid.*, 1846, 317.
8. *Ibid.*, 1848, 521.
9. *Ibid.*, 1847, 452.
10. *Ibid.*, 1853, 692.
11. *Ibid.*, 1858, 27-28.
12. *Ibid.*, 1859, 655.
13. *Ibid.*, 1852, 218.
14. *Ibid.*, 1865, 562.
15. *Ibid.*, 1852, 165; see also 1857, 614; 1859, 212; 1862, 396.
16. *Ibid.*, 1841, 313.
17. *Ibid.*, 1856, 595-96.
18. *Ibid.*, 1859, 233.
19. *Ibid.*, 1857, 351-52.
20. *Ibid.*, 1863, 168-69.
21. *Ibid.*, 1864, 341.
22. *Ibid.*, 1847, 384.
23. *Ibid.*, 1851, 467-68.
24. *Ibid.*, 1853, 212-13.
25. *Ibid.*, 1853, 341-42.
26. *Ibid.*, 1851, 581-82.
27. *Ibid.*, 1861, 559.
28. *Ibid.*, 1864, 127.
29. *Ibid.*, 1864, 510-13.
30. Garrison, *op. cit.*, 226.
31. See F. S. Chapin, *Contemporary American Institutions* (New York: Harper & Brothers, 1935), and W. H. Sewell, "A Short Form of the Farm Family Socioeconomic Status Scale," *Rural Sociology* VIII (1943), 161-70.
32. Reported in *Louisville Courier Journal,* August 23, 1931.

Chapter VII

1. *Millennial Harbinger,* 1846, 1.
2. *Christian Baptist,* IV, 323.
3. W. E. Garrison and A. T. De Groot, *The Disciples of Christ,* (St. Louis: Bethany Press, 1948), 324ff.
4. Cf. D. W. Medearis and F. E. Rector, *Facts About Our Churches and a Changing America,* (Department of Church Development and Evangelism, United Christian Missionary Society).
5. *Millennial Harbinger,* 1842, 4.
6. *Ibid.,* 1842, 523.
7. As quoted in Garrison, *op. cit.,* 186.
8. *Millennial Harbinger,* 1847, 201.
9. *Ibid.,* 1849, 272-73.
10. *Ibid.,* 1849, 92.
11. *Ibid.,* 1858, 222-23.
12. As quoted in Garrison, *op cit.,* 193.
13. *Millennial Harbinger,* 1847, 649.
14. *Ibid.,* 1840, 4 (italics mine); see also *ibid.,* 1846, 58.
15. *Ibid.,* 1840, 221.
16. *Ibid.,* 1841, 480.
17. *Ibid.,* 1843, 213-14.
18. *Ibid.,* 1843, 282; see also *ibid.,* 1849, 288; *ibid.,* 1853, 508.
19. *Ibid.,* 1850, 335.
20. *Ibid.,* 1851, 695.
21. *Ibid.,* 1856, 491.
22. *Ibid.,* 1856, 550.
23. *Ibid.,* 1865, 449; see also *ibid.,* 1846, 373.
24. *Ibid.,* 1845, 27.
25. *Ibid.,* 1855, 343.
26. *Ibid.,* 1848, 414 (letter of W. F. Arny).
27. *Ibid.,* 1850, 487-88.
28. *Ibid.,* 1860, 388-89.
29. *Ibid.,* 1856, 172-73.
30. *Ibid.,* 1856, 671.
31. *Ibid.,* 1864, 3-4.

Chapter VIII

1. *Lard's Quarterly,* April, 1865.
2. *Millennial Harbinger,* 1866, 505.
3. *Ibid.,* 1866, 497-98.
4. *Ibid.,* 1868, 140.
5. *Ibid.,* 1868, 219.
6. *Ibid.,* 1868, 128.
7. As quoted in Garrison, *op. cit.,* 232.
8. *Millennial Harbinger,* 1867, 475-76.
9. *Ibid.,* 1868, 36.
10. *Ibid.,* 1870, 324.
11. *Ibid.,* 1867, 207-8.

12. *Ibid.,* 1869, 140.
13. *Ibid.,* 1868, 285-86.
14. *Ibid.,* 1868, 161.
15. *Ibid.,* 1869, 290-91.
16. *Ibid.,* 1869, 380 (T. D. Butler).
17. *Ibid.,* 1870, 286 (C. Loos).
18. *Ibid.,* 1866, 109.
19. *Ibid.,* 1866, 5.
20. *Ibid.,* 1867, 601.
21. *Ibid.,* 1869, 406.
22. *Ibid.,* 1870, 397.
23. *Ibid.,* 1866, 63-64.
24. *Ibid.,* 1866, 133-34.
25. *Ibid.,* 1870, 718.

Chapter IX

1. E. S. Ames., *Undenominational Religion,* (Pamphlet, 1938).
2. *Christian-Evangelist,* LXXV, (1937), 311.
3. *Ibid.,* LXXXI, (1943), 671.
4. *Ibid.,* LXXXV, (1947), 763.
5. On the Amish, see J. Gillin, *The Ways of Man,* (New York: Appleton-Century-Crofts, 1948), 209-20.
6. *Christian-Evangelist,* XCIV, (1956), 979.
7. *Ibid.,* XCV, (1957), 203.
8. *Ibid.,* 1256.
9. *Ibid.,* LXXVI, (1938), 1260.
10. *Ibid.,* LXXVII, (1939), 1270.
11. R. K. Merton, *Social Theory and Social Structure,* (Glencoe, Illinois: The Free Press, 1949), 151. Used by permission.
12. A. W. Fortune, *World Call,* X, (1928), No. 3, 7.
13. Annie Davidson, *Missionary Tidings,* XXIV, (1906-07), 307.
14. *Ibid.,* XXX, (1912-13), 274.
15. *World Call,* I, (1919), No. 5, 3.
16. *Ibid.,* No. 10, 1.
17. *Ibid.,* III, (1921), No. 9, 4.
18. *Ibid.,* IV, (1922), No. 7, 3.
19. H. B. McCormick, *ibid.,* VI, (1924), No. 2, 30-31.
20. *Ibid.,* No. 3, 22, 24.
21. Fred W. Wolff, *ibid.,* VII, (1925), No. 12, 15.
22. H. H. Peters, *ibid.,* IX, (1927), No. 10, 5.
23. Howard Short, *Christian-Evangelist,* XCVI, (1958), 62-63.
24. Stephen J. England, *ibid.,* XCIV, (1956), 1189-90.
25. On this point, see the address of George Combs, "The Mission of the Disciples," *World Call,* XVI, (1934), No. 10, 27.
26. A. A. Honeywell, *Christian-Evangelist,* LXVII, (1930), 445.
27. *Ibid.,* LXXII, (1935), 1026.
28. *Ibid.,* LXXXII, (1944), 83.
29. Mrs. W. W. Wharton, *Missionary Tidings,* XXIV, (1906-1907), 243.
30. F. E. Lumley, *ibid.,* XXXI, (1913-14), 234.

31. *World Call,* I, (1919), No. 1, 3.
32. *Ibid.,* No. 6, 26.
33. *Ibid.,* II, (1920), No. 5, 11ff.
34. *Ibid.,* III, (1921), No. 8, 37-38.
35. *Ibid.,* No. 9, 49.
36. Stephen E. Fisher, *ibid.,* IV, (1922), No. 10, 9.
37. *Ibid.,* VI, (1924), No. 9, 5.
38. Alva Taylor, *ibid.,* XI, (1929), No. 1, 27.
39. James Crain, *ibid.,* XVI, (1934), No. 5, 20.
40. Earle Marion Todd, *Christian-Evangelist,* LXXVIII, (1940), 83-84.
41. *Ibid.,* LXXII, (1935), 41.
42. *Ibid.,* XCVI, (1958), 434.
43. *World Call,* XX, (1938), No. 11, 23.
44. Barton Hunter, *ibid.,* XXXVIII, (1956), No. 11, 17.
45. *Ibid.,* No. 1, 24-25.
46. *Missionary Tidings,* XXVI, (1908-1909), 216-17.
47. H. C. Armstrong, *World Call,* I, (1919), No. 2, 27-28.
48. *Christian-Evangelist,* LXVII, (1930), 42.
49. *Ibid.,* LXIX, (1932), 1673.
50. *World Call,* XIX, (1937), No. 1, 3.
51. *Christian-Evangelist,* LXXXI, (1943), 213.
52. Ronald E. Osborn, *World Call,* XXXIII, (1951), No. 2, 16.
53. M. E. Sadler, *ibid.,* XXVIII, (1946), No. 8, 9, 24.
54. *Ibid.,* XXV, (1943), No. 1, 18.
55. Harrold McFarland, *Christian Standard,* LXXXVI, (1950), No. 39, 13.

Chapter X

1. *Christian Standard,* LXXII, (1937), 271.
2. W. S. Willis, *Christian-Evangelist,* LXXV, (1937), 461.
3. Richie L. Davis, *ibid.,* 498.
4. J. E. Catron, *ibid.,* 626.
5. C. B. Tigner, *ibid.,* LXXVIII, (1940), 171.
6. M. Lee Sorey, *ibid.,* LXXXVIII, (1950), 218.
7. *Christian Standard,* LXXXVII, (1951), No. 41, 8.
8. *Ibid.,* XC, (1954), No. 21, 2.
9. W. R. Warren, *World Call,* IX, (1927), No. 1, 5-6.
10. W. R. Walker, *Christian Standard,* LXXXIX, (1953), No. 14, 7.
11. *Ibid.,* XCII, (1956), 674. Cf. also *ibid.,* LXXXI, (1945), 276; *ibid.,* XC, (1954), No. 50, 8.
12. Harrold McFarland, *ibid.,* LXXXIII, (1947), 63.
13. *Ibid.,* 402.
14. *Ibid.,* 594.
15. William E. Harris, *ibid.,* LXXI, (1936), 975.
16. Edward H. Kolbe, *ibid.,* XCIII-A, (1958), 82.
17. Annie E. Davidson, *Missionary Tidings,* XXV, (1907-1908), 301-302.
18. J. H. Jowett, *Missionary Review of the World,* June 1918.
19. J. T. Wooddy, *Christian Standard,* LXV, (1930), 527.
20. *Ibid.,* LXIX, (1934), 495-96. Cf. also *ibid.,* LXX, (1935), 102.

21. *Ibid.,* LXXVIII, (1943), 323.
22. L. W. Klinker, *ibid.,* LXXVII, (1942), 787.
23. *Ibid.,* LXXVIII, (1943), Cf. also *ibid.,* LXXX, (1944), 131.
24. *Ibid.,* LXXXII, (1946), 611.
25. Ray Downen, *ibid.,* LXXXIX, (1953), No. 7, 5-6.
26. *Ibid.,* No. 29, 2.
27. *Ibid.,* XCI, (1955), 306.
28. *Ibid.,* LXXXIV, (1948), 107.
29. *Ibid.,* 154.
30. *Ibid.,* LXVII, (1932), 183.
31. Dean Hays, *ibid.,* 431.
32. *Ibid.,* LXXXIV, (1948), 794.
33. *Ibid.,* 346.
34. *Ibid.,* LXXX, (1944), 674.
35. *Ibid.,* 691. Cf. also *ibid.,* LXIX, (1934), 680; S. S. Lappin, *ibid.,* LXXVII, (1942), 78; LXXV, (1949), 730.
36. H. H. Watson, *Christian-Evangelist,* XCV, (1957), 1592.
37. W. R. Walker, *Christian Standard,* LXIX, (1934), 189.
38. *Ibid.,* LXX, (1935), 927.
39. *Ibid.,* 975.
40. Joseph W. Helms, *Christian-Evangelist,* LXXII, (1935), 1325.
41. Edwin V. Hayden, *Christian Standard,* XC, (1954), No. 33, 8.
42. *World Call,* XV, (1933), No. 8, 13-14. Cf. also, *Christian Standard,* LXXXI, (1945), 258; *ibid.,* LXVIII, (1933), 798.
43. *Christian-Evangelist,* LXVII, (1930), 545. Cf. also *ibid.,* 902; Joseph H. Dampier, *Christian Standard,* LXXXVII, (1951), No. 21, 11-12.
44. Charles O. Lee, *World Call,* XVII, (1935), No. 1, 12, 27.
45. *Christian Standard,* LXXXVIII, (1952), No. 41, 7. Cf. also C. H. Phillips, *ibid* No. 52, 3.
46. *Ibid.,* LXXXIX, (1953), No. 5, 8.
47. *Christian-Evangelist,* XCV, (1957), 1550.
48. *Ibid.,* LXVII, (1930), 91.
49. Gentry Reynolds, *Christian Standard,* LXV, (1930), 479.
50. Edward J. Cain, *ibid.,* LXVII, (1932), 527.
51. Nell A. Keifer, *Christian-Evangelist,* LXXI, (1934), 1423.
52. *World Call,* XV, (1933), No. 3, 23. Cf. also C. V. Dunn, *Christian-Evangelist,* LXX, (1933), 145; Carl V. Covey, *ibid.,* LXVIII, (1931), 1623.
53. *Ibid.,* 1326.
54. *Ibid.,* LXXVI, (1938), 429.
55. *Ibid.,* LXVIII, (1931), 320; and U. W. Smith, *ibid.,* LXXI, (1934), 260.
56. *Christian Standard,* LXIX, (1934), 511.
57. William Ward Ayer, *Baptist Standard,* October 27, 1956.
58. O. P. Spiegel, *Christian-Evangelist,* LXVIII, (1931), 567; G. W. Hootman, *Christian Standard,* LXIX, (1934), 19; *ibid.,* LXXII, (1937), 27-28; B. H. Coonradt, *ibid.,* 267; *ibid.,* 482; J. F. Reimann, *ibid.,* 796; Melvin P. Traxler, *ibid.,* LXXXIV, (1948), 739, 744; *ibid.,* LXXXV, (1949), 58.

59. *Christian-Evangelist,* LXXII, (1935), 354.
60. *Ibid.,* 439.
61. C. E. Lemmon, *ibid.,* 441.
62. Letter, Corvallis, Montana, *ibid.,* 417. (Blanks mine.)
63. U. H. Gatchell, *ibid.,* 485.
64. *Christian Standard,* LXX, (1935), 268.
65. *Ibid.,* 364.
66. William F. Rugg, *ibid.,* LXXII, (1937), 940.
67. W. A. Welsh, *Christian-Evangelist,* XCVI, (1958), 59-60.
68. *Christian Standard,* LXVIII, (1933), 458.
69. Timothy Tarwater, quoted by F. D. Kershner, *Christian-Evangelist,* LXXI, (1934), 581.
70. Henry H. Blankenship, *ibid.,* LXXIV, (1936), 1251.
71. *Christian Standard,* XCII, (1956), 344.
72. J. E. Reynolds, *Christian-Evangelist,* LXXI, (1934), 1452; Henry A. Littlehelp, *Christian Standard,* LXXII, (1937), 197; *ibid.,* XC, (1954), No. 38, 2; Henry Young, *Christian-Evangelist* XCVI, (1958), 1439, 1466.
73. *Christian Standard,* LXXXIX, (1953), No. 19, 8.
74. *World Call,* I, (1919), No. 9, 9. Cf. also *Christian Standard,* LXV, (1930), 330; letter to F. D. Kershner, *Christian-Evangelist,* LXX, (1933), 181.
75. *World Call,* II, (1920), No. 4, 21.
76. *Ibid.,* No. 9, 3. Cf. also *ibid.,* IX, (1927), No. 8, 3; *Christian-Evangelist,* LXVII, (1930), 219.
77. John H. Booth, *World Call,* IV, (1922), No. 11, 8.
78. *Christian-Evangelist,* LXVIII, (1931), 527.
79. T. F. George, *ibid.,* LXXV, (1937), 258; R. B. Hurt, *ibid.,* LXXVII, (1939), 1121; *Christian Standard,* LXXIV, (1939), 1175.
80. Joseph M. Smith, *Christian-Evangelist,* LXXVI, (1938), 159.
81. *Ibid.,* XCVI, (1958), 466.
82. *Christian Standard,* XCI, (1955), 402.
83. *Ibid.,* LXV, (1930), 694.
84. *Ibid.,* LXVI, (1931), 706. Cf. also *Christian-Evangelist,* LXIX, (1932), 1383.
85. *Christian Standard,* LXX, (1935), 663.
86. Marion Browning, *Christian-Evangelist,* LXXV, (1937), 658.
87. *Christian Standard,* LXXXIII, (1947), 162.
88. *Ibid.,* LXXXVI, (1950), 186.
89. *Ibid.,* LXXXVII, (1951), No. 31, 10.
90. James G. Van Buren, *ibid.,* XC, (1954), No. 16, 7.
91. *Ibid.,* LXVI, (1931), 331.
92. P. H. Welshimer, *ibid.,* LXXVI, (1941), 332, Cf. also *ibid.,* 887.
93. W. A. Fite, *Christian-Evangelist,* LXXXII, (1944), 189.
94. P. H. Welshimer, *ibid.,* 237.
95. C. J. Sharp, *Christian Standard,* LXXXVII, (1951), No. 4, 11. Cf. also *ibid.,* LXXXIII, (1947), 18.
96. Lonnie E. Dever, *ibid.,* LXXXVII, (1951), No. 24, 11.
97. *Ibid.,* LXXXVIII, (1952), No. 9, 10.

98. William E. Sweeney, *ibid.,* No. 30, 3.
99. *World Call,* XIV, (1932), No. 12, 10.
100. A. T. DeGroot, *Christian-Evangelist,* LXXIV, (1936), 414.
101. *Ibid.,* LXXXII, (1944), 639.
102. W. E. Garrison, *ibid.,* LXXXIII, (1945), 187.
103. J. P. Sanders, *ibid.,* XCIV, (1956), 828-29.
104. James G. Van Buren, *Christian Standard,* LXXXVIII, (1952), No. 31, 9. Cf. also *ibid.,* No. 45, 2.
105. *Ibid.,* LXVII, (1932), 882.
106. *Ibid.,* LXVIII, (1933), 30.
107. *Ibid.,* LXIX, (1934), 343.
108. *Ibid.,* 427.
109. Joseph W. Helms, *Christian-Evangelist,* LXXII, (1935), 1102; *Christian Standard,* LXXI, (1936), 663; G. M. Walker, *Christian-Evangelist,* LXXVII, (1939), 87; J. H. Blunt, *Christian Standard,* LXXVI, (1941), 279; Charles E. Mills, *ibid.,* LXXXII, (1946), 363; Donald A. Nash, *ibid.,* LXXXVII, (1951), No. 35, 15; W. R. Walker, *ibid.,* XCII, (1956), 806.
110. R. C. Foster, *ibid.,* LXXXVI, (1950), No. 47, 12.
111. R. E. Elmore, *ibid.,* LXXI, (1936), 536.
112. Resolution adopted at Annual Meeting, The Christian Restoration Association, *Christian-Evangelist,* LXXV, (1937), 1297; *Christian Standard,* LXX, (1935), 567; D. N. Gillett, *ibid.,* LXXIII, (1938), 47; C. V. Dunn, *Christian-Evangelist,* LXXIV, (1936), 861-62; J. F. Rosborough, *Christian Standard,* LXXI, (1936), 167; Ralph Eller, *Christian-Evangelist,* LXXVI, (1938), 773; U. H. Gatchell, *ibid.,* 111; W. H. Book, *ibid.,* LXXVIII, (1940), 511.
113. *Christian Standard,* LXXVII, (1942), 919; W. H. Book, *ibid.,* LXXVIII, (1943), 15; E. Lee Williams, *ibid.,* 70.
114. W. R. Walker, *ibid.,* XC, (1954), No. 32, 6; Fred W. Smith, *ibid.,* LXXXVII, (1951), No. 5, 13-14.
115. James G. Van Buren, *ibid.,* LXXXVIII, (1952), No. 36, 3.
116. *Ibid.,* No. 51, 2.
117. *Ibid.,* No. 43, 2.
118. *Christian-Evangelist,* LXXVI, (1938), 15ff.
119. *Ibid.,* XCIV, (1956), 1216-17, 1224.

Chapter XI

1. *Millennial Harbinger,* 1862, 127.
2. Albert Terrill Rasmussen, *Christian Social Ethics: Exerting Christian Influence,* page 11, copyright 1956 by Prentice-Hall, Inc., Englewood Cliffs, N. J. Reprinted by permission of the publisher.
3. *Christian-Evangelist,* XCIV, (1956), 1116.
4. *Ibid.,* LXVII, (1930), 1330.
5. *Ibid.,* LXX, (1933), 438.
6. *Ibid.,* LXVIII, (1931), 1486.

7. Harold Lunger, *The Political Ethics of Alexander Campbell,* p. 108, copyright 1954 by Bethany Press and reprinted by permission. Quotation within the citation is from *Millennial Harbinger,* 1845, 108.
8. *World Call,* XIV, (1932), No. 7, 3.
9. *Missionary Tidings,* XXXII, (1914-15), 480-81.
10. *Christian-Evangelist,* LXIX, (1932), 904.
11. "A Theologically Biased View of Protestant Politics," *Religion in Life,* XXI, (1952), 57. Used by permission of William Miller.
12. *Christian-Evangelist,* XCVI, (1958), 1079, 1098.
13. *Ibid.,* 1204-05.
14. Louise Moseley, *World Call,* XXXII, (1950), No. 5, 11, 16. Cf. also James Crain, *ibid.,* XX, (1938), No. 10, 8; Willard Shelton, *Christian-Evangelist,* LXXV, (1937), 1554; *ibid.,* LXX, (1933), 566; F. E. Davison, *World Call,* XIV, (1932), No. 8, 14, 23; C. E. Lemmon, *ibid.,* No. 8, 15, 23.
15. Nikolai Berdyaev, *The Destiny of Man,* (London: Geoffrey Bles, 1937), 197. Used by permission.
16. Eugene Ogrodowski, *Christian-Evangelist,* LXXIX, (1941), 137.
17. "Problems Protestantism Faces in Contemporary American Society," *Christianity and Society,* XVII, (1952), 8-14. Statements of major points are Underwood's, but he is not responsible for the interpretations derived. Used with the author's permission.
18. E. Parker, D. Barry, and D. Smythe, *The Television-Radio Audience and Religion,* (New York: Harper & Brothers, 1955), 396. Used by permission.
19. W. Schramm, *Responsibility in Mass Communication,* (New York: Harper & Brothers, 1957), 3. Used by permission.
20. Lunger, *op. cit.,* 269-71.
21. Reprinted by permission from James West: *Plainville, U.S.A.,* Columbia University Press, 1945.
22. Roger Shinn, *Social Action,* XXII, (Sept., 1955), 7-10, 13. Used by permission.
23. *Ibid.,* XX, (Feb., 1954), 30-31.
24. Marvin E. Smith, *World Call,* XXVIII, (1946), No. 11, 21.
25. *Ibid.,* XXXIV, (1952), No. 7, 16, 18.
26. *Ibid.,* No. 8, 5.
27. Barton Hunter, *ibid.,* XXXVII, (1955), No. 9, 14-15.
28. J. Oscar Lee and Alfred S. Kramer, *ibid.,* XXXIV, (1952), No. 7, 13-14.
29. *Millennial Harbinger,* 1842, 13.

INDEX